Women in Parliament

Ireland: 1918-2000

To my parents, John and Sarah McNamara,
and my family dear as life

To my father, Joseph Mary, and my mother, Eva
and to my family close at heart

Women in Parliament

Ireland: 1918-2000

Maedhbh McNamara
and
Paschal Mooney

WOLFHOUND PRESS

Published in 2000 by
Wolfhound Press Ltd
68 Mountjoy Square
Dublin 1, Ireland
Tel: (353-1) 874 0354
Fax: (353-1) 872 0207

British Library Cataloguing in Publication Data
A catalogue record for this book is available from the British Library.

ISBN 0-86327-759-4

10 9 8 7 6 5 4 3 2 1

The authors and publisher are grateful to the women surveyed and their families for
permission to reproduce photographs used in this book. The pictures of Constance
Markievicz (p. 71) and Linda Kearns-MacWhinney (p. 170) are reproduced courtesy
of the National Library of Ireland. The Central Catholic Library is acknowledged for
permission to reproduce pictures of Mary MacSwiney (p. 80), Ellen Desart (p. 160)
and Nora Connolly-O'Brien (p. 178). G.A. Duncan is acknowledged for permission to
reproduce the picture of Eleanor Butler (p. 174). Lensman is acknowledged for
permission to reproduce the picture of Jane Dowdall (p. 178). The publishers have
made every reasonable effort to contact the copyright holders of photographs
reproduced in this book. If any involuntary infringement of copyright has occurred,
sincere apologies are offered and the owners of such copyright are requested to
contact the publishers.

Cover photographs: Mary Robinson (courtesy *The Irish Times*), Constance Markievicz
(courtesy the National Library of Ireland), Margaret Collins O'Driscoll (courtesy her
family), Maureen O'Carroll (courtesy her family), Mary Harney (courtesy Mary
Harney)
Cover Design: Graham Thew
Typesetting and book design: Wolfhound Press
Printed and bound by MPG Books Ltd., Bodmin, Cornwall

Contents

My husband said that if I became a politician, it would be grounds for annulment.

LIZ O'DONNELL

Women don't vote for women; most of them vote for me.

BERTIE AHERN, KILLARNEY, 1990

This is women now. You cannot even give way to someone who wants to give information.

ALBERT REYNOLDS, DÁIL DEBATES, VOL. 437, COL. 10–11, 9 DECEMBER 1993
(HEARD BY POLITICAL CORRESPONDENTS AS 'THERE'S WOMEN FOR YOU.')

Mr Noonan: *Does the Acting Chairman have any intention of calling those women in the back of the House to order?*

Ms Hanafin: *Deputies.*

Dr McDaid: *The Deputy is in trouble.*

Acting Chairman: *I was under the impression the Deputy was enjoying*
(Mr Briscoe)   *the interruptions.*

Mr Quinn: *That is Deputies for you.*

DÁIL ÉIREANN OFFICIAL REPORT, 3 DECEMBER 1997

Acknowledgements

We wish to express our profound gratitude to those who have helped us with our research:

— The Members of the Oireachtas who made room in their crowded schedules to participate in the study and provide information and photographs.

— Her Excellency President McAleese for writing the Foreword.

— Her Excellency Mary Robinson for providing the Preface.

— Senator Maurice Hayes, Kieran McLoughlin, Lisa Betts and Kingsley Aikins of the Ireland Funds, whose generous funding enabled the research to be undertaken.

— The Ceann Comhairle and Office of the Houses of the Oireachtas, in particular the Clerks of the Dáil and Seanad, Kieran Coughlan and Deirdre Lane, Maureen Kilkenny; Marie Buckley, Veronica Dunne, Dr Adrian Kelly, Dr David O'Donoghue, Verona Ní Bhroinn, Micheál O'Rourke, Alan Murphy and Antoinette Doyle.

— Kathleen Redmond, who turned a dreadful manuscript into a legible text with patience, skill and unflagging good humour.

— Oireachtas Library and Research Section colleagues headed by helpful Maura Corcoran; Jim Fisher who shared his impressive IT expertise, Jean O'Brien and Antoinette Mernagh whose computer advice was invaluable; Charlotte Cousins, John Kelly and Joan Flynn, who gave excellent research assistance. Dr Patrick Melvin's and Séamus Haughey's scholarship, wit, forbearance and philosophical acuity make work a delight.

— Our Trinity Policy Institute authors, for their consummate professionalism: Úna Nic Giolla Choille, Dr Yvonne Galligan and Professor Kathleen Knight.

— Relatives of former members of the Oireachtas or the Northern Ireland Assembly: Ruairí Brugha and the Brugha family, Éilis O'Carroll, Fiona O'Carroll and Patricia O'Carroll, Sister Kathleen Rice, Finbarr Dowdall, Charles Doggett, Mary Buckley and Carol Cotter, Bernard Browne, Constance and Helen Cassidy, Jurgen Mantel, Deputy Gerry Reynolds, Mary Savage, Maureen Kirwan, Una Mulhearn, Pól Ó Murchú, Diana Taggart and Lucille MacGinley.

— Colleagues in the world of knowledge who always turn up trumps: Elizabeth McNamara, Kay O'Neill, Ciara McCaffrey and Carolyn O'Keeffe of Trinity College Library; Pauline O'Donnell, Malachy Moran, Amy Kerr and Shay de Barra of RTÉ Reference Library; Brian McKenna of the National Library of Ireland; George Woodman and Samantha McCombe of the Northern Ireland Assembly Library.

— Niamh Stephenson and Philip Hannon of the Fianna Fáil Press Office; Zoë Healy, P.J. O'Meara and Niall Ó Muilleoir of the Fine Gael Press Office; Tom Butler and Tony Heffernan of the Labour Party Press Office; and Jack Murray of the Progressive Democrats Press Office.

— Those whose advice opened doors: Mary Gallagher, Mary Flaherty, Senator Joe O'Toole, Gerry McNamara, Senator David Norris, Aisling Maguire, Enda Dowling, Sarah and John McNamara, Brian Ó Cléirigh, Senator Des Hanafin, Stephen Collins, Orla Spring and Chris Giblin.

— Bob Doyle of Irish Microfilm Systems.

— Our publishers, Séamus Cashman and Emer Ryan, who kindly guided us through the publishing experience.

— Those whose encouragement and amiability heartened us so: Sr Mary Roche, Sr Camilla Roche, the McNamara family, Mary and John Brosnan, Bridie and Michael O'Connell, Edmund and Rosemarie Roche, James Roche, Nano and Pat Nolan, Carmel Lambert and Gerard MacMichael, Mary and Michael Russell, Noreen Walshe, John and Brenda McNamara, Anne and Tommy Griffin, Catherine Kelly, Sheila and Graham Harrison.

— Margaret Cooney, Elizabeth Breen, Joan Kenny, Vera and Bill O'Connor for their splendid help.

— Alexandra and Aengus Byrne for their angelic forbearance.

— Maria, Siobhán, Andrew, Niall and Brian Mooney for their kindness.

— Our greatest debt is to Seán Byrne, whose unparalleled understanding, wit and support makes everything possible, and Sheila Mooney for her essential inspiration, advice and fortitude.

Foreword

This past century has seen the blossoming of women's talents in every sphere of Irish life, in a way that would have been unimaginable a hundred years ago.

We owe a great deal of gratitude, in particular, to the Irish women who broke new ground as public representatives in past generations. It took a lot of courage and determination at a time when the range of opportunities open to most women was narrowly confined — and attitudes were even narrower. We take pride in the achievements and effectiveness of their successors — the women who are involved in political life in Ireland today.

It must, however, be a matter of concern that participation rates remain disappointingly low. We need to do our utmost to change that, not just as a matter of equality, but also because Irish society as a whole will otherwise be the poorer for it. We need the insights and experiences of women to inform our policy-formation and decision-making processes. And we need to understand and seek to change the factors which discourage women from entering and remaining in politics.

This book will provide valuable information on these issues, especially as perceived by women parliamentarians themselves. I commend all those who have contributed to and compiled the directory and I hope that the next hundred years will see many more young women putting their gifts to use in public life.

Mary McAleese
President of Ireland

Preface

I welcome the publication of a book that highlights the part played by Irish women in political life. It is an important part of the story of Irish development which too often focuses on the contribution of men. Yet, women have been in the vanguard of the struggle to achieve the full participation of all citizens in political activity. I think back to remarkable women like Hanna Sheehy Skeffington. And Constance Markievicz who, in 1918, became the first woman to be elected to the House of Commons. Many women whose names are less well known have fought long and hard to champion the legal and political status of women in Ireland. There should be proper recognition of the rich contribution which Irish women, North and South, have made and continue to make.

As High Commissioner for Human Rights, I see it as a top priority to achieve the abolition of every vestige of discrimination against women and to bring about true equality. An essential component is to increase the participation of women in all areas of decision-making and public life.

The role of women in Irish society has changed dramatically over the past forty years. Today women are active in every walk of life. But there is a big deficit to make up before it can be said that women are adequately represented at political level. At present only 13 per cent of Dáil Deputies and 15 per cent of elected local representatives are women. I look forward to the day when women's participation in all levels of government will be an unremarkable feature of public life. We will know that there is true equality when the last obstacles are overcome, when women are as free to make mistakes as men and not to have it blamed on their gender!

If the representation of women in public life in Northern Ireland is less strong than in the South, we should not lose sight of the crucial role which the women of both communities have played in nurturing the peace process and promoting reconciliation. No political arrangement can last unless it has support at grassroots level. The women of Northern Ireland have shown that they can make a special contribution to peace-building and conflict resolution.

Mary Robinson
United Nations High Commissioner
for Human Rights

Introduction

Women, Ideals and *Realpolitik*

Ireland, like almost all societies, is male-dominated. In contrast to other European democracies, in Ireland progress towards increasing the participation of women in the economy and society has been slow. Women are under-represented in the Irish political system, the state institutions, the formal economic system and the churches. According to the All Party Oireachtas Committee Report on the Constitution:

> *Even casual observation of the Irish political system reveals that there is marked gender imbalance among public representatives. This is another systems weakness because it means that the knowledge, experience and sensibility of women are largely absent from the process through which the state seeks to express the values of its people.*[1]

As a new group entering politics, women have had an uphill struggle to gain a foothold in the public realm. The fact that they have been consistently under-represented in parliament indicates the existence of systematic barriers blocking women's progress in political life. Since women constitute half the citizens of a country, their absence from decision-making denotes a failure on the part of democratic institutions to represent the major interests in society. The conclusion of the first century in which women represented their fellow citizens in parliament in a significant number of countries is an appropriate moment to celebrate the achievements of the trailblazers. Pioneering women, who entered political life and parliament from the beginning of the twentieth century, changed the rules and expectations and eased the path of those who followed. Their experiences in challenging biases and cultural blockages are of great political and historical significance. This book describes and evaluates the experiences of those Irish women.

The parliamentarians featured in this book stand out because they have confronted assumptions about gender that are more tenacious than we like to think. The most grotesque of these assumptions is the traditional belief that men are more suited to leadership than women — 'by nature'. Changes on society's surface often conceal deeper perceptions of women as intrinsically second-class citizens. This perception is apparent in the political disadvantages attached to being a woman. The fact that politics is overwhelmingly male at decision-making levels has been accepted as natural for so long that sexism has become subconscious.

The difficulty faced by women in gaining a high vote in Ireland is shown by the fact that only one woman ranks among the top 50 vote-getters in the period 1918–2000. Of the deputies elected during that period, Eithne Fitzgerald, who received the highest first-preference vote in the 1992 election, ranked only fifteenth for the whole period.[2] In the general election of 1997, the highest woman vote-getter, Theresa Ahearn, received 0.96 of the quota in comparison to the highest male vote-getter, Bertie Ahern, with 1.70 of the quota.[3] The twentieth woman vote-getter, Marian McGennis, gained 0.44 of the quota in comparison with the twentieth male vote-getter, Eamon Ó Cuiv, who won 1.03 of the quota.[4]

In addition to the unconscious bias in favour of male politicians, many women entering politics are at an economic disadvantage compared to men. Even young Irish women, who have had equal access to education and training, earn just 86 per cent of average male earnings.[5] The average Irish woman earns 73 per cent of average male hourly earnings. This is an obstacle for aspiring politicians who need to finance a car, a telephone, childcare, sponsorships and raffle tickets, drink-buying, and the cost of advertising clinics in the local paper. It is difficult for women to be selected to contest elections in Ireland, and it is even more difficult for them to win election to parliament and to retain a seat once elected.[6] Women's rate of incumbency (retention of seat in parliament) is markedly lower than that of men in Irish political life.[7] Until recently, women, in order to succeed in politics, have had to convince the electorate that they are 'as good as' men, that they possess the gravitas assumed to be inherent in their male counterparts. The women featured in this book are highly visible as models of strength and self-esteem, ambition and action. They have changed people's perceptions of women's capacities.

However, recent research has shown that women get fewer votes than men because they are less likely to be incumbents — rather than because they are women. The incumbency effect dominates all others. The best thing to be in an Irish election is a male incumbent and the worst thing to be is a female challenger. It is, however, far better to be a female incumbent than a male challenger. There is no significant negative effect attached to being a woman *per se*. This suggests a vicious circle in which women are less likely to be nominated because they are less likely to be incumbents or, if challengers, less likely to be experienced. Being less likely to be nominated, they are, in turn, less likely to become incumbents, or to gain experience of fighting elections.[8,9] The under-representation of women in parliamentary life is an aspect of the gender deficit which characterises decision-making at every level. Women possess half the talent, expertise and skills, and a nation which relies on only half its resources can expect to realise only half its potential, as President McAleese told the Mexican Senate.[10] A balanced participation by women and men in decision-making might produce different ideas, values and styles of behaviour suited to a fairer world for everybody.

We inhabit a lopsided world in which annual expenditure on basic health, nutrition, water and sanitation amounts to £15 billion compared to military expenditure of £538 billion. The UN has resources of under $2 a year per person, compared to the $150 per person spent annually on armies and armaments worldwide. Research indicates that men are greater supporters of military expenditure, while women tend to prefer health and education expenditure. A broader range of women in positions of political power might lead to many countries becoming more prosperous and more peaceful. The strength, resilience and ingenuity of women are usually cited in the context of their endurance of poverty and war; sufficient women in positions of power could deploy those qualities to prevent poverty and war.

*

Women won the right to enter parliament in 1918 while Ireland was still part of the United Kingdom. The first woman to be elected to British Parliament was an Irish woman, Constance Markievicz, who had participated in the 1916 Rising. Constance Markievicz was one of the large number of Sinn Féin MPs elected in 1918 who did not take their seats in Westminster but formed themselves into the first Dáil. Since 1918 women's share of Dáil seats has grown from 1 per cent to a peak of 13.8 per cent. Three broad phases in the participation of women in the Dáil and Seanad since 1918 can be identified. These are Republican Women, 'A Vote for the Widow' and Feminist Women.

Republican Women

Newly emancipated women drawn into parliamentary life via the fight for independence came mainly from a highly nationalist background. By unanimously taking the anti-Treaty side they opted out of the possibility of governing in the early years of the fledgling state. These women's formative years had been spent in a society where women did not have the vote. Several were active in the cross-fertilising organisations of suffragism, nationalism and socialism. They had distinguished themselves in their original occupations; some had broken into professions from which women had been excluded or they had successfully established new enterprises. This was a period of political gains for women, which raised their expectations. The British government's reform of local authorities from 1898 had allowed women to take up elected positions as poor-law guardians and members of urban and rural district councils. Two women who were important political figures in the early years of the state, Kathleen Clarke and Jenny Wyse Power, had gained their first political experience at municipal level.

Women's military role in the armed conflict of the Easter Rising, War of Independence and Civil War gave them experience in working alongside men, taking risks in courier and intelligence work. They also organised relief in the absence of male leaders, in addition to their traditional role of nursing the wounded and providing shelter. A promise of equality for all citizens was contained in the 1916 Proclamation, and the draft 1922 Free State constitution contained Article 3, which stated 'Every person, without distinction of sex ... shall ... enjoy the privileges and be subject to the obligations of ... citizenship'. These provisions were inserted as a result of women's activism and lobbying, rather than because of the magnanimity of the State's 'founding fathers'.

Despite the achievement of having women's rights recognised in the 1916 Proclamation and the 1922 Constitution, these women's hostility to the Treaty made them seem uncompromising, willing to shed blood in pursuit of an ideal rather than engage in the compromises of *realpolitik*. Some writers such as the pro-Treaty historian, P.S. O'Hegarty, blamed women for the divisiveness and violence that plagued the Civil War period and its aftermath.[11] This view was not supported by the events of the time, but the horrors of the Civil War gave rise to the need for a scapegoat. Women were an easy and obvious target.[12] The Civil War had a negative effect on male perceptions of women's right to participate in political life, and this perception was translated into legislation enacted by successive Free State governments, which placed obstacles in the way of women's participation in politics.

'A Vote for the Widow'

The late 1920s and 1930s was a conservative period in Irish politics, characterised by a reversal of women's rights. During the fifty years from 1922 to 1972, the average Dáil contained only four women, 3 per cent of Deputies. From the 1930s to the 1960s, the women elected were, with a few exceptions, widows or other relatives of deceased members. Only seven women were elected to the Dáil in the period 1922–37. Some had been active themselves in the struggle for independence, but a few were new to politics. Pensions for the widows and children of deceased TDs were not introduced until 1968 by the *Oireachtas Allowances to Members (Amendment) Act, 1968*, so there may have been an economic factor in the decision of some widows to stand for election. Some had large families (Margaret Collins-O'Driscoll, for example, had fourteen children, eleven of whom survived; Maureen O'Carroll had ten children and no household help) and the trip to Dublin from a rural area was taxing. Unless a by-election was involved, a widow was not guaranteed an easy route to a party nomination. According to one Oireachtas contemporary, 'I remember Cecilia Lynch telling me about the great struggle she had to be accepted as a candidate when her husband died.'[13]

These women gave priority to their constituency activity over their legislative function, and their contributions to debates were infrequent. For example,

Mary Reynolds, who still holds the record for most elections won by a woman, won nine elections between 1932 and 1957, yet confined herself largely to parliamentary questions. Loyalty to their parties determined the response of these deputies. Only Margaret Collins-O'Driscoll and Helena Concannon contributed to debates to a significant degree, supporting the conservative policies of their parties. The disconcerting feature of the late 1920s and 1930s was the introduction of statutory discrimination on the basis of sex. Legislation was introduced limiting women's access to higher posts in the civil service, to jury service, to information on birth control and to employment in industry.[14]

During the debate on the *Juries Act, 1927*, which sought to exempt women from jury service, a suggestion was made that equality reform had been imposed by the *British in the Sex Disqualification Act, 1919*. The debate revealed attitudes and values among the political élite regarding the place of women. There was a sense that woman's role was in the domestic domain. Opponents of the bill were dismissed as 'self-appointed', a 'truculent minority' who held 'advanced' or 'intellectual' opinions. They were accused of displaying a 'dog in the manger' attitude towards those in the home. It must be said that a majority of 'ordinary' women probably felt represented by those who supported the Bill.

As early as the debate on the draft 1922 constitution Kevin O'Higgins, the Minister for Home Affairs, tried to weaken the concept of equality for women. In the context of recently gained women's rights, the reversal of women's rights was shocking to activists. Bridget Redmond ineffectually attempted, in the debate on the 1937 Constitution, to change the part of Article 41 which said that 'woman by her life within the home gives the State a support without which the common good cannot be achieved' to include all women, in or out of the home. The rolling back of rights for women has been explained as a reaction to their intransigence in relation to the national issue.[15] Their experience, however, prefigures that of British women who replaced men in the workforce during the Second World War and were then expected to go back to the home when the men returned from fighting.

The unimpressive legislative record of women TDs during this phase has been lamented,[16] but it is useful to place their efforts in a context of a social and political climate which was inimical to the participation of women. Painful aspects of women's experience were not unknown to these women TDs — for example, unwanted pregnancy and homespun attempts at abortion. The climate was such that such matters could not even be mentioned, let alone placed on the political agenda.

Feminist Women

Influenced by the ideas of the second wave of the women's movement, as interpreted by organisations such as the Women's Political Association and Woman

Elect, women began to stand in the 1970s as candidates in their own right, supported by campaigns such as 'Why Not a Woman?' In 1973, Ireland joined the European Economic Community, which put the equal representation of women on the agenda in a constructive way. The equality legislation required by the EEC gave women more employment opportunities and, therefore, greater independence.

Women began to contest elections in increasing numbers and the proportion of women elected rose gradually from 4.1 per cent in 1977 to 12 per cent in 1997. The 1977 election was a turning point. In December 1979 a woman (Máire Geoghegan-Quinn) was appointed to cabinet level for the first time since the foundation of the State. (Constance Markievicz had been Minister for Labour in the pre-Independence first Dáil of 1919). Máire Geoghegan-Quinn was followed over the next two decades by seven more women. The first woman President, Mary Robinson, who as a lawyer and senator had achieved major advances in individual rights, was elected in 1990. Since the 1970s, women have been speaking out often on issues of vital concern, and taking courageous and sometimes unpopular positions which have led to legislative change.

The Experience of Women in Seanad Éireann, 1922-1937

While women were elected members of the Dáil from 1918, they were nominated to the Seanad in its early years by the leader of the Dáil, then named President of the Executive Council. The Seanad was obliged to accommodate minority opinion in Ireland, which essentially meant the non-Catholic and non-nationalist community. Two women members of the first Seanad, the Countess of Desart and Alice Stopford Green who were Jewish and Anglo-Irish Protestant respectively, voted, like William Butler Yeats, in favour of divorce.

The women nominated to the 1922–1937 Seanad were highly gifted and distinguished by their contribution to cultural, economic or political life. Jennie Wyse Power had been active in the Ladies' Land League (1881–2), in local government and in numerous political organisations, as well as running businesses and rearing children who themselves contributed to public life. She was 'having it all' long before the term was coined, and remained a member of the Seanad until it was abolished in 1936. Ellen Odette Cuffe, Countess of Desart, a London-born Jewish woman, had founded a woollen mill, workers' garden village, theatre and hospital in Kilkenny and was a supporter of the Irish language. Alice Stopford Green was a noted historian, and Eileen Costello was a London teacher who moved to Tuam, County Galway, converted to Catholicism and collected folk songs in Irish. Kathleen Clarke (a well-known nationalist) and Kathleen Browne (a self-proclaimed Blueshirt) joined the Seanad in 1928 and 1929.

A notable feature of these women was their commitment to women's equality. They could work together to promote[17] women's issues despite their political differences. Jennie Wyse Power and Eileen Costello were strong in their opposition to the *Civil Service Regulation (Amendment) Bill, 1925*. This legislation sought to confine state examinations for senior civil service positions to men. Wyse Power regretted that the bill was introduced by men who participated in a fight with women at a time 'when sex and money were not considerations'.[18] She and Costello convinced the Seanad to reject the bill at Second Stage and hold up its introduction for twelve months. Wyse Power had worked in the republican courts set up during the War of Independence and was staunch in her opposition to the *Juries Act, 1927*.

The subject of birth control was introduced during the debate on the *Censorship of Publications Bill, 1928*, providing for a five-person censorship board. Until then, people had the possibility of access to written information about contraceptives — access which was denied upon the 1929 enactment of this Bill. The women of the Dáil and Seanad did not participate to a significant degree in the birth-control debate or the general debate about censorship. Margaret Collins-O'Driscoll, the only woman in the Dáil, indicated her support for the Bill. Her position probably reflected the views of the majority of Catholic women who unquestioningly accepted Catholic teaching on contraception.

Senators Wyse Power, Browne, Clarke, Costello and Desart supported the *Illegitimate Children (Affiliation Orders) Bill, 1929*. This was designed to improve the status of unmarried mothers by providing the mother with the right to seek financial maintenance from the father for the upkeep of her child. The debate in the Dáil was remarkable for the attention given to the dilemma facing the putative father. Concern for his plight surpassed concern for the plight of the mother. Unmarried mothers were described as 'hardened sinners'. Even the Minister, Fitzgerald-Kenney, spoke of the 'considerable number of immoral women in the world'.[19] Some senators referred to the hardships facing unmarried mothers, which, in some cases, impelled them to infanticide.

The *Criminal Law Amendment Bill, 1934* addressed the issues of prostitution, contraception and the age of consent. Kathleen Clarke opposed a contraceptive ban on the grounds that it would drive the question of birth control underground. On the question of raising the age of consent to fifteen in the case of indecent and sexual assault, Wyse-Power, Clarke, Browne and Costello proposed raising it to eighteen, arguing (without success) that this would give greater protection to girls and women.

The *Conditions of Employment Bill, 1935* gave power to the Minister for Industry to restrict the employment of women in industry. The view that a woman's place was in the home permeated the debate. Jennie Wyse Power told the House that girls who had lost their jobs in industry had said to her, 'When our own men are in power, we shall have equal rights',[20] a belief which she said showed 'their lack of experience'. Although her party (Fianna Fáil) was in government, Kathleen Clarke argued against sections of the bill that restricted women's employment and was supported by Wyse Power and Browne in her attempts to have them deleted. She called for solidarity from the trade union movement in seeking equal pay — a very radical demand. She described herself as a nationalist and not a feminist; her inspiration was the equality promised in the 1916 Proclamation. She was unhappy that references to housework were 'sneered at' by male senators. Clarke said that if the Minister were to prevent women from doing such work, he would have her support.[21]

The Post-1937 Senate

The 1937 Constitution initiated a new system of election to the Seanad. Of the sixty members, forty-three were elected from five vocational panels, six were elected by the graduates of the National University of Ireland and University of Dublin (Trinity College), and eleven were nominated by the Taoiseach of the day. Members of the Dáil and Seanad and county councils constitute the bulk of the electorate for the panels, with the result that panel members, despite their ostensibly vocational character, have tended to be party politicians.

It is worth noting that the Taoiseach, who can nominate eleven senators, could, if he wished, nominate eleven women, or 18.3 per cent of senators. When added to elected women, eleven women senators would bring the proportion of women in the Irish parliament close to 30 per cent. No Taoiseach since 1937 has nominated more than three women.

The universities have the best record on gender balance. In fifteen of the twenty Seanad elections to date, they have returned one or two women, that is, 15 per cent to 33 per cent of their seats. In a sixteenth election, in 1981, they returned three women, a full 50 per cent of their representatives — Gemma Hussey, Mary Robinson and Catherine McGuinness (all of whom proceeded to high office). Prominent among the women nominated by the Taoiseach to the Seanad were the presidents of the Irish Countrywomen's Association (ICA). The fact that four successive presidents of the Irish Countrywomen's Association were nominated by Taoisigh is a recognition of the contribution by that organisation to women's educational and social development.

Women's Participation in the Dáil and Seanad since 1937

From the foundation of the state, the obstacles to women's participation in the Dáil and Seanad reflected the weak position of women in Irish society, and the increasing numbers of women in political life contributed to improving the position of women. Most of the women in the pre-1937 Dáil and Seanad had been involved in the struggle for independence or were nominated members of the minority non-Catholic community. It was not until 1954 that the first Labour woman deputy, Maureen O'Carroll, was elected to the Dáil. She raised in the Dáil her concerns about infringements of the law concerning the adoption of Irish babies by US couples — a policy whose full repercussions became apparent in the 1990s. Maureen O'Carroll also raised the issue of rising prices and food quality, which were of great concern to women.

No Dáil has had no woman member (though the first Dáil (1919–1921) and the sixth (1927–1932) each returned only one woman deputy, Constance Markievicz and Margaret Collins-O'Driscoll, respectively). It is significant that Ireland elected a woman to parliament in 1918, the first occasion when it was possible to do so. This is a remarkable achievement, as women got the vote as well as the right to stand for parliament only in 1918 when the *Parliament (Qualification of Women) Act* was passed. The *Representation of the People Act, 1918*, extended the vote to women of the age of 30 years and over, all adult males and to soldiers over 18 years of age. No British woman was elected in 1918 and the first woman MP to take her seat, Nancy Astor, was not elected until 1919.

The election by Irish voters of Constance Markievicz as the first woman MP in the UK parliament seemed like a promising beginning for Irish women in parliament but proved to be no more than an historical curiosity. Since the first Dáil of 1919, women have won only 176 of the 4,120 Dáil seats or 4.27 per cent of the seats filled in the twentieth century. Of 1,064 TDs in Dáil Éireann to date, only sixty-three of them have been women, just 5.83 per cent of the total. Fifty-seven women have been Senators out of a total of 624, that is 8.81 per cent. Of the eight Presidents to date, two have been women. Women have never comprised more than 13.8 per cent of Dáil membership or 18.3 per cent of Seanad membership although they constitute 51 per cent of the population.

One factor that, in a modest way, has favoured the election of women is the occurrence of by-elections.[22] Parties have often found it expedient to nominate a relative of a deceased or retiring TD for the ensuing by-election; this can help to avoid friction in the constituency organisation and attracts a sympathy vote. A relative who was involved in the late deputy's constituency work may have access to that deputy's networks and thus be well qualified to take over the former incumbent's role. The first time a party successfully nominated any relative of the departed TD at a by-election was in 1945, when Fianna Fáil's Honor Mary Crowley retained her husband's seat — also her late father's seat — in Kerry South. The pattern has been of widows, sons or daughters being nominated to contest the by-election caused by the departure of a male TD.

Of the 119 seats to be filled at by-election the vacancies in 116 cases have been caused by the departure of a male TD, and twelve of these vacancies have been filled by women, while men have won all three by-elections caused by the deaths of women TDs, giving women a 'net gain' of nine seats. Women's capture of twelve of the 119 by-election seats (10 per cent) represents over twice the proportion of all Dáil seats they have taken since 1918. Eight of the successful women by-election candidates have been relatives of a male TD whose death created the vacancy. Four were widows and three daughters; an eighth, Mary Upton, is a sister; a ninth, Myra Barry (1979), was the daughter of a sitting TD in the constituency who had decided to retire at the next election; and a tenth, Cecilia Keaveney (1996), was the daughter of a former TD for the constituency. In May 2000 Ellen Ferris was nominated by Labour to contest her late husband's seat in Tipperary South, but she failed to win it. Gallagher has found that TDs winning by-elections have fared at least as well as those they replace. Of the by-election winners who were related to the TD whose departure caused the vacancy, Eileen Desmond and Máire Geoghegan-Quinn were two of the six who became cabinet ministers while their deceased relative had not.[23]

Women Parliamentarians and Women's Issues

It could be suggested that men can adequately represent women's interests in parliament. However, this argument does not take account of the fact that men's economic, social and political experiences are significantly different from those of women. Most male parliamentarians enjoy economic and social power before being elected and cannot have a full understanding of the needs and requirements of women whose life experience is completely removed from their own. Well-intentioned as some may be, the representation they can give will be that of an outsider looking in. Many deputies believe that the Hepatitis C tragedy,[24] in which 1,600 people were infected by blood and blood products, would have been handled differently by a woman Minister. Deputy Kathleen Lynch's contribution to the Dáil debate on this topic was indeed notable — she herself had received Anti-D treatment and described her own fear and horror.[25]

Women from different political parties have expressed their perception of male representatives' failure to understand women's problems. 'Men often see things from a different point of view,' Senator Cathy Honan told *The Irish Times*. 'It was brought home to me most forcibly when the Kilkenny incest case was being discussed in the Seanad — when all I could hear were these men blaming the mother, because she hadn't left. I couldn't believe my ears. They had money in their pockets and cars under their backsides — what could they possibly know about a woman in her situation?'[26] Deputy Breeda Moynihan-Cronin told *The Irish Times* that she works closely with the local Rape Crisis Centre and sees many battered wives. 'They come to me because I'm a woman, especially in rural areas where the doctor is a man, the priest is a man, the Guard is a man.'[27] Máirín Quill spoke of the jolt she received on her first day in the Dáil, looking around at 'these executive-type men sitting in the chamber'. To Deputy Quill they 'seemed incongruous representatives for the thousands of women I'd met on housing estates and in supermarkets throughout the canvass', many of whom were trapped by poverty, unemployment and early pregnancy.[28]

There is some evidence that women take their role as legislators more seriously than men do. *The Sunday Tribune*, taking amount of time speaking in the Chamber as a crude measure of this, has counted the number of minutes each Deputy has spoken, and reports that women, on average, spend more time speaking than men.[29]

Several of the women who entered the Dáil and Seanad in the 1970s and 1980s — such as Mary Robinson, Nuala Fennell, Monica Barnes and Gemma Hussey — had begun their careers in public life campaigning on women's issues and had significant success in bringing those issues onto the political agenda and introducing legislative change. The most celebrated was Mary Robinson who, as a lawyer, had taken cases to the Supreme Court and the European Court of Justice on equal treatment of women under the tax code and access to contraception. The women deputies and senators who made improving the lot of women central to their political work did not come to politics as relatives of male deputies or from a family tradition of involvement in a mainstream party. They became involved in parties in order to further the causes in which they believed. In some cases the parties sought them because of the high regard in which they were held for their campaigning work.

At the close of the second millennium, the United Nations[30] found that half of Ireland's citizens — its women — are worse off relative to men than in any other developed country, as well as less likely to be in positions of power in business or politics. Ireland has the second highest proportion of people living in poverty in the industrialised world and women are more likely to be poor than men. Ireland also has the highest level of functional illiteracy of seventeen industrialised states, and the second-highest level of long-term unemployment. Although remarkable growth rates over the past decade have made Ireland a comparatively wealthy country, this rapid growth has increased inequality. Irish society now faces a fundamental choice as to whether we wish to be a society like the US where affluence for a minority co-exists with poverty and degradation for a significant proportion of the population, or a social market economy which combines efficient markets with generous social provision. The role of women in decision-making is fundamental to the transformation of society and it is significant that the most advanced societies are those in which women have the greatest role in decision-making.

To ensure greater participation by women in decision-making a gender perspective must be introduced into all areas of policy-making. Experience has shown that guaranteeing legal rights and supporting small positive-action programmes were not of themselves sufficient mechanisms to achieve equality for men and women. Mainstreaming of a gender perspective in all policies and programmes was an important outcome from the UN Fourth World Conference on Women held in Beijing in 1995.

New opportunities are opening up for women as political parties aim to have more women stand for election. However, traditional electoral politics is in decline in Ireland as in most Western countries as people focus instead on single issues. Can women renew flagging politics? Women have been to the forefront in community development, attracted by the bottom-up approach facilitated by the European Union whose generous funding of this sector has by-passed representative politics. At this level, women have been empowered. Voluntary organisations have had input into policy in a power structure parallel to the traditional body politic, in the shape of Area Partnerships, LEADER programmes, cross-border networks. This sector is well established, but Government will have firmer control over it as European funding is set to diminish.

The profiles of women parliamentarians in this book show that such involvement is an ideal prerequisite for electoral politics. Yet women seem not to be translating this experience into a greater participation in national politics. Representation of women has reached a plateau, according to the most recent local and national election figures. International experience suggests that real changes in political culture can be achieved only when a certain critical mass is achieved. In the case of women's representation, that mass appears to be about 30 per cent. The new devolved parliaments in Scotland (with 38 per cent women members) and Wales (with 40 per cent) have passed that threshold by using twinning and quotas in selecting candidates. Increased representation for women was achieved by these policies.

The Irish incumbency research suggests that a short-term policy of imposing quotas for women candidates would, by generating more women incumbents and more experienced women challengers, counter the indirect negative effects for women candidates. Since there seems to be no specific prejudice by Irish voters against women candidates, the existence of a larger experienced pool of women politicians would obviate the need for quotas in the longer term.[31] In another possible scenario, men could desert parliamentary politics for more lucrative opportunities in the private sector, leaving opportunities for women.

Voices will be needed in the Oireachtas to bring forward challenging viewpoints. The women featured in this book have changed perceptions. They have made the idea of women leaders more real to everyone.

Notes
1. All Party Oireachtas Committee on the Constitution: second progress report: Seanad Éireann, Pn. 3835, Dublin: Stationery Office, 1997, p.7.
2. See Donnelly, Sean, *Elections '97*, Dublin: 1998.
3. Ibid.
4. Ibid.
5. Eurostat, *A Statistical Eye on Europe*, Luxembourg: Office for Official Publications of the European Communities, 1999.
6. Gallagher, Yvonne and Rick Wilford, 'Women's Political Representation in Ireland' in Galligan, Yvonne, Eilis Ward and Rick Wilford, *Contesting Politics: Women in Ireland, North and South*, Oxford: Westview, 1999.
7. Darcy, Robert, 'The Election of Women to Dáil Éireann: A Formal Analysis', *Irish Political Studies 3*, 1988.
8. Ibid.
9. Galligan, Yvonne, Michael Laver and Gemma Carney, 'The Effect of Candidate Gender on Voting in Ireland, 1997', *Irish Political Studies*, Volume 14, PSAI Press, 1999.
10. *The Irish Times*, 7 April, 1999.
11. O'Hegarty, P.S., *The Victory of Sinn Féin*, Dublin: Talbot Press, 1924.
12. Valiulis, Maryann Gialanella, 'Free Women in a Free Nation: Nationalist Feminist Expectations for Independence', in Farrell, Brian (ed), *The Creation of the Dáil*, Dublin: Blackwater/Radio Telefís Éireann, 1994.
13. Personal communication by Oireachtas contemporary, June 1999.
14. Clancy, Mary, 'Aspects of Women's Contribution to the Oireachtas Debates in the Irish Free State, 1922–1937' in Luddy, Maria and Cliona Murphy, *Women Surviving*, Swords, 1989.
15. Valiulis, op. cit.
16. Manning, Maurice, 'Women in National and Local Politics 1922–77' in MacCurtain, Margaret and Donncha Ó Corrain, (eds), *Women in Irish Society: The Historical Dimension*, Dublin: Arlen House, 1978.
17. See Clancy, Mary, 'Shaping the Nation: Women in the Free State Parliament, 1923–1937', in Galligan, Yvonne, Eilis Ward and Rick Wilford, *Contesting Politics: Women in Ireland, North and South*, Oxford: Westview, 1999.
18. *Seanad Reports*, vol.6, cols. 256–9, 17 December 1925.
19. *Dáil Éireann Official Report*, Vol. 13, col. 708, 29 March 1930.
20. *Seanad Reports*, vol. 20, col. 1248, 27 November 1935.
21 *Seanad Reports*, vol. 20, col. 1390, 11 December 1935.
22. Gallagher, Michael, 'By-elections to Dáil Éireann 1923–96: The Anomaly that Conforms', *Irish Political Studies*, Volume 11, 1996.
23. Ibid.
24. See *Report of the Expert Group on the Blood Transfusion Service Board*, Dublin: Stationery Office, 1995.
25. *Parliamentary Debates Official Report*, Volume 466, 12 June 1996, Hepatitis C Compensation Claims: Motion.
26. *The Irish Times*, 26 May 1997.
27. Ibid.
28. *The Irish Times*, 27 March 1987.
29. *Sunday Tribune*, 26 September, 1999, 21 June 1998.
30. United Nations, *Human Development Report*, 1998.
31. See Galligan, Yvonne, Michael Laver and Gemma Carney, op. cit.

Pathways to Power:
Women in the Oireachtas 1919–2000
Yvonne Galligan, Kathleen Knight and Úna Nic Giolla Choille
in association with Maedhbh McNamara and Senator Paschal Mooney

Introduction

When we discuss the representation of women in the Dáil and Seanad, it is useful to do so in a comparative context. In doing so, we can see a particular pattern in women's representation over time falling into three phases. The first period is a long one, generally dating from post-1945 until the 1970s and 1980s, when women account for less than 10 per cent of parliamentarians. This is followed by a growth in women's representation to 20 per cent or over within a decade. The third period is characterised by a women's parliamentary membership rising to one-third or more. Only the Nordic countries and the Netherlands have achieved this high level of women's representation in parliament to date. New Zealand and Australia are likely to break the one-third barrier in the coming decade. In the context of this three-stage pattern of development, Ireland is now in the second phase. With women's representation in the Dáil standing at 13 per cent in September 2000, the challenge is to win one-fifth or more parliamentary seats before 2010. Meeting this target is a complex task, and one that calls for a deep understanding of women's relationship with the political world. Our study of the parliamentary careers of women members of the Oireachtas is designed to throw light on this matter. In doing so, it will provide important information on women's views of political life, which can inform a strategy for the advancement of women in Irish politics.

In this survey, we ask women parliamentarians[1] how they view their participation in political life, what obstacles they have encountered and what sources of support have given them the confidence to follow a career in politics. We ask them to identify their policy interests, to reveal their ambitions for holding high office, and to suggest ways of helping women to enter and remain in political life.

The core of this study is a comprehensive postal survey of living Irish women parliamentarians.[2] The survey is supplemented by an examination of biographical data on all women parliamentarians, based on the information contained in the Directory part of this book. This discussion of the survey and biographies is organised into three sections. Part one constructs a profile of Irish women parliamentarians over time, drawing on the information in the biographical database. It considers this profile in the comparative context, looking in particular at political parties and the significance of coming from a political family. The next section examines the influences that encourage women to take the plunge into electoral politics, and identifies the factors women politicians have experienced as significant barriers to entry into politics. Again, the experiences of Irish women representatives are compared with those of women politicians in other countries. In the final section, we see how Irish women parliamentarians view their political careers — their achievements, opportunities and ambitions. We conclude our study by drawing attention to the need to increase significantly the number of women entering the Oireachtas if a modest 20 per cent representation of women is to be achieved, and also to the factors that need to be addressed to reach this target.

Women in the Oireachtas: How Many?

To begin our study of Irish women parliamentarians, let us first of all examine their numerical representation.[3] Figure 1 provides an overview of the number of women in the Oireachtas over nineteen general elections from 1938 until 1997. At no time between 1938 and 1973 did the number of women parliamentarians exceed ten. Indeed, it was only in 1964, after four by-elections had returned a woman in each case, that women's representation in the Oireachtas as a whole reached ten. The preceding general election in 1961 had seen only three women elected to the Dáil and three more take seats in the Seanad.

Figure 1: Women in Each Oireachtas, 1938–1997

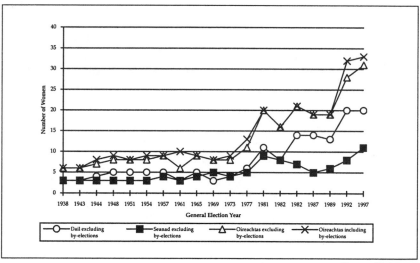

Source: Database

Notes:
1.   Presidents are included as well as Dáil and Seanad members.
2.   See also the general notes to the database tables.
3.   As regards the line 'Oireachtas including by-elections', each Oireachtas is attributed to the year in which it started, i.e., the year the underlying general election was held; for example, by-election victors who became members of the 1961–1965 Oireachtas are allocated to the year 1961.

The increase in the number of women members began in 1977. The general election of that year returned eleven women (5 per cent) to the Oireachtas (six to the Dáil and five to the Seanad), with two more elected in the course of the term (Table 1). This trend continued into the early 1980s, with twenty women (9 per cent) taking their seats in the Oireachtas in 1981, eleven of these in the Dáil. The number of women in the Oireachtas ranged from sixteen to twenty-one for the rest of that decade. A further significant numerical increase took place in 1997, with thirty-one women in total (14 per cent) taking seats in the Oireachtas. This increase was a result of the larger number of women returned to the Seanad on this occasion.

Table 1: Number of Women Members in Selected Oireachtais
1938–1997

Oireachtas Session Beginning	Dáil excl. BE	Seanad excl. BE	Oireachtas excl. BE	Oireachtas incl. BE	Total Oireachtas Members	% of Women Members excl. BE
1938	3	3	6	6	198	3.0
1943	3	3	6	6	198	3.0
1944	4	3	7	8	198	3.5
1948	5	3	8	9	207	3.9
1957	5	4	9	9	207	4.3
1961	3	3	6	10	204	2.9
1965	5	4	9	9	204	4.4
1969	3	5	8	8	204	3.8
1973	4	4	8	9	204	3.9
1977	6	5	11	13	208	5.3
1981	11	9	20	20	226	8.8
1982 (Feb)	8	8	16	16	226	7.1
1982 (Nov)	14	7	21	21	226	9.3
1987	14	5	19	19	226	8.4
1989	13	6	19	19	226	8.4
1992	20	8	28	32	226	12.4
1997	20	11	31	33	226	13.7

Source: Database of women members
compiled by the Policy Institute from directory entries.

Notes
1.   BE denotes by-elections.

See also general notes to database tables.[4]

Comparisons with Women in Other Legislatures

Comparative literature on women's representation in parliaments generally focuses on the lower or more directly elected house. In the Irish case this is the Dáil. Appendix 1 gives us a picture of women's representation in the Dáil and in a range of other lower houses of parliament in established democracies. Clearly, the pattern of women's representation in the Dáil is at a rate consistently lower than that of the Scandinavian countries, where today women hold between 36 and 42 per cent of parliamentary seats. It is also lower than that of women in English-speaking democracies such as New Zealand, Australia, Canada and the UK. In these countries, women hold between 18 and 29 per cent of seats in parliament. With women holding 13 per cent of the Dáil seats, Ireland's level of female parliamentary representation is similar to that of the USA. It is however, a better record than that of women legislators in Italy (11 per cent), France (11 per cent) and Greece (6 per cent). Taking women's parliamentary presence in global terms, women constitute 14 per cent of lower-house membership world-wide — a figure equivalent to that of women's representation in the Dáil.

Figure 2: Women in Lower Houses of Parliament in Selected Countries, 2000

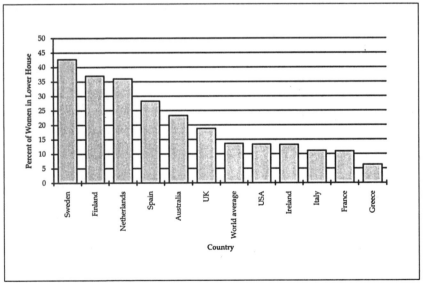

Source: Inter-Parliamentary Union, www.ipu.org/parline, extracted from database as of 28 April 2000.

Appendix 1 gives a more complete picture of women's legislative representation over time. It is clear that, in general, the participation of women in national assemblies has been growing since the 1970s, led by the Nordic countries. Ireland and the USA broke the 10 per cent threshold in the mid 1990s, ahead of the United Kingdom and France. The pattern of women's legislative representation in both countries, however, appears to be set to mirror the relatively gentle increase of the first stage. This is unlike countries such as Canada, Australia, Belgium and Spain, all of which fit into the pattern of a rapid increase in women's parliamentary presence once the 10 per cent threshold has been breached.

Women in the Oireachtas: A Profile

Although women do not have a substantial presence in the Oireachtas, there are more women in parliament today than at any other time in our history. Let us now look at what kind of woman obtains a seat in the Oireachtas today and compare her profile with that of previous women members. We do this by looking at characteristics such as age, marital status, family size, education, connections with politics and party affiliation.

Age

In Table 2 we can clearly see the changing age structure of women politicians on their entry to the Oireachtas. With the exception of the 1950s, the majority of women entering parliament for the first time were between 30 and 49 years of age. In the 1980s and 1990s, 70 per cent or so of women parliamentarians were in this age category, compared to about half of women taking their seats for the first time in the 1960s and 1970s. The proportion of women in the older age groups on first entry to the Oireachtas has declined — the last person aged 60 or more was elected in the 1950s. This was Nora Connolly O'Brien, daughter of James Connolly, who was nominated to the Seanad by Éamon de Valera in 1957 when she was 64 years of age.

Table 2: Ages of Female Members at First Entry to the Oireachtas, by Decade of Entry, 1919 to 1999

Decade	First-Entry Women in Decade	Age Category at First Entry					
		20–29	30–39	40–49	50–59	60–79	% aged 30–49
1919–1929	14	0	2	5	3	4	50
1930–1939	7	1	2	4	0	0	85
1940–1949	3	1	2	0	0	0	66
1950–1959	7	2	0	3	1	1	43
1960–1969	7	1	3	1	2	0	57
1970–1979	11	4	1	5	1	0	55
1980–1989	27	5	9	10	3	0	70
1990–1999	28	4	9	11	4	0	71
Total	104	18	28	39	14	5	64

Source: Database of women members
compiled by the Policy Institute from directory entries.

The 1970s was the decade of young women politicians — 36 per cent of those on first entry to parliament were under 30 years of age; by the 1990s they constituted just 14 per cent of new female legislators. Both older and younger women now comprise a smaller proportion of new women parliamentarians than four decades ago. Newly arrived women politicians today are concentrated in their thirties and forties at first entry, in contrast to the position at the foundation of the State when there was a small group of women diversified over the entire age range.[5]

Marital Status

Two separate and strong trends can be observed in recent decades with regard to marital status on first entry to parliament (Table 3). The first trend is for the proportion of married women to increase from 28 per cent in the 1950s to 46 per cent in the 1970s and to over 80 per cent in the 1980s and 1990s. This is not surprising, given the middle-aged profile of women first entering the Oireachtas in recent decades. The second striking feature is the absence of widows entering parliament: widows have not been elected in over twenty years, signalling a clear decline in the customary seat transmission from deceased husband to wife. The last widow to be elected to the Dáil was Eileen Lemass. She was elected to the new constituency of Dublin Ballyfermot in 1977, having failed to hold her late husband's seat in the Dublin South West by-election in 1976.[6] Thus, women taking their seats for the first time in the Oireachtas today are most likely to be married, although single women also continue to be elected.

Table 3: **Marital Status of Female Members at First Entry to the Oireachtas,
by Decade of Entry,
1919 to 1999**

Decade	First-Entry Women in Decade	Family Status		
		Married	Single	Widowed
1919–1929	14	6	4	4
1930–1939	7	2	2	3
1940–1949	3	1	0	2
1950–1959	7	2	3	2
1960–1969	7	3	1	3
1970–1979	11	5	4	2
1980–1989	27	23	4	0
1990–1999	28	23	5	0
Total	104	65	24	15

Source: Database of women members
compiled by the Policy Institute from directory entries.
Notes:
1.   Family Status categories used were married, single or widowed at first entry.

Family Size

Given the universal decline in family size in the past thirty years, we would expect this trend to be reflected in the number of children born to women politicians. While 43 per cent of women elected in the 1950s had families of four or more children, only 14 per cent of women first elected in the 1960s and 1990s had families of this size (Table 4). Although 26 per cent of new women parliamentarians in the 1980s had families of four or more children, the trend towards smaller families among female politicians is in line with the general pattern of smaller family size in Ireland.

Table 4: Number of Children per Female Member,
by Decade of Entry,
1919 to 1999

Decade	First-Entry Women in Decade	No Children		1–3 Children		4 or More Children	
		%	number	%	number	%	number
1919–1929	14	(57)	8	(21)	3	(21)	3
1930–1939	7	(71)	5	(0)	0	(29)	2
1940–1949	3	(67)	2	(0)	0	(33)	1
1950–1959	7	(43)	3	(14)	1	(43)	3
1960–1969	7	(43)	3	(43)	3	(14)	1
1970–1979	11	(36)	4	(46)	5	(18)	2
1980–1989	27	(18)	5	(56)	15	(26)	7
1990–1999	28	(29)	8	(57)	16	(14)	4
Total	104		40		42		22

Source: Database of women members
compiled by the Policy Institute from directory entries.

Notes
1.   With time, those entering in the 1990s without children may be expected to have children in accordance with the general demographic trend over recent years of increased average age of females at birth of first child. The four females who entered in the 1990s at the age of twenty-nine or less were in 1999 still under the age of thirty-three.

2.   Percentages had in some cases to be rounded up or down to sum to 100 per cent, owing to the small number of entries in each category.

A second interesting trend over time is the proportion of new women parliamentarians who have no children. Again, this is decreasing from a high of 67 per cent of new female entrants with no children in the 1940s to a low of 18 per cent in the 1980s. In the 1990s, just under 30 per cent of new women members were childless. This is partly explained by the fact that five of the nine new women parliamentarians were unmarried at the time of their election. It is possible that some of these women will become mothers in time while continuing to have a parliamentary career. Of the new parliamentarians in the 1990s who were mothers, Mary Kelly, with six daughters, had the largest family, while Joan Burton had one daughter at time of entry. The record for the female parliamentarian with the largest family goes to Margaret Collins-O'Driscoll (eldest sister of Michael Collins), who had fourteen children on her election in 1923.

Education

A third dimension to this picture of women Oireachtas members over time is the increase in their level of educational attainment (Table 5). This has increased steadily over the century. In the early years of the State there was quite a gap in formal educational qualifications among political women. Some women parliamentarians had not gone further than primary school, while half of the women elected in the first decade of the new state were educated to third level and

Table 5: Highest Level of Education Completed by Female Oireachtas Members,
by Decade of Entry,
1919 to 1999

Decade	First-Entry Women in Decade	Highest Education Level Completed[1]					
		Primary	Secondary	Third Level	Post-Third Level[1]	Third Level or greater[2]	NA[1]
1919–1929	14	1	2	6	1	7	4
1930–1939	7	1	4	1	1	2	0
1940–1949	3	0	1	2	0	2	0
1950–1959	7	0	2	4	0	4	1
1960–1969	7	0	3	3	1	4	0
1970–1979	11	0	1	8	2	10	0
1980–1989	27	0	7	14	6	20	0
1990–1999	28	0	3	18	7	25	0

Source: Database of women members
compiled by the Policy Institute from directory entries.

Notes:
1.   The categories used were Primary, Secondary, Third Level, Post-Third Level (for a second qualification obtained in a third-level institution) and 'NA'. For the latter cases, there was insufficient information in the directory to enter any education level in the database.
2.   This refers to the percentage of total female first entrants in any decade with education greater than third level, e.g., the sum of columns third level and post-third level expressed as a percentage of the total first-entry women in the decade.

further. By the 1940s, however, all women members had completed second-level education. Apart from the 1930s, the educational standard of women entering parliament for the first time remained consistently high. Once again, the 1970s stand out, with over 90 per cent of new women members being educated to third level or higher. This is closely matched by the newcomers of the 1990s, with 89 per cent of this group being educated to degree and post-graduate level.

Inherited Seats and Political Families

Family connections to politics have been found to play an important part in women's electoral opportunities. What is not often appreciated, however, is the changing nature of this family relationship. Our survey clearly shows a shift from the widow's inheritance to daughters taking the place of fathers in parliament (Table 6). In the period 1922–1977, twelve widows were elected to seats previously held by their husbands. Daughters begin to inherit the political mantle from the 1970s, with ten becoming members of the Oireachtas between 1973 and 1997. There were no widows elected or appointed to Oireachtas membership after the 1970s. As will be discussed below, the daughter-successor is now the most common form of seat inheritance among women (see also footnote regarding the rarer phenomenon of brother–sister seat transmission).

Table 6: Immediate Political Family Connections of Female Oireachtas Members, by Decade of Entry, 1919 to 1999

Decade	First-Entry Women in Decade	Family Connection with Immediate Predecessor Member[1,3]		
		Widows	Daughters	Not Immediate Successors
1919–1929[2]	14	—	—	14
1930–1939	7	3	0	4
1940–1949	3	2	0	1
1950–1959	7	2	0	5
1960–1969	7	3	0	4
1970–1979	11	2	2	7
1980–1989	27	0	3	24
1990–1999	28	0	5	23
Total	104	12	10	82

Source: Database of women members
compiled by the Policy Institute from directory entries.

Notes
1.   The definition of an immediate family connection with predecessor member is of a female member who succeeded a family member in the next succeeding general or by-election, in either house. This excludes any female members who did not 'succeed' exactly under these terms. Examples of these cases would include women who had a family connection with a member of a previous Dáil or Seanad which was not the immediately preceding one, or who had a family background in politics, or who succeeded a family member but with a gap of more than one election or who had a family member currently or

subsequently sitting in either house when they were elected for the first time. Further detail on these wider connections may be found in Appendix 3.

2.   In the 1920s, there were technically no female successors since there was no immediately preceding Irish Parliament. For the record, the family and political backgrounds of these first female members was as follows: sisters of those active in politics (2); widows of those active in politics (3); mothers of those active in politics (1); daughters of those active in politics (1); and those with no family connections in politics (7).

3.   In October 1999, Mary Upton's election was an additional instance of immediate succession to a family member (Pat Upton), the connection being sister–brother in this case.

Party Affiliation

The final element in this profile of Irish women parliamentarians is that of party affiliation (Table 7). There are three interesting trends to observe with respect to the party attachment of new women parliamentarians. The first, and most consistent trend, is the dominance of Fianna Fáil and Fine Gael in obtaining seats for women in parliament. Indeed, the entire complement of new women entrants in the 1930s came from these parties. Although the dominance of the two larger parties was challenged by Labour in the 1950s and 1960s, the pattern reverted to type in the 1970s, when ten of the eleven new women entrants came from either Fianna Fáil or Fine Gael. In the 1990s, smaller parties

Table 7: Political Party Affiliation of Female Oireachtas Members,
by Decade of Entry, 1919–1999

Decade	First-Entry Women in Decade	Party[1]					
		FF/SF	FG/CG	Labour	PDs	DL	Other[2]
1919–1929	14	8	4	0	0	0	2
1930–1939	7	5	2	0	0	0	0
1940–1949	3	2	0	1	0	0	0
1950–1959	7	3	1	2	0	0	1
1960–1969	7	3	1	2	0	0	1
1970–1979	11	7	3	0	0	0	1
1980–1989	27	7	13	1	4	0	2
1990–1999	28	8	5	9	2	2	2
Total	104	43	29	15	6	2	9

Source: Database of women members
compiled by the Policy Institute from directory entries.

Notes
1.   The political party categories listed in the table refer to the political party affiliation of female members as at first entry, rather than the political party of which they are now members, or the party of which they have been members for the majority of their careers. Some members have changed their affiliations during their political careers. The FF/SF category includes Sinn Féin members in the 1920s and 1930s, while the FG/CG category includes Cumann na nGaedheal members in the 1920s and 1930s. Labour and Democratic Left members have been allocated separately depending on the party affiliation as at date of election; any members elected to the merged Labour party (the two parties merged in December 1998) have been allocated to that party.

2.   The other category covers small parties and independents.

began to promote women for office, and for the first time in the history of the state, less than one half (46 per cent) of new women legislators came from Fianna Fáil and Fine Gael. Labour accounted for 32 per cent of new women parliamentarians in the 1990s, with the Progressive Democrats and Democratic Left combined bringing in another 14 per cent of the new women to the Oireachtas. While it is not clear whether this trend will continue, it does highlight the fragmentation of the party system that occurred in the 1990s and the scope for smaller parties to bring new women into the legislature.

The Importance of Recruitment

As Duerst-Lahti (1998) points out in the case of the United States, efforts to increase the proportion of women in legislatures are critically dependent upon both increasing the number of new entrants and retaining women incumbents. In Ireland, women's representation has seen rapid increases in the past twenty years, driven by significant numbers of women entering parliament for the first time, particularly in the 1980s. Figure 3 compares the number of women in any Oireachtas with the number of first entrants in that Oireachtas for every year since 1969 (the underlying data are contained in Appendix 3). The three major leaps in women's representation, in 1977 (from nine to thirteen), in 1981–82 (the three elections taken as one saw a further increase to 26), and in 1992 (to 32), were all accompanied by significant increases in the number of first entrants (9 in 1977, 16 in 1981, and 17 in 1992). In any Oireachtas where women's representation

Figure 3: Women in Selected Oireachtais, 1969–1997

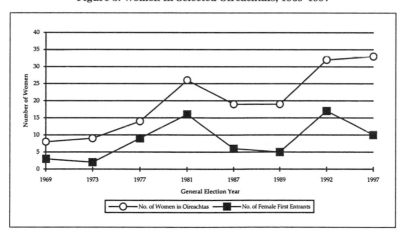

Source: Database of women members compiled by the Policy Institute from directory entries.

1. Presidents are included as well as Dáil and Seanad members.
2. See also the general notes to the database tables.
3. For the purposes of this figure, the three elections in June 1981, February 1982 and November 1982 are treated as one. See table in Appendix 3 for the data underlying this table.

remained static, or declined — say, in 1989 or in 1997 — the number of first entrants was static or lower than the number entering the previous Oireachtas.

It stands to reason that efforts to increase the overall representation of women — for example, to return a target of 20 per cent women in the elections in the first decade of this millennium — will require a dramatic increase in the number of first entrants. There is also good reason to suspect that retirements of women politicians will be greater in the coming decades given the later age at first entry of female parliamentarians in the 1980s and 1990s. Three of the current crop of thirty-three female members are over sixty, while another eight are over fifty. If, for example, all female members over fifty-five (eight members as of September 1999) were to retire at the next election, then, excluding the possibility of seat losses by current female members and retirements for other reasons apart from age, at least twenty female first entrants would be required to bring the Oireachtas proportion up to 20 per cent.[7] Twenty new entrants would require a doubling of the number of first entrants over the 1997 election. This need for new female entrants to the Oireachtas poses a significant challenge to political parties to recruit and select sufficient numbers of women, and then ensure that they are elected. Achieving this target will require a sophisticated understanding of how and why women become involved in politics. It will also quite probably require targeted initiatives designed to encourage women's involvement in politics and to assist in overcoming the obstacles they face. Motivation, support and barriers to participation are issues we address in the next section.

Factors Influencing Oireachtas Entry

Our biographical database has allowed us to construct a profile of Irish women parliamentarians. The woman TD or Senator today is likely to be between 30 and 39 years of age on first taking her seat. She is also likely to be married, be a mother of between 1 and 3 children, have a third-level education and belong to either Fianna Fáil or Fine Gael. She is also likely to hold her seat without the advantage of prior family connections to the Oireachtas, but if she comes from a political family, she is most likely the daughter of a male former parliamentarian.

Now that we have a broad picture of women's participation in the Oireachtas, we will try to see what motivates Irish women to enter parliament, what are their sources of support and what obstacles they encounter in pursuing their political careers. This information is gleaned from our in-depth questionnaire administered to women members of the Oireachtas, retired and current. It is linked once again with the wider literature on women's political participation.

Influences

When asked to rate the importance of a variety of influences on their entry to parliament, the importance of party stands out. Whether it was through being active in a political party or through being invited by a party to stand for election, it is clear that three out of every five women politicians (60 per cent) received encouragement from the parties (Table 8). Over one-third (36 per cent) of the surveyed members gave party activism the highest rating as a motivating force in their entry to the Oireachtas. An additional quarter (24 per cent) gave the specific invitation of a party the highest rating. The two party-related influences were not particularly overlapping. Party activists were not always 'invited' to stand, while women receiving party overtures were not necessarily party activists at the time of receiving the invitation. These different routes of recruitment provide an important insight into the role of the political parties as channels to parliamentary life. On the one hand, parties provide socialisation experience for women interested in politics. On the other, since it is generally perceived that women are less likely to think of themselves as potential candidates, party invitations provide a very specific motivation for entering the political fray. One way or another, this finding emphasises the vital role of political parties in assisting and encouraging women in their parliamentary ambitions. This is not a phenomenon unique to Ireland. In a recent wide-ranging study of women politicians, Interparliamentary Union found that political parties provided the channel for over three-quarters (78 per cent) of women politicians to enter parliamentary life (IPU 2000: 83–4).

Table 8: Most Important Influences Motivating Women's Entry to the Oireachtas

Factor (1)	Mean of Ratings	Nos. Giving 5 Rating	% Giving 5 Rating
Party Activism	2.6	22	36
Women's Issue Activism	2.3	18	29
Family Background	2.2	19	31
Invitation from Party	2.0	19	31
Community Activism	2.0	9	15
Political Issue	1.6	10	16
Retention of Family Seat	1.0	11	18

Source: Replies to question 13 of the Survey. N=61.

Notes
1.   On this question, respondents were given a scale of zero to 5 for a list of influences. A zero response indicated that the factor had no influence; a 5 rating indicated that the factor was very influential. Respondents could identify as many of the factors as applied and could identify other influences beyond those listed. Further detail is given in Appendix 3.
2.   Of total respondents, 36 per cent identified party activism as a motivating factor while 31 per cent identified invitation from party; however, 7 per cent of those who gave the second factor had also identified the first. This gives a net figure of 60 per cent (36 per cent plus 24 per cent) of all respondents who had identified either one or other or both of these party-related motivating factors.

Other influences identified as motivating women to stand for election were seen to be almost as important as party. Having a family background in politics also highlights a crucial site of socialisation to politics. In political families, electoral ambitions are more likely to be seen as an acceptable activity for women as well as for men. This is not necessarily the same as retaining a family political seat, a factor identified by only 18 per cent of our respondents as being important. In both cases, party affiliation is acquired in tandem with the motivation to seek a seat. What these factors tell us is that the influence of a political family background is something that can be transmitted from one generation to another. Political seats, on the other hand, are not always transferable between generations and, as we have seen (Table 6), today there are proportionally fewer women in political life through a family seat inheritance than there were three decades or more ago.

The final influences of importance identified by our survey are activism in women's issues, activism in the community, and interest in a specific political issue. Rather like the political family legacy discussed above, an involvement in campaigning for women's rights or other community political issues brings certain women into politics through socialising them into the ways of the political world. Involvement with women's groups was identified as an important route to parliament for 29 per cent of our survey members, community activism and issue involvement were identified as important by a further 15 per cent each. These factors point to an alternative route to socialisation to electoral politics — a route not necessarily brokered by the parties. Thus, two general distinct channels of entry into politics have emerged from our analysis — one which is dominated by party politics including political family background; and a second 'grassroots' path which ultimately must be linked with party activity for electoral success. One or more of these influences was foremost in bringing the majority of parliamentarians we surveyed into politics and into the Oireachtas.

Sources of Support for a Political Career

If party involvement, family background and political activism are the main socialising influences pushing women towards the Oireachtas, they receive support for this activity from a number of sources. In broad terms, sources of support can be divided into two categories — personal and political. In the personal category, husbands were a very important source of support for over half (52 per cent) of our parliamentarians, followed by friends (38 per cent), mothers (32 per cent) and children (26 per cent). The importance of these personal sources of support may be a reflection of the difficulties many women face with family responsibilities. It is possible that the willingness of a husband to take on additional responsibilities at home, the availability of near friends or a mother who can step in if needed, or children who have learned to accept their mothers' preoccupation with a demanding career (and even assist her with it on occasions) may be crucial to a woman's ability to devote herself to politics.

Outside the circle of family and friends, the political party (34 per cent) was given the highest average rating as a source of support. This is consistent with our previous findings on the importance of the party in influencing women to run. Women's groups (21 per cent) and community groups (11 per cent) were the other major sources of support identified in the survey. Interestingly, only one respondent identified business associates as a major source of support. This points to an important difference in the political backgrounds of current male and female politicians more generally, since men have traditionally been able to translate a network of business contacts into political support (Conway et al., 1997).

Table 9: Most Important Sources of Support
for Women's Political Careers

Source of Support	Mean of Ratings	Nos. Selecting 5 Rating	% Selecting 5 Rating
Personal			
Husband	3.1	32	52
Friends	2.9	23	38
Mother	2.3	20	32
Children	1.9	16	26
Political			
Party	3.0	21	34
Women's Groups	1.8	13	21
Community Groups	1.3	7	11
Business Associates	1.5	1	2
Religious Group	0.5	1	2

Source: Replies to question 14 of the Survey. N=61.

Notes
On this question, respondents were given a scale of zero to 5 for a list of possible sources of support. A zero response indicated that the source of support was not at all important; a 5 rating indicated that the source of support was very important. Respondents could identify as many of the factors as applied and could identify other sources of support beyond those listed. Further detail is given in Appendix 3.

Barriers to a Political Career

We also asked our respondents to rate their perceptions of sources of difficulty for women in general as they consider becoming members of the Oireachtas. Once again, the personal takes precedence over the political. Over two-thirds (67 per cent) of those surveyed rated family-care responsibilities as the most important source of difficulty (Table 10). Somewhat surprisingly, a third of our parliamentarians rated husbands as a most important source of difficulty for women in general. Apparently, while the majority of women in the survey had the benefit of supportive husbands themselves, they also realised that the lack of a supportive spouse would make it difficult for a woman to have a political career. Other personal sources of difficulty included educational constraints, peer pressure and a traditional family upbringing, but these were modest in comparison with the perceived problems of balancing the demands of family life with a political career. These demands were exacerbated when the politician was based outside Dublin. In the view of one respondent:

> *Politics is difficult for women — particularly rural women — living away from family; family responsibilities are also a burden.*

(DIRECT QUOTE FROM SURVEY)[8]

Another observed that:

> *Often the most difficult obstacle to overcome in entering political life is the 'personal choice' involved in potentially compromising family security and stability. Women tend not to make space for themselves — riddled with guilt about neglected families.*

A third gave a graphic description of the reality of balancing family and political responsibilities:

> *The biggest issue for women politicians arises if she has young children. I have two [school-going] children.... This week, on Tuesday morning, as I was about to leave for Dublin, my housekeeper took ill. Because it was not school time, I brought them with me and left them in my sister's house in Dublin. The Seanad sat until 10.15 on Tuesday evening and until 9.30 on Wednesday night. My husband's job is equally demanding, he too was away on Tuesday night. The added pressure is enormous.*

Turning to the political barriers to women's involvement in parliamentary life, lack of funding received the highest rating as a difficulty for women in general, and was rated as most important by nearly half (49 per cent) of our respondents. The second major source of difficulty, that of party politicians' attitudes (20 per cent), is a complex issue. It could be construed as a reaction by an established group anxious to protect their position, for it is the case that every seat taken by a women in parliament is one less opportunity for a man. It could also reflect the perception of conservative views on gender roles in political life. On the whole, negative attitudes by party politicians to women's political participation are likely to consist of a mix of these two factors. One respondent described how women politicians have to struggle against male reluctance to accept their authority:

One of the constant problems encountered by women who are elected is that even with experienced women there are still male colleagues who don't accept a suggestion or proposal from a woman member until a man has actually suggested it and the idea becomes the property of 'the man' who robbed the woman's suggestion.

The other major sources of difficulty — general discrimination against women and voters' attitudes — appear to be embedded in traditional perceptions of gender roles in political life. This is illustrated by the experience of one politician who wrote:

When I was first elected, a journalist reported my election as 'an obscure young suburban housewife has had a surprise victory'. I don't think I ever heard a new male candidate being referred to as an obscure young (or not so young) estate agent or teacher.'

Are these findings on the influences, supports and obstacles encountered by Irish women parliamentarians similar to those experienced by women legislators in other countries? In general, the answer is yes. There is now an extensive appreciation of the central role played by parties in helping or hindering

Table 10: Most Important Sources of Difficulty Experienced
in Achieving Political Office

Source of Difficulty	Mean of Ratings	Nos. Selecting 5 Rating	% Selecting 5 Rating
Personal			
Family Care Responsibilities	4.3	41	67
Husband	3.2	20	33
Educational Constraints	1.3	2	3
Peer Pressure	0.8	3	5
Family Upbringing	0.3	1	2
Political			
Lack of Funding	3.9	30	49
Party Politicians' Attitudes	2.2	12	20
Discrimination against Women	1.4	6	10
Voters' Attitudes	1.3	6	10
Media Portrayal of Women	1.1	1	2

Source: Replies to question 16 of the Survey. N=61.

Notes
On this question, respondents were given a scale of zero to 5 for a list of possible difficulties perceived by them as experienced by women in general in politics. A zero response indicated that the difficulty was not an obstacle at all; a 5 rating indicated that the difficulty was a great obstacle. Respondents could identify as many of the factors as applied and could identify other difficulties beyond those listed. Further detail is given in Appendix 3.

women's electoral opportunities. Specific aspects of party behaviour and ideology have been found to impact on women's chances of selection for parliament. These consist of three main factors: party ideology, the attitude of party leaders to women in politics and party selection processes. In addition, other factors, such as the nature of the electoral system, social attitudes towards women in power, the consistent presence of women in parliament over time, and constituency size interact with party to shape an environment that is accepting, or otherwise, of women in political life.

Recent national and international studies identify these issues as important. A study of women seeking election to state-level parliaments in the United States finds that women are less successful in constituencies where voters have traditional attitudes towards women's roles in society, and are more successful in constituencies with high seat-turnovers and multi-member constituencies (Carey et al., 1998: 107–116). In an international study, Caul (1999: 79–98) examines sixty-eight parties in twelve advanced industrial democracies and finds that women are more successful in getting elected to parliament when they belong to left-wing parties (in particular, new left parties), when there is a solid number of women serving at national executive level in parties, when the rules of selection are clearly stated and complied with, and when gender targets or quotas are in operation.

This comparative research reflects the findings of Galligan and Wilford (1999) for Ireland, who conclude that parties with secular and progressive outlooks are more likely to encourage women into political careers than parties of the centre or right. They also find a clear distinction between old and new parties, with the latter more aware of the need to include women as legislators. In a world-wide study of women's representation in parliament, Reynolds (1999: 547–72) concurs with these findings, pointing out the importance of parties sympathetic to the promotion of gender balance in parliament, the presence of women in political life over time, and a culture that is not overly hostile to women holding power. All studies also stress the importance of the electoral system being reasonably fair to women. The Irish electoral system has been found not to discriminate unduly against women (Galligan, Laver and Carney, 1999). Compared with other electoral systems, the Irish system has been found to be somewhere in between the list proportional system, which can be designed to favour women, and the plurality system of the UK, which actively militates against the election of women candidates (Reynolds, 1999: 556–7).

Explaining women's under-representation in politics in Northern Ireland, research by Miller, Wilford and Donoghue (1996) suggests that there are three important issues to consider. First, women do not seek political office of their own accord and often need to be invited to do so. Second, women's family responsibilities need to be taken into account in considering a career in politics.

Third, political parties do not readily provide women with the opportunity to enter politics. These findings neatly reflect the perceptions of women parliamentarians in our survey, where party invitation to stand for election was a significant influence in a number of cases, and where family obligations were seen as constituting a major difficulty for women wishing to become legislators. In the Republic, Randall and Smyth (1987: 200–201) identified family commitments and lack of personal finance as important constraints on women's political ambitions — issues also raised by the women politicians we surveyed.

In sum, then, the obstacles experienced by Irish women in entering politics are similar to those experienced by women in other countries. While these findings are cold comfort, identifying these obstacles opens up the possibility of removing the barriers through specific actions. Although the family and funding barriers are rooted in deep cultural attitudes towards women's role in society, there is room to introduce measures that would counter them, at least to some extent. Parties in particular can play an important role in this regard through the introduction of family-friendly practices and financial mechanisms for women who wish to become politicians. Quotas and targets, though controversial, are proven ways of increasing the presence of under-represented groups in parliament, though their effect can best be seen over time. In addition, clear and transparent selection rules and procedures and a commitment to representative democracy by parties, combined with the above conditions, offer women the prospect of equal political opportunities with men.

Experiences of Political Life

Once women enter parliament, the next interesting question to explore is their attitudes towards their political role. Do they give primary importance to their legislative tasks or do constituency duties figure more prominently in their understanding of parliamentary representation? Will women from an earlier generation of parliamentarians have a different view of their political activity from women elected in more recent times? We sought to explore these issues in a number of ways, examining their personal identification of their most significant achievements as politicians, then evaluating their policy interests and finally analysing their political ambitions.

Most Significant Achievement

The literature on parliamentary politics in Ireland raises the question as to whether national politicians see their role as legislators or as constituency servers. In a famous phrase, Chubb (1963) described the activities of elected representatives as being one of 'persecuting civil servants', suggesting that the majority of TDs spent most of their time on constituency business. Gallagher and Komito (1999: 206–231) point to the extensive constituency case-load borne by Irish parliamentarians, but point out that this level of brokerage is not unique to Ireland and that it is an integral part of the job of being a public representative. When one examines the extent to which women engage in constituency work, it is clear that this form of public work is as important for political women as it is for political men. However, what is also clear is that older generations of women politicians were more likely to lay a heavier emphasis on serving constituency needs than present-day women (Dolan and Ford 1998: 75).

Irish women parliamentarians are open to the same constituency demands as their male counterparts. However, when asked to identify their most significant Oireachtas achievement, only three (5 per cent) mentioned constituency-related activities (Table 11). This is not to say that constituency work is irrelevant to women TDs. Far from it. One woman parliamentarian graphically described the demands of constituency life in the following terms:

In the fifties a TD in rural Ireland had to be affable, approachable, always available, have an open house at all times (day and night), know all his or her constituents (preferably by first name), attend every funeral in the constituency (they were great supporters you were told), answer every letter and deliver the goods (get results). Most of the letters were in connection with applications for jobs, grants, pensions, sheep-dipping tanks, special allowances, road improvements, and so on. Many of these people were entitled to what they were seeking but believed that only a letter from a TD would do the job. If you had enough clout to acquire them something to which they were not entitled you were assured of success in the next election. People were desperately poor and deprived.

(see footnote 8)

Four decades later, the need for a parliamentarian to be available to constituents was as strong as ever:

Once you get elected you instantly become public property. You are on call 24 hours a day, 365 days a year…. As a TD you become responsible for whatever it is that any one of your 100,000 constituents wants you to be responsible for. They will raise these issues with you when you are out shopping, relaxing in the pub on Sunday night or at any other time they happen to run into you. Alternatively they might decide to, and indeed often do, call to your home to discuss their problems….

(MÁIRE GEOGHEGAN-QUINN, QUOTED IN GALLAGHER AND KOMITO, 1999: 207)

However, the routine nature of constituency tasks does not lend itself to an evaluation of political achievement. Single legislative initiatives or promotion to higher office (for example, becoming a cabinet minister) are more tangible ways of reckoning political success. For this reason, twenty-four members (56 per cent) identified specific policy and legislative initiatives as their most significant contribution to Irish political life. An additional nine respondents (20 per cent) measured their achievement in terms of career progression, moving from being a backbencher to being committee chairperson, to ministerial office or to other weighty political positions.

Table 11: Oireachtas Achievements

Oireachtas Achievement Category	Percentage of Responses	No. of Responses	Detail on Type of Achievement Classified under this Category
Legislative	36	17	Piloting a bill (whole or part of) amending it or voting against a provision
Policy Initiative	20	8	Drafting/suggesting/implementing a specific policy scheme, new policy orientation or report
Career	20	7	Achieving political office such as Minister, Minister of State, Chair of an Oireachtas Committee, Seanad Cathaoirleach etc.
Constituency-related	5	2	Being elected, doing constituency work
Vague/Unspecific	18	10	Typical responses involved raising awareness on women or work done on furthering a general issue
Total	100	44	

Source: Replies to question 12 of the Survey. N=61; non-respondents were 17.

Notes
The question was an open-ended one as follows: 'For which Oireachtas achievement would you most like to be remembered?' The classification scheme for responses given to this question was drawn up by the Policy Institute.

The personal satisfaction of being a legislator was captured by one respondent who remarked:

I was on duty non-stop in the Seanad for two consecutive days and nights doing legislative work for which I will probably never get any recognition or credit, but which I enjoy and consider I am good at — and it's my job.

Other members pointed to the constraints on being a legislator, such as the demands of party discipline:

I personally found the whip system very difficult. You became a cog in a parliamentary wheel. Too often the expedient became party point-scoring, or the populist issue rather than social need, public good or moral imperative.

The lack of time for considered reflection on policy matters was also raised:

Membership of the Dáil gave me greater insight into the working of govern-
ment and politics. The biggest disappointment I found was that politicians
rarely do any long-term strategic planning on policy and other issues. They
are always compelled by the numbers of calls on their time to think short-term,
[to take] fire-brigade action to deal with the immediate crisis.

In sum, women members of the Oireachtas, and female TDs in particular, are attentive to the dual role of being an elected representative. On the one hand, they are mindful of their constituency duties and believe that brokerage plays an important part in being re-elected. On the other hand, they are conscious of their role as legislators. Exactly what their legislative interests are is explored in the next section.

Policy Interests

The literature on women's parliamentary representation points to three trends. The first, and possibly the most significant, is that women and men politicians do not hold significantly different policy priorities overall. Women and men in Canadian politics, for instance, share common policy concerns, with the economy and finance being given priority by both groups, followed by social policy (Tremblay, 1998: 449–50). Legislative studies of the US Congress also emphasise the lack of significant evidence pointing to women having priorities different from those of men (Dolan and Ford, 1998). Nonetheless, when the policy interests of male and female parliamentarians are analysed more closely, there is a small and clear difference in the importance female and male parliamentarians attach to specific issues. Repeated studies in the US and elsewhere have shown that while women and men see the economy as a major policy interest, more men than women emphasise the importance of economic issues. In the same way, while both women and men parliamentarians see social policy as another major area of policy interest, more women than men identify it as a significant concern.

The second finding from the literature is that women's issues are not a major policy interest for either women or men. This is found to be the case in Canada (Tremblay, 1998) and in Britain (Norris, 1996). However, while it is of minor policy interest in the overall context of parliamentary concerns, policy matters relating to women are much more likely to be of importance to women legislators than to their male colleagues (Thomas, 1999: 128–48). Furthermore, the majority of women legislators are in favour of allocating a higher priority to women's issues, while men are found to be more selective in their prioritising of women's issues — giving them a high priority on some occasions, a low one at other times (Tremblay, 1998; Barry, 1991).

A third trend evident in research on gender differences in politics shows women taking more parliamentary initiatives than men on women's issues. Drawing together a range of studies on gender and parliamentary activity, Dolan and Forde (1998) conclude that women spend more time than men promoting women's rights legislation, and are more likely than men to list women's distinctive concerns as their top legislative priorities. Additional research in the USA and Africa confirms these findings (Goetz, 1998; Swers, 1998; Norton, 1999). In the case of Canada, Tremblay (1998: 463) finds that 'while women's issues represent a relatively minor field of interest for both women and men in Canada's House of Commons, they occupy a clearer place in the political universe of a larger proportion of female MPs ... female MPs in Canada integrate women's issues in their mandate of political representation in a more overt manner than their male colleagues'.

Table 12: Major Policy Interests Identified by Survey Respondents

Subject Selected[1]	Number Indicating this Subject as Choice 1, 2 or 3	Rank	Per Cent of Cases Indicating this Subject as Choice 1, 2 or 3
Environment/Local Government	23	(1)	44%
Education	21	(2)	40%
Health	16	(3)	31%
Social, Family and Children's Affairs	13	(4)	25%
Equality	10	(5)	19%
Law, Crime and Justice	10	(5)	19%
Sectoral economic (2)	9	(7)	17%
Women	7	(8)	13%
Social Inclusion	6	(9)	12%
Cross-Border/ N Ireland	5	(10)	10%
Economics	5	(10)	10%
Arts	4	(12)	8%
Foreign Affairs	4	(12)	8%
Regional and Local Development	3	(14)	6%
Other	12	NA	NA
Total	**148**	**NA**	**NA**

Source: Survey replies to question 19 of the Survey. N=61; 16 respondents left one, two or three of the three selections blank, with 35 such fields as a result.

Notes
1.   In reply to the open-ended request: 'Please list your three major policy interests'. The Policy Institute reclassified/merged the responses into major categories for ease of analysis.
2.   Includes agriculture, marine, small business.

These findings give us some indicators for analysing the policy priorities of women members of the Oireachtas. Our observations are limited by the fact that we did not examine the policy perceptions of male legislators. However, in our examination of the policy interests of Irish women politicians, we should be able to draw conclusions as to whether they are more or less likely to support women's issues than women in other parliaments.

The survey asked women parliamentarians to list their three major policy interests. Table 12 sets out the responses to this question. It is a multiple response table, combining the answers to the three policy items across a number of different categories.[9] 'Per Cent of Cases' provides the most interesting perspective on the question. This is the percentage of respondents who mentioned the policy area in any of the three responses. We find that more than two of every five women (44 per cent) identify planning and the environment as an important policy interest. This is followed by education (40 per cent), health (31 per cent) and social and family affairs (25 per cent). Law, crime and justice, and equality were each mentioned by 19 per cent of respondents. Women's issues are specifically mentioned as a policy interest by only 13 per cent of women parliamentarians. Social inclusion and cross-border issues were each mentioned by almost 10 per cent of respondents. The categories of arts, economics and foreign affairs are mentioned least frequently, at about 8 per cent each.

It is immediately clear that Irish women parliamentarians are similar to, yet different from, their international colleagues in terms of their policy interests. On the one hand, there is less expressed interest in economic affairs among Irish women parliamentarians than among their counterparts elsewhere. However, this is balanced by a stronger interest in environmental, planning and development issues. On the other hand, the number of Irish women TDs and Senators who spontaneously rate women's affairs as a high priority is similar to the level of interest in this subject shown by female politicians in other jurisdictions. This finding suggests that, overall, Irish women parliamentarians may not have distinctive policy priorities different from those of men. Further research is needed to see how, and to what extent, issues of women, children and family are prioritised in the Oireachtas by women legislators.

Political Ambitions

There is a general presumption that women politicians have become more ambitious over time. This is a rather contentious view, based on the observation that, in the past, women parliamentarians concentrated on nursing their constituencies and did not make a significant contribution to legislative activity. While a study of the legislative record may indicate that women parliamentarians in earlier decades reserved their contributions to debates on their particular policy interests, it must be remembered that political life at the time was less

**Table 13: Highest Office (HO) Achieved by Female Members
by Decade of First Entry to the Oireachtas,
1919 to 1999**

Decade	First-Entry Women in Decade	Nos. Subsequently Achieving					
		HO[1]	Minister/ Minister of State/Tánaiste	Committee Chair	Committee member[3]	Other	
1919–1929	14	3	1	1	1		0
1930–1939	7	1	0	0	1		0
1940–1949	3	1	0	0	0	Council of State Member	1
1950–1959	7	1	0	0	0	Assistant Party Whip	1
1960–1969	7	5	1	0	2	President Leas Cathaoirleach	1 1
1970–1979	11	8	4	0	3	Cathaoirleach	1
1980–1989	27	16	6	4	6		0
1990–1999[2]	28	13	5	0	6	President	1
Totals	**104**	**48**	**17**	**5**	**19**		**6**

Source: Database of women members
compiled by the Policy Institute from directory entries.

Notes
1. For the purposes of this exercise, high office (HO) was defined as positions arising in Government, Oireachtas or State, and included the following: Minister, Tánaiste, Minister of State (included under the Minister/Tánaiste heading) Committee chair (separate heading), membership of the Council of State, Party Whip, President, Cathaoirleach and Leas Cathaoirleach (the last five are included in the 'other' category).

2. The appointment of Mary Hanafin as Minister of State in late 1999 brings the 1990–1999 figure for the category 'Minister/Minister of State/Tánaiste' to six, or 21 per cent of the 1990s intake.

3. As regards Committee membership, all four women nominated to various committees from 1930 to the end of the 1970s served on committees related to the provision of services for Oireachtas members (such as for the library, restaurant, and procedures and privileges). Only in 1969 was the first female member nominated to a substantive policy-making or legislative committee; this was Evelyn Owens, who served on the Committee on Statutory Instruments. In the 1980s, women began to be nominated to various committees: women's rights, marriage breakdown, crime, small business and public accounts.

See also general notes to database tables.

'professionalised' than it is today. Thus, it is not surprising that women parliamentarians today are more assertive in their legislative activities while also being concerned with constituency matters. If politics is now viewed in career terms, it can be expected that motivated women will seek to achieve high political office. In our study, we sought to gain some insight into this view by exploring women's achievement of high office and their expectations of political promotion.

First, we examined women's achievement of political office over time. From Table 13, it is clear that, with some significant exceptions, the thirty-eight women who entered the Oireachtas between 1920 and the end of the 1960s tended to languish on the back benches. One of the first to break this mould was Mary Robinson, who was elected to the Seanad in 1969 and became President in 1990. Of the eleven women first elected in the 1970s, five (45 per cent) reached positions of high political importance as they continued their careers.[10]

This pattern of women holding high office has continued, with ten (37 per cent) of the twenty-seven women who first entered parliament in the 1980s holding ministerial office or chairing parliamentary committees. Of the twenty-eight women coming to parliamentary life in the 1990s, seven (25 per cent) have already become holders of important political positions.[11] The breakdown between the positions is as follows: Cabinet Ministers (one or 3.5 per cent), Junior Ministers (five or 18 per cent) and President (one or 3.5 per cent). The pattern for the 1990s may currently underestimate women's achievements because of the time lag between first entry to parliament and appointment to higher office and the reality of promotional progression through political offices, from Committee Chair to Junior Minister to Senior Minister. However, if the pattern of the 1980s continues, it can be expected that at least a third of women entering the Oireachtas in the 1990s will achieve high office in the current decade, and that the high offices to which women are appointed will become more senior over time (taking into account that the vast majority of female ministers within the 1990s first entrants are still Junior Ministers).

It is clear, then, that women parliamentarians have a reasonable chance of being promoted to higher political office during their time in the Oireachtas. The question now is how this expectation matches with their personal ambitions and expectations. We approached the question of ambition by asking respondents what political offices they would like to hold in the future. This was followed up by asking what offices they expected to achieve. Respondents were free to identify as many posts as they wished in both cases. The contrast between ambition and expectation is portrayed in Figure 4. It is clear that the members surveyed were ambitious, but that this ambition was tempered with caution in assessing their prospects for holding further office. The most desired positions were a full ministry (62 per cent), a junior ministry (43 per cent) and committee chairperson (36 per cent). The least favoured positions were Ceann Comhairle (11 per cent), Cathaoirleach (13 per cent) and party leader or deputy leader (18 per cent each). In between, ambitions of becoming Taoiseach (25 per cent), President (23 per cent) and EU Commissioner (21 per cent) were expressed.

There is no doubt that women parliamentarians see their legislative role as extending beyond that of a backbench politician. When asked to assess realistically the possibility of holding any of these offices, however, a large gap emerged between ambition and expectation in relation to all but one of these posts. The position that women felt was, in real terms, most available to them was that of junior minister (39 per cent). In this case, the gap between ambition and expectation was minimal; however, in our findings on high office, this would appear to be an overly optimistic assumption, given the positions achieved by the 1990s first entrants, 18 per cent of whom are currently junior ministers. The second most accessible post was, in their view, that of committee chair (23 per cent), while only about half of those who would wish to hold a full ministerial position (33 per cent) considered it a realistic possibility. After that, the pattern is more disappointing — no woman believed that she would ever become party leader, Taoiseach or President, while only a tiny proportion saw themselves as becoming an EU Commissioner (2 per cent), a party deputy leader (3 per cent), or a speaker of either house of the Oireachtas (5 per cent in each case). This very significant gap between the offices women parliamentarians would like and expect to hold suggests a high level of frustrated ambition among women legislators. It is clear that women parliamentarians feel that parliamentary politics underutilises their talents and capabilities.

Figure 4: High Office Ambitions v. Expectations of Women Oireachtas Members in Survey

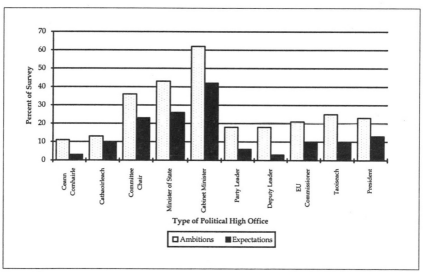

Source: Survey.

The wide gap between ambition and expectation of holding higher office surprised and intrigued us, so we decided to examine the responses of current and retired politicians to see whether any more light was shed on this matter. In this instance, we focused on the ambition of both categories of parliamentarian

— the positions they would like, or would have liked, to hold. This information is presented in Figure 5. There are two striking points to be made about this chart. The first is that women who are in the Oireachtas at present are much more ambitious than their retired equivalents when they were in parliament.

**Figure 5: High Office Ambitions of Women Oireachtas Members in Survey:
Currently Serving v. Retired Members**

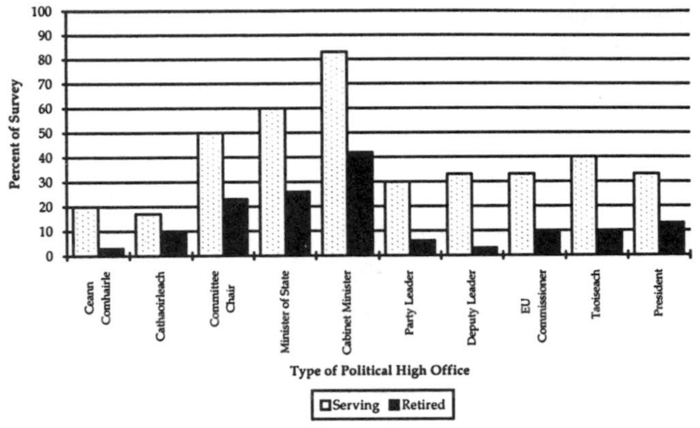

Source: Survey.

More than four in every five women (83 per cent) who currently hold a seat in the Oireachtas want to be a full minister, 60 per cent would like to become junior ministers and 50 per cent aspire to being a committee chairperson. In fact, across all positions, their level of ambition is much higher than that seen in Figure 4. This is understandable, as the opportunity to realise their ambition could yet be presented to them, given the unpredictable nature of politics. Parallel with this finding is the much lower level of ambition held by retired women politicians during their careers — although the preferences remain in the same order: minister, junior minister and committee chair as the main choices. No doubt, the lower ambition of former parliamentarians relates to the restricted opportunities for women politicians to progress in the political world at the time. However, this points to another significant finding. Earlier, we discussed the fact that women politicians appeared to concentrate on their role as constituency carers rather than as legislators. This chart indicates that these parliamentarians also harboured significant ambitions across all of the higher offices. For instance, over two-fifths (42 per cent) would have liked to have been a minister, over a quarter (26 per cent) would have accepted a junior ministry. Yet, in reality, only a tiny minority of this group managed to get beyond being a backbench TD or Senator. So, they tended to their constituency duties because higher office was, for all practical purposes, out of their reach. Thus, to dismiss earlier generations of women politicians as having little ambition beyond nursing their constituencies is a superficial interpretation of the realities of political life for women at the time.

Table 14: Women Politicians Most Admired by Survey Respondents

Rank/(Number of Responses)[1]		Woman Admired[2]
1	(10)	Mo Mowlam
2	(9)	Mary Robinson
3	(7)	Mary Harney
4	(4)	Mary O'Rourke
5	(3)	Máire Geoghegan-Quinn
6	(2)	Liz O'Donnell
6	(2)	Gro Harlem Bruntland

Source: Survey replies to question 41 of the Survey.

Notes:
1. The results presented are for single responses only since the survey sought one response. Some respondents gave more than one response.

2. Total survey respondents = 61. Non-responses were 15 leaving valid votes of 46. In addition, single votes were received for Mary Banotti, Monica Barnes, Hillary Clinton, Nora Owen, President McAleese and Indira Ghandi, while three respondents suggested 'all women'.

Finally, given the importance of role models in shaping women's expectations of political life, we asked our respondents to name the female politician they most admired (Table 14). Mo Mowlam, Mary Robinson and Mary Harney were the three most admired female political figures. Clearly, respondents were conscious of the contributions of these women to political life on the island of Ireland in recent times. In addition, it is quite likely that most, if not all, respondents met, or worked with, one or more of these women in the course of their political careers. Thus, for the majority of our respondents, the role models adopted were drawn from a category of political women who were successful within an Irish context in the recent past. These were women with whom respondents could identify, and the measure of whose achievements they could appreciate. Indeed, in choosing these three women in particular, it is likely that respondents were selecting politicians whose record of achievement was seen as being within their capabilities, and who, therefore, were useful as role models. International figures (with the single exception of Gro Harlem Bruntland) and historical women were not identified as 'most admired', possibly because of remoteness of political context and time.

Conclusions

This study of Irish women parliamentarians has confirmed some impressions and has yielded some new information regarding this élite group of women in Irish society.

The first section of our study places women's representation in the national assembly in a comparative context. It also concentrates on building up a social and demographic profile of women legislators. We find that women comprise 51 per cent of the population of Ireland, yet their representation in the Oireachtas is only 14 per cent. This is very low in comparison with other EU and English-speaking countries. Despite the increase in the number of women entering the Oireachtas in recent decades, we conclude that the prospects for further advances in women's representation are poor. We will come back to this point shortly. Of the women who do make it to parliament, they are concentrated in middle age, are married, have small families, are well-educated and belong mainly to Fianna Fáil and Fine Gael.

The second part of our research examined the context of women's routes to parliament. The one overriding conclusion to be drawn from this section emphasises, once again, the importance of political parties in bringing women into public office. This can take two forms: women's party membership and activism can lead them to desire a political career, while parties often invite high-profile women leaders from women's and community politics to stand for them at election time. The influence of party is supported by two other important social-ising agencies — the political family and activism on women's issues. These factors interact with party to create opportunities for women to pursue political careers.

Although parties are the gatekeepers to political office, our research also identified supports and barriers to women's political representation. Personal supports — of family and friends — were the most important for successful women politicians, with party offering a secondary source of support. However, in other circumstances, women in political life found that the balancing of family responsibilities with public duties was a difficult issue, exacerbated fur-ther when the constituency base was outside Dublin. The second major difficulty for women seeking political office was the lack of funding for political campaigns: male colleagues were seen to have access to non-party electoral funding that was denied to women. In the light of recent public revelations on electoral funding, moves by the parties to regulate donations to party campaigns should go some way towards redressing this issue for political women.

In part three, we examined where women's policy interests lay once they became members of the Oireachtas. Here, we found that women are concerned with broad social policy and planning matters. The absence of a substantial interest in economic affairs is disquieting, given the central role of economic ministries and committees in shaping Irish society. Interesting, too, was the fact that the women we surveyed did not give a very high priority to women's affairs, reflecting the policy priorities of women legislators in some other countries.

We also discovered that women politicians today are very ambitious, and aspire to hold high public office to a greater degree than did their predecessors. We found that ambition is tempered by realism: the highest office most current members expect to achieve is that of junior minister. What our study also revealed was that retired women politicians in their time were much more ambitious than was hitherto realised, but that they served at a time when the opportunities for women to advance to high office were restricted.

Looking to the future, our research suggests that we cannot be complacent about women's participation in political life. There is no guarantee that the number of women in the Oireachtas is going to increase significantly without clear and positive intervention by parties. An increase in the numbers of women in the Oireachtas to reach a modest one-fifth of parliamentary represen- tation is only possible with a coherent, focused party strategy. This plan must include targeted attempts to deal with the difficulties of family and funding that particularly militate against women politicians.

The key to increasing women's representation is to focus on building on the number of women entering parliament for the first time, as well as maintaining and supporting existing women parliamentarians. On present figures and trends, the number of women in the Oireachtas is likely to remain static, at best, in the coming years. Women's representation could even decline in the near future. It is clear that women have to be encouraged to become involved in politics. Parties, Fianna Fáil and Fine Gael in particular, need to establish and implement unequivocal commitments to bringing more women into political life, to select- ing them as candidates, to making sure that they win or are appointed to seats in the Oireachtas, and to putting them into positions of high office.

In spite of all the difficulties faced by women in their political careers, the abiding impression we gained was one of strong, committed parliamentarians determined to give their best both to their families and to their country. We leave the last word on the matter to one current woman legislator who asked herself a fundamental question:

Why do I do this? That's a very good question. And yes, it is harder for women. On the other hand, it is the most challenging — and most satisfying — thing I have ever done.

Biographies of Authors

YVONNE GALLIGAN is a Reader in politics at Queen's University, Belfast where she is also Director of the Centre for the Advancement of Women in Politics. Her research interests are comparative public policy and gender politics. She has published extensively on women in politics, is author of *Women in Politics in Contemporary Ireland* (1998) and contributing co-editor of *Contesting Politics: Women in Ireland, North and South* (1999).

KATHLEEN KNIGHT is currently Visiting Associate Professor at Barnard College, Columbia University in New York. She joined this research project while a Visiting Lecturer at the Department of Political Science at Trinity College, University of Dublin in 1998–1999. She wishes to personally thank Professors Michael Laver and Michael Marsh for the opportunity to undertake teaching and research in Ireland.

ÚNA NIC GIOLLA CHOILLE is Senior Research Officer with the Policy Institute at Trinity College. A civil servant previously with the Revenue Commissioners and the Department of Finance, she spent over four years in the Houses of the Oireachtas, working on applied policy research with various Committees. She is currently editor of the series 'Studies in Public Policy', the Institute's publication outlet aimed simultaneously at readers in the academic world and also those interested in policy formulation, implementation and review.

Acknowledgements

The TCD Policy Institute authors (Yvonne Galligan, Kathleen Knight and Úna Nic Giolla Choille) sincerely wish to acknowledge the financial support of the Ireland Funds, without which they would have been unable to become involved in the project. They had the assistance of a number of people as research assistants and accordingly thanks are also due to the following: Sian Muldowney and Jayne Mollard for questionnaire management, Fiachra Kennedy for database compilation and associated statistical analysis and Gemma Carney for drafting tables and graphs and also checking entries.

Notes

1. We define parliamentarians and members of the Oireachtas as those who serve, or have served, in the Dáil, Seanad or presidency. When we want to talk about their membership of one particular house, we identify it by name.

2. The methodology used was a postal survey of all current and retired Oireachtas members of which there were 70 in all. Responses were received from 61 members, indicating a response rate of 87 per cent. Four reminders were issued before the close of the survey on 30 September 1999. The survey consisted of 41 questions, designed to elicit a mix of open and scaled responses. Further details on the methodology used and on the compilation of the database of all Irish female parliamentarians since 1922 is contained in Appendix 2.

3. This information was extracted from the bibliographical data contained in this directory.

4. General notes to database tables

   (1) For the purposes of all tables deriving from the database, Oireachtas women members comprise all female members, including Presidents (Constitution Article 15.1.2). In tables indicating first entrants in a particular decade, all women who became members during the decade, whether elected to the Dáil or Seanad, in general or by-elections or nominated by the Taoiseach, and also Presidents, are included.

   (2) In tables indicating first entrants in a particular decade, the first decade is always the eleven years from 1918 to 1929.

   (3) The compilation of the database was completed on 30 September 1999 and it therefore excludes any female members elected since then. The additional female member elected since then would bring the total for the 1990s to thirty-four members and twenty-nine first entrants.

5. More detailed information on age is available in Appendix 3.

6. However, in October 1999, a direct seat transmission took place between brother and sister, when Mary Upton was elected to the Dáil in the by-election consequent on the death of her brother, Pat. Previous instances of brother–sister connections relate to sisters of men active in the 1919–1923 period, such as Mary McSwiney, Margaret Mary Pearse and Margaret Collins-O'Driscoll, who were also active in politics themselves and were elected to Dáil Éireann subsequently.

6. This by-election took place in the Dublin South West constituency that was later reorganised. The last widow elected to the Seanad was Tras Honan, in August 1977. Her husband, a former senator, had died in 1976.

7. Calculated as follows: 33 incumbents less 8 'age-related' retirements leaves 25 who we assume would carry on in politics. Assuming they were to go forward and retain their seats, a further 20 new members added to this 25 would bring the female total to 45, which amount to 20 per cent of 226 Oireachtas members. On the other hand, if new entrants only cancelled out 'age-related' retirements (i.e., totalled eight), it is likely that

women's membership would decline, after account was taken of further reductions due to seat losses, non 'age-related' retirements and Taoiseach's nominees not being nominated again.

8. Any quotes following, unless indicated otherwise, were derived from replies to the open-ended question 41 in the survey, which sought general comments on politics, and details on respondents' experiences during their careers in political life. Some respondents were willing to disclose their names while others wished to have their quotations cited anonymously. For the purposes of consistency and research integrity and to provide the greatest degree of confidentiality for all respondents, the authors therefore decided that all quotations would be cited on a non-attributable basis.

9. 'Count' is the number of times each policy area was mentioned across all three responses. 'Per cent of responses' is the number of responses in each category (count) divided by the total number of responses (137).

10. Máire Geoghegan-Quinn, first elected in 1975, became Minister for Justice in 1993; Mary Harney, first appointed to the Seanad in 1977, became Tánaiste and Minister for Enterprise, Trade and Employment in 1997; Síle de Valera, first elected in 1977, became Minister for Arts, Heritage and the Gaeltacht in 1997; Gemma Hussey, first elected in 1977, became Minister for Education in 1982 and Tras Honan, first elected to the Seanad in 1977, became the first woman Cathaoirleach of that house in 1982.

11. The President is included as the office is technically part of the Oireachtas (Article 15.1.2, Bunreacht na hÉireann). Mary McAleese did not serve in the Oireachtas prior to her election as president. The 'seven' detailed in the text refers to the position at time of writing (September 2000) and therefore includes Mary Hanafin.

Appendix 1

Women Members of Parliament in Selected Countries,
1945–2000 (%)

Country	% of Women Elected to Lower House in Year											
	1945	1950	1955	1960	1965	1970	1975	1980	1985	1990	1995	2000
Sweden	7.8	9.6	12.2	13.8	13.3	14.0	21.4	27.8	31.5	38.4	40.4	42.7
Denmark	5.4	7.9	9.5	9.5	9.5	10.6	15.6	23.5	26.3	33.0	33.5	37.4
Finland	9.0	9.0	14.0	15.0	16.5	16.6	23.0	26.0	30.5	31.5	33.5	37.0
Norway	4.7	4.7	4.7	6.7	8.0	9.3	15.5	23.9	34.4	35.8	39.4	36.4
Netherlands	(4.0)	2.0	4.0	5.3	6.7	5.3	5.3	14.7	18.7	21.3	22.7	36.0
New Zealand	2.5	3.8	5.0	5.0	6.3	4.8	4.6	8.7	12.6	16.5	21.2	29.2
Spain	0.4	0.3	0.3	0.3	0.5	1.1	1.1	6.9	6.3	14.6	16.0	28.3
Australia	1.3	0.8	0	0	0	0	0	2.4	5.4	6.8	8.8	26.8
Belgium[1]	0	3.3	4.2	4.2	3.3	3.8	6.6	7.5	7.5	9.0	12.0	23.3
Switzerland[2]	0	0	0	0	0	0	7.0	10.5	11.0	14.0	17.5	23.0
Canada	0.4	0.4	1.5	1.9	1.5	0.4	3.4	5.0	9.6	13.3	18.0	19.9
UK	3.8	3.3	3.5	3.9	4.4	4.1	4.3	3.0	3.5	6.3	9.2	18.4
USA	0	1.6	2.7	3.9	2.8	2.3	3.7	3.7	5.0	6.4	11.0	13.3
Ireland	2.9	3.4	3.4	3.4	3.5	2.1	2.8	4.1	7.8	7.8	12.0	13.2
Italy	0	7.8	5.6	4.2	4.6	2.7	3.8	8.4	7.6	12.9	15.1	11.1
France	5.6	7.0	3.7	1.5	1.9	2.1	2.7	4.3	7.1	6.9	6.4	10.9
Japan	0	2.6	1.7	1.5	1.5	1.6	1.4	1.8	1.6	2.3	2.7	4.6
Greece	0	0	0.3	1.3	0.7	—	2.0	3.3	4.3	6.7	6.0	6.3

Source: Inter-Parliamentary Union 1995; www.ipu.org/parline.
Figures for 2000 are extracted from IPU database as of 28 April 2000.

Notes
  The figures represent the proportion of women returned to the lower house of parliament in each country at the election closest to the end of each five year period. Thus,
  for example, the 39.4 per cent of women in the Norwegian parliament in 1995 is actually
  the figure for women returned in the election in September 1993. In the same vein,
  Finland had its highest representation of women in 1991, when 39 per cent women were
  returned to parliament. This is not included, as the 1995 election result supersedes it in
  this table.
  The first election after WW2 in the Netherlands took place in 1946
  The Greek parliament was suspended from 1967 until 1975.

1. All women were given the right to vote in 1948 and voted for the first time in the 1949
   general election.

2. Swiss women were given the right to vote and to stand for election in 1971.

Appendix 2
Survey and Database Methodology

Questionnaires were posted to all seventy women members of the Oireachtas who in June 1999 were still living, and this total included both members currently serving and those who had retired from politics. The questionnaires were sent with an introductory letter after the close of the session in June 1999 and the survey closed at the beginning of October. The research team did not take on board any relevant political developments after this deadline. In particular, the election of Mary Upton and promotion of Mary Hanafin to Minister of State were not included in our analysis but are referred to in the text and/or tables, where appropriate.

Completed questionnaires amounted to 61, giving a valid number (N) for the survey of 61, so that after four months a response rate of 87 per cent was achieved, including three questionnaires completed by personal interview. Four reminders had been sent over this period.

The questionnaire included a number of fixed-format and open-ended questions covering such areas as committees of service, major accomplishments and memorable incidents, ambitions and expectations, support and barriers for women's political careers and a number of policy proposals aimed at different means of achieving additional representation by women. A variety of demographic information was also collected, including marital status at the time of entry, number of children, level of education, and the like.

All response scale items were collected in the same format. This is a 0 to 6 scale with labelled end-points. Alpha for the five funding items was .82. Analysis was conducted using SPSS and Excel.

The authors also compiled a database of information relating to personal and political characteristics of the 104 Irish women parliamentarians since 1918. The raw material used came only from the directory, and a sizeable number of derived variables were then calculated using this biographical material, such as decade of first entry, constituency type, length of parliamentary service, etc. The database contained 154 fields for 104 cases, with over 16,000 entries as a result.

The database was used separately to characterise all members over time, but also merged with survey responses for living members responding to the survey. The database was then used as back-up and quality control for both the survey responses and the database entries. For example, matters such as Oireachtas career, party affiliation, etc., could be cross-checked between both sources to check for errors and inconsistencies.

Valid N for the portions of analysis based upon the database is 104. This number represents the total of all women serving in the Irish parliament since its original session in 1919.

Appendix 3
Detailed Tables Referred to in the Text

Table A.1: Ages of Female Members at First Entry to the Oireachtas, by Decade of Entry, 1919 to 1999

Decade	First-Entry Women in Decade	Age Category at First Entry: Numbers and Percentages[1]					
		20–29	30–39	40–49	50–59	60–79	% aged 30–39
1919–1929	14	0	(14) 2	(36) 5	(21) 3	(28) 4	50
1930–1939	7	(14) 1	(29) 2	(57) 4	(0) 0	(0) 0	85
1940–1949	3	(33) 1	(66) 2	(0) 0	(0) 0	(0) 0	66
1950–1959	7	(29) 2	(0) 0	(43) 3	(14) 1	(14) 1	43
1960–1969	7	(14) 1	(43) 3	(14) 1	(28) 2	(0) 0	57
1970–1979	11	(36) 4	(9) 1	(45) 5	(9) 1	(0) 0	55
1980–1989	27	(22) 5	(33) 9	(37) 10	(9) 3	(0) 0	70
1990–1999	28	(14) 4	(32) 9	(39) 11	(14) 4	(0) 0	71
Total	104	18	28	39	14	5	64

Source: Database of women members compiled by the Policy Institute from directory entries.

Notes
1. Percentages in age category for each decade are in brackets.
See also general notes to database tables.

Table A.2: Marital Status of Female Members at First Entry to the Oireachtas, by decade of Entry, 1919 to 1999

Decade	First-Entry Women in Decade	Family Status (1)		
		Married	Single	Widowed
1919–1929	14	(42) 6	(29) 4	(29) 4
1930–1939	7	(29) 2	(29) 2	(42) 3
1940–1949	3	(33) 1	(0) 0	(67) 2
1950–1959	7	(29) 2	(42) 3	(29) 2
1960–1969	7	(43) 3	(14) 1	(43) 3
1970–1979	11	(46) 5	(36) 4	(18) 2
1980–1989	27	(86) 23	(14) 4	(0) 0
1990–1999	28	(82) 23	(18) 5	(0) 0
Total	104	65	24	15

Source: Database of women members compiled by the Policy Institute from directory entries.

Notes
1. Percentages had in some cases to be rounded up or down to sum to 100 per cent, owing to the small number of entries in each category.

See also general notes to database tables.

**Table A.3: Highest Level of Education Completed by Female Oireachtas Members,
by Decade of Entry, 1919 to 1999**

Decade	First-Entry Women in Decade	Highest Education Level Completed[1,2]										
		Primary		Secondary		Third Level		Post Third Level[1]		Third Level or Greater		NA[1]	
1919–1929	14	(7)	1	(14)	1	(43)	1	(7)	1	(50)	7	(43)	4
1930–1939	7	(14)	1	(57)	1	(14)	1	(14)	1	(29)	2	(43)	0
1940–1949	3	(0)	0	(33)	1	(67)	1	(0)	0	(67)	2	(0)	0
1950–1959	7	(0)	0	(29)	1	(57)	1	(0)	0	(57)	4	(43)	1
1960–1969	7	(0)	0	(43)	1	(43)	1	(14)	1	(57)	4	(0)	0
1970–1979	11	(0)	0	(9)	1	(73)	1	(18)	1	(91)	10	(0)	0
1980–1989	27	(0)	0	(26)	1	(52)	1	(22)	1	(74)	20	(0)	0
1990–1999	28	(0)	0	(11)	1	(64)	1	(25)	1	(89)	25	(0)	0

Source: Database of women members
compiled by the Policy Institute from directory entries.
Notes
1. The categories used were Primary, Secondary, Third Level, Post Third Level (for a second qualification obtained in a third-level institution) and NA. For the latter cases, there was insufficient information in the directory to enter any education level in the database.
2. Percentages had to be rounded to sum to 100 per cent owing to the small number of entries in each category.
See also general notes to database tables.

**Table A.4: Political Family Connections of Female Oireachtas Members,
by Decade of Entry, 1919 to 1999**

Decade	First-Entry Women in Decade	Family Connection with Person Active in Politics[1]					
		Widows[1]	Daughters[1]	Other Political Family Connections		Percentage/ Number without Connections	
1919–1929[2]	14	3	1	Sister	2	(50)	7
				Mother	1		
1930–1939	7	3	0	Sister	1	(43)	3
1940–1949	3	2	0	—		(33)	1
1950–1959	7	2	3			(29)	2
1960–1969	7	3	0	Niece	1	(43)	3
1970–1979	11	2	2	Granddaughter	1	(55)	6
1980–1989	27	0	9	Grandniece	1	(63)	17
1990–1999	28	0	9	Greatgrandniece	1	(64)	18
Total	104	15	24		8	(55)	57

Source: Database of women members compiled by the Policy Institute
from directory entries.
Notes
1. The definition of family connection with predecessor member is of a female member who succeeded a family member in the next succeeding general or by-election, in either House (classed as 'immediate successors in the main text'), who had a family connection with a previous member, who had a family background in politics, who succeeded

a family member but with a gap of more than one election or who had a family member currently or subsequently sitting in either House when they were elected for the first time.
2. In the 1920s, those with relatives active in local politics or during the 1916–1922 period have been classed as 'successors' for the purposes of this table only.

See also general notes to database tables.

Table A.5: Number of Women Members in Selected Oireachtais, 1938–97

Oireachtas Session Beginning	No. of Women incl. By-elections	No. of Women First Entrants incl. By-elections
1969	8	3
1973	9	2
1977	13	9
1981	20	12
February 1982[1]	16	2
November 1982[1]	21	2
1981/1982/1982[1]	*26*	*16*
1987	19	6
1989	19	5
1992	32	17
1997	33	10

Source: Database of women members compiled by the Policy Institute from directory entries.

Notes
1.   In this table, the outcomes of the three elections held in June 1981, February 1982 and November 1982 are given separately. The outcomes of the three elections are treated as one in the line in italics.

See also general notes to database tables.

**Table A.6: Ages of Female Members in the Oireachtas,
1979 and 1999**

Year	Age Category at First Entry[1]					
	20–29	30–39	40–49	50–59	60–79	Percentage aged 30–39
1979	(29) 4	(7) 1	(43) 6	(7) 1	(14) 2	50
1999	(3) 1	(18) 6	(45) 15	(24) 8	(9) 3	64

Source: Database of women members compiled by the Policy Institute from directory entries.

Notes
1.   Percentages in age category for each decade are in brackets.

See also general notes to database tables.

Table A.7: Most Important Influences Motivating Entry to the Oireachtas

Factor[1]	Mean of Ratings	Standard Deviation from Mean	No. Giving 0 Rating	Percentage Giving 0 Rating	No. Giving 5 Rating	Percentage Giving 5 Rating
Party Activism	2.6	2.3	25	41	22	36
Women's Issue activism	2.3	2.2	22	36	18	29
Family Background	2.2	2.3	25	46	19	31
Invitation from Party	7.0	2.3	32	53	19	31
Community Activism	2.0	2.3	29	48	9	15
Political Issue	1.6	2.0	33	54	10	16
Retention of Family Seat	1.0	2.0	47	77	11	18

Source: Replies to question 13 of the Survey. N=61.

Notes

1. On this question, respondents were given a scale of zero to 5 for a list of influences. A zero response indicated that the factor had no influence; a 5 rating indicated that the factor was very influential. Respondents could identify other influences beyond those listed.

Table A.8: Most Important Sources of Support for Oireachtas Entry

Source of Support[1]	Mean of Ratings	Standard Deviation from Mean	No. Giving 5 Rating	Percentage Giving 5 Rating
Personal				
Husband	3.1	2.3	32	52
Friends	2.9	2.1	23	38
Mother	2.3	2.3	20	32
Children	1.9	2.2	16	26
Political				
Party	3.0	1.9	21	34
Women's Group	1.8	2.1	13	21
Community Group	1.3	1.8	7	11
Business Associates	1.5	1.1	1	2
Religious Group	0.5	0.3	1	2

Source: Replies to question 14 of the Survey. N=61.

Notes

1. On this question, respondents were given a scale of zero to 5 for a list of possible sources of support. A zero response indicated that the source of support was not at all important; a 5 rating indicated that the source of support was very important. Respondents could identify other sources of support beyond those listed.

Table A.9: Most Important Sources of Difficulty Experienced in Achieving Political Office Identified by Survey Respondents

Source of Difficulty[1]	Mean of Ratings	Standard Deviation from Mean	No. Selecting 5 Rating	Percentage Selecting 5 Rating
Personal				
Family-Care Responsibilities	4.3	1.5	41	67
Husband	3.2	1.9	20	33
Educational Constraints	1.3	1.7	2	3
Peer Pressure	0.8	0.8	3	5
Family Upbringing	0.3	0.7	1	2
Political				
Lack of Funding	3.9	1.5	30	49
Party Politicians' Attitudes	2.2	2.0	12	20
Discrimination Against Women	1.4	1.7	6	10
Voters' Attitudes	1.3	1.8	6	10
Media Portrayal of Women	1.1	1.4	1	2

Source: Replies to question 16 of the Survey. N=61.

Notes

1.   On this question, respondents were given a scale of zero to 5 for a list of possible difficulties perceived by them as being experienced by women in general in politics. A zero response indicated that the difficulty was not an obstacle at all; a 5 rating indicated that the difficulty was a great obstacle. Respondents could identify other difficulties beyond those listed.

Bibliography

Barry, Jim, *The Women's Movement and Local Politics: The Influence of Councillors in London*, Aldershot: Avebury, 1991.

Carey, John M., Richard G. Niemi and Lynda W. Powell, 'Are women state legislators alike?' in Sue Thomas and Clyde Wilcox (eds), *Women and Elective Office: Past, Present and Future*, New York: Oxford University Press, 1998.

Caul, Miki, 'Women's Representation in Parliament: The Role of Political Parties', *Party Politics*, 5:1, 1999, pp. 79–98.

Chubb, Basil, '"Going about Persecuting Civil Servants": The Role of the Irish Parliamentary Representative', *Political Studies*, 11:3, 1963, pp. 272–86.

Conway M. Margaret, Gertrude A. Steuernagel and David Ahern, *Women and Political Participation*, Washington, DC: Congressional Quarterly Press, 1997.

Dolan, Kathleen and Lynne E. Forde, 'Are All Women State Legislators Alike?' in Sue Thomas and Clyde Wilcox (eds), *Women and Elective Office: Past, Present and Future*, New York: Oxford University Press, 1998.

Duerst-Lahti, Georgia, 'The Bottleneck: Women Becoming Candidates' in Sue Thomas and Clyde Wilcox (eds), *Women and Elective Office: Past, Present and Future*, New York: Oxford University Press, 1998.

Gallagher, Michael and Lee Komito, 'The Constituency Role of TDs' in John Coakley and Michael Gallagher (eds), *Politics in the Republic of Ireland*, 3rd edition, London: Routledge and PSAI Press, 1999.

Galligan, Yvonne and Rick Wilford, 'Gender and Party Politics in the Republic of Ireland' in Yvonne Galligan, Eilís Ward and Rick Wilford (eds), *Contesting Politics: Women in Ireland, North and South*, Boulder, Colorado: Westview Press and PSAI Press, 1999.

Galligan, Yvonne, Michael Laver and Gemma Carney, 'The Effect of Candidate Gender on Voting in Ireland, 1997', *Irish Political Studies*, 14, 1999, pp. 118–22.

Goetz, Anne Marie, 'Women in Politics and Gender Equity in Policy: South Africa and Uganda', *Review of African Political Economy*, 76, 1998, pp. 241–262.

Inter-Parliamentary Union website: Parline @ www.ipu.org.

Inter-Parliamentary Union, *Women in Parliaments 1945–1995: A World Statistical Survey*, 'Reports and Documents' No. 23, Inter-Parliamentary Union, Geneva, 1995.

Inter-Parliamentary Union, *Democracy Still in the Making: A World Comparative Study*, 'Reports and Documents' No. 28, Inter-Parliamentary Union, Geneva, 1997.

Inter-Parliamentary Union, *Politics: Women's Insight*, 'Reports and Documents' No. 36, Inter-Parliamentary Union, Geneva, 2000.

Miller, Robert, Rick Wilford and Freda Donoghue, *Women and Political Participation in Northern Ireland*, Aldershot: Avebury, 1996.

Norris, Pippa, 'Women Politicians: Transforming Westminster?', *Parliamentary Affairs*, 49, 1996, pp. 89–102.

Norton, Noelle H., 'Uncovering the Dimensionality of Gender Voting in Congress', *Legislative Studies Quarterly*, 24:1, 1999, pp. 65–86.

Randall, Vicky and Ailbhe Smyth, 'Bishops and Bailiwicks: Obstacles to Women's Political Participation in Ireland', *Economic and Social Review*, 18:3, 1987, pp. 189–214.

Reynolds, Andrew, 'Women in the Legislatures and Executives of the World: Knocking at the Highest Glass Ceiling', *World Politics*, 51: 4, 1999, pp. 547–72.

Swers, Michele L., 'Are Women More Likely to Vote for Women's Issue Bills than their Male Colleagues?' *Legislative Studies Quarterly*, 23:3, 1998, pp. 435–48.

Thomas, Sue, *How Women Legislate*, New York: Oxford University Press, 1994.

Tremblay, Manon, 'Do Female MPs Substantively Represent Women? A Study of Legislative Behaviour in Canada's 35th Parliament', *Canadian Journal of Political Science*, 31:3, 1998, pp. 435–65.

The Dáil

First Dáil

Polling Day: 14 December 1918   *69 SEATS*

The 1918 general election was the last all-Ireland general election to the United Kingdom Parliament at Westminster. The Sinn Féin members of the House of Commons became members of the first Dáil Éireann, which met in Dublin on 21 January 1919.

The first Dáil Éireann, 'Parliament of Ireland', consisted of elected Sinn Féin representatives who refused to take their seats in the British House of Commons. Only twenty-seven out of sixty-nine were able to attend the first meeting — most of the rest were in prison. Éamon de Valera, who had escaped from Lincoln Jail, was elected President of the Dáil, and he made Countess Markievicz Minister for Labour. The first session approved the Constitution, the Declaration of Independence, and the Democratic Programme. On 10 September 1919 the Dáil was declared a dangerous association, and was banned; subsequent meetings were held in secret.

General Election

Women Elected
MARKIEVICZ, CONSTANCE GEORGINA DE (DUBLIN, ST PATRICK'S)

Constance Markievicz, née Gore-Booth

DATE/PLACE OF BIRTH: 4 FEBRUARY 1868/BUCKINGHAM GATE, LONDON
PARTY: SINN FÉIN
CONSTITUENCY: DUBLIN, ST PATRICK'S
DÁIL/SEANAD: 1ST, 2ND DÁIL (14 DECEMBER 1918-15 JUNE 1922), 4TH, 5TH
    DÁIL (27 AUGUST 1923-5 JULY 1927 (DEATH))
AGE AT ENTRY TO DÁIL: 50
FAMILY: MARRIED TO COUNT CASIMIR DUNIN-MARKIEVICZ; ONE DAUGHTER
EDUCATION: GOVERNESS AT HOME. SLADE SCHOOL, LONDON; PARIS
OCCUPATION: REVOLUTIONARY
CAREER:
Minister for Labour, 2 April 1919-9 January 1922. Founder Member, United Arts Club, 1907. Member, President, Theatre of Ireland company. Member, Inghinidhe na hÉireann, 1908. Member, Sinn Féin, 1908 – its executive, 1909. Founder, Fianna na hÉireann, 1909. Member,

Irish Citizen Army, 1913. Member, President, Cumann na mBan, 1914. Honorary president, Irish Women Workers' Union, 1917.

PUBLICATIONS:
James Connolly's Policy and Catholic Doctrine, 1924. *Prison Letters of Countess Markievicz*, London: Virago, 1987 (reissue, with new introduction, of 1934 Longmans Green edition)

DATE OF DEATH: 15 JULY 1927

ADDRESS: 1 FRANKFORT AVENUE, RATHGAR; FRANKFORT HOUSE, RATHGAR (LAST ADDRESS)

CONSTANCE GORE-BOOTH was born to Sir Henry Gore-Booth, landowner and Arctic explorer, and his wife Georgina, daughter of Colonel Charles Hill of Tickhill Castle, Yorkshire. Eva Gore-Booth, the poet, was her sister. The family was descended from Sir Paul Gore, a soldier of fortune who established himself in Ireland in 1597 and from whom was also descended the family of Al Gore, the American Vice-President. During the 1750s there were nine Gores, almost certainly all cousins, in the Irish parliament, according to Sir Josslyn Gore-Booth. (See Dodd, John, 'Gore blimey', *The Spectator*, 22 January 2000).

She was educated privately at Lissadell Court, the family estate in County Sligo, in which W.B. Yeats set his poem, 'In Memory of Eva Gore-Booth and Con Markiewicz'. In 1887 she was presented at court to Queen Victoria, studied art at the Slade School in London in 1893 and in Paris (1898–1900). In London on 29 September 1900 she married the painter, Count Casimir Dunin-Markievicz, son of a Polish landowner in the Ukraine. Constance's only child, Maeve Alys, was born in November, 1901 and the Markieviczs settled in Dublin in 1903.

Drawn to the nationalist movement through her interest in the Abbey Theatre and the Gaelic League, Constance found back numbers of the *Peasant* and *Sinn Féin* journals which sparked her interest in the nationalist movement. She was, with her husband and Ellen Duncan, a founder member of the United Arts Club in 1907. She entered Sinn Féin politics in 1908. She joined Inghinidhe na hÉireann, a feminist society founded by Maud Gonne and wrote for its journal, *Bean na hÉireann*, which brought her into contact with the Irish suffragettes.

In 1909 she founded Na Fianna, an organisation for boys, to whom she taught drilling and the use of arms. Patrick Pearse said that without the Fianna, there would have been no Volunteers in 1913, and the Easter Rising of 1916 would have been impossible. Attracted to socialism by her sister, Eva, Constance met the Irish labour leaders, James Connolly and James Larkin, helped the 1913 Lockout of Dublin workers by running a soup kitchen in Liberty Hall, and joined the Citizen Army, organised by Connolly. In a lecture to the Irish Women's Franchise League in 1915 she recommended women to 'dress suitably in short skirts and strong boots, leave your jewels in the bank and buy a revolver ... take up your responsibilities and be prepared to go your own way depending for safety on your own courage, your own truth and your own common sense'.

In the 1916 Easter Rising Constance served with the Irish Citizen Army company at the College of Surgeons, Dublin, second in command to Commandant Michael Mallin. After laying down arms, she was court-martialled in Kilmainham Gaol, and was sentenced to death. She was reprieved, however, and her sentence was commuted to penal servitude for life in Aylesbury Gaol. Released in the general amnesty of June 1917, the Countess converted to Catholicism and was made honorary president of the Irish Women Workers' Union. Sligo city declared her a freeman in August 1917.

Having been re-arrested in May 1918, she contested the December 1918 general election from Holloway prison, and won a seat in St Patrick's Division, Dublin. She was the first British woman Member of Parliament. In accordance with Sinn Féin policy, she did not take her seat in Westminster. (Later, she visited the Members' vestibule to look at the peg reserved for her hat and coat.) A member of the first Dáil Éireann which met on 21 January 1919, she was released from Holloway on 10 March and was appointed Minister for Labour on 2 April 1919, becoming the first woman cabinet minister in Western Europe.

When Madame Markievicz was made Minister for Labour she came rushing home to tell me. I asked her how she managed it, as I had noticed that the present leaders were not over-eager to put women into places of honour or power, even though they had earned the right to both as well as the men had, having responded to every call made upon them throughout the struggle for freedom. She told me she had to bully them; she claimed she had earned the right to be a Minister as well as any of the men, and was equally as well fitted for it, educationally and every other way, and if she was not made a Minister she would go over to the Labour Party.

(CLARKE, KATHLEEN, *REVOLUTIONARY WOMAN: KATHLEEN CLARKE 1878–1872: AN AUTOBIOGRAPHY,* EDITED BY HELEN LITTON, DUBLIN: O'BRIEN PRESS, 1991)

Constance Markievicz's first Dáil assignment was as a member of a committee appointed by Arthur Griffith to consider prisoners of war and kidnapped children. This Dáil inquiry obtained their release, and the committee was able to report the return home of the kidnapped children. Proscribed as a member of illegal organisations, she served a prison sentence in Cork in 1919 and was also on the run. However, she continued her work in her Labour ministry, where she also had responsibility for social welfare. Her department was concerned with setting up Conciliation Boards and arbitrating labour disputes, surveying areas and establishing guidelines for wages and food prices. From February 1921 the Ministry organised an economic boycott of Belfast as a protest against tests of political and religious beliefs which were often made conditions of employment there.

While imprisoned in Mountjoy (January–July 1921) she was returned un-opposed with all other nominees to the Second Dáil on 19 May 1921, was re-appointed Minister for Labour on 26 August 1921 (though, alas, this was no longer a full Cabinet post) and served as Minister until 9 January, 1922. The Ministry's activities now included agricultural disputes involving the harvest bonus on several farms, disagreements in factories, offices and stores. Even where the authority of the Dáil was not officially recognised, cases were arbi-trated by the Republican boards. Markievicz reported in December that on 15 September the Tyrone County Council (which functioned under the British Local Government Board, not the Local Government Department of Dáil Éire-ann), had submitted to the arbitration of the Labour Ministry a dispute between itself and the quarry workers employed by it.

When arbitration failed, she threatened to use military force against reli-gious bigotry, telling a Catholic quarry manager in the north that unless intimidation against a Protestant workman ceased, the matter would be put into the hands of the Republican police.

Countess Markievicz opposed the Anglo–Irish Treaty of 1921 and toured America in April and May 1922 to enlist support for the Republican cause. Defeated in the 1922 general election, she secured a seat in Dublin Borough South in the August 1923 election when the Civil War had ended, but she abstained from taking her seat as a Sinn Féin republican. Briefly on hunger strike after her arrest for advocating republicanism in November 1923, she wrote a pamphlet, *James Connolly's Policy and Catholic Doctrine* (1924), and a play, *Broken Dreams*. She joined Fianna Fáil when it was founded by De Valera in 1926, and left Sinn Féin which had divided after the IRA had split from it. She also resigned from the IRA women's army, Cumann na mBan, thereby abandon-ing violence and embracing parliamentary democracy. Having been re-elected to the Dáil (1927), she died in a public ward of Sir Patrick Dun's Hospital, in Dublin, on 15 July, 1927, supported by Casimir, her stepson and her daughter. Accorded a public funeral, for which the working class people lined the street, she was buried at Glasnevin cemetery.

Constance Markievicz was shortlisted as a Woman of the Millennium by UK *Guardian* readers (*The Guardian*, 25 January 1999).

Second Dáil ————————————————————————————

General Election to the Parliament of Southern Ireland/ Second Dáil 1921

128 SEATS

Nomination day: 24 May; no election contested

General elections to the parliaments of Northern Ireland and Southern Ireland were provided for in the *Government of Ireland Act, 1920*, which established the two parliaments. The Sinn Féin members of the Southern Ireland house of commons abstained from attendance and, on 16 August 1921, together with one abstentionist Sinn Féin member of the Northern Ireland house of commons, constituted themselves as the second Dáil Éireann.

Women Elected

CLARKE, KATHLEEN (SINN FÉIN, DUBLIN, MID)

ENGLISH, DR ADA (SINN FÉIN, NATIONAL UNIVERSITY OF IRELAND)

MACSWINEY, MARY (SINN FÉIN, CORK CITY)

MARKIEVICZ, CONSTANCE DE (*SEE P. 71*) (SINN FÉIN, DUBLIN SOUTH) (SECRETARY FOR LABOUR RE-APPOINTED 26 AUGUST, 1921)

O'CALLAGHAN, KATHLEEN (SINN FÉIN, LIMERICK CITY & LIMERICK EAST)

PEARSE, MARGARET (SINN FÉIN, DUBLIN)

Kathleen Clarke, née Daly

DATE/PLACE OF BIRTH: 1878/LIMERICK

PARTY: SINN FÉIN

CONSTITUENCY: MID-DUBLIN

DÁIL/SEANAD: 2ND DÁIL: 19 MAY 1921-15 JUNE 1922, 5TH DÁIL: 9 JUNE 1927-14 SEPTEMBER 1927. 3RD, 4TH, 5TH TRIENNIAL PERIODS, SEANAD (6 DECEMBER 1928-29 MAY 1936)

AGE AT ENTRY TO DÁIL: 43

FAMILY: NIECE OF JOHN DALY, SISTER OF EDWARD DALY. MARRIED TO THOMAS J. CLARKE; THREE SONS.

OCCUPATION: BUSINESSWOMAN (DRESSMAKING, SHOPKEEPING)

CAREER:

Married Thomas Clarke, first signatory to the Republican Proclamation, 1916. Arrested in May 1916 and released after her husband's execution (3 May 1916). Formed first Committee of Republican Prisoners' Dependent Fund, May 1916. Deported, May 1918, to Holloway Jail. Founder Member, Vice-president, Cumann na mBan, 1913-26; Member, Sinn Féin Executive, 1917-26; received freedom of city of Limerick, 1921. Alderman, Dublin Corporation, 1922-5. President of Children's Court and last President of Court of Conscience, 1920; District Justice, Sinn Féin Courts and occasionally Circuit Court Judge, 1920 to dissolution of Republican Courts. Chair, Peace Committee set up in the Dáil, 1921-2; Member, Dublin Corporation, 1930-39; candidate for office of Lord Mayor of Dublin, 1932, 1934, 1935, 1936, 1937, 1938. First woman Lord Mayor of Dublin, June 1939 and June 1940. Elector for Senate, 1st and 2nd Senate, after passing of new Constitution. *Particular policy interest*: opposition to Treaty.

PUBLICATIONS:

Revolutionary Woman: Kathleen Clarke 1878-1872: An Autobiography, Helen Litton (ed.) Dublin: O'Brien Press, 1991. Ruane, Medb, 'Kathleen Clarke', in *Ten Dublin Women*, Dublin: Women's Commemoration and Celebration Committee, 1991.

DATE OF DEATH: 1972

ADDRESS: ST RAPHAEL'S, 92 CLONTARF ROAD, DUBLIN

KATHLEEN CLARKE (née Daly) was the third of nine daughters of Edward Daly, Fenian, and was a niece of John Daly, Fenian prisoner and Mayor of Limerick. Her brother, Edward Daly, was executed on 4 May 1916. She was apprenticed as a dressmaker and opened her own business at the age of eighteen. When she sold it five years later, it had become one of the busiest dress warehouses in the city of Limerick. She married Thomas J. Clarke on 16 July 1901, the day after her arrival in New York. Their first son, Daly, was born in 1902, by which time Tom had become an American citizen and a key member of Clann na Gael, under the leadership of John Devoy. The couple ran a candy store and farmed a market garden before returning to Ireland late in 1907, determined to work for Irish independence.

The Clarkes' second son, Tom, was born in 1908, and the following year they opened a second shop at 75A Parnell Street. Tom brought out the first edition of his newspaper, *Irish Freedom*, in October, 1910. The same year, Kathleen gave birth to their third son, Emmett.

Their goal was to create an Irish republic, which would be established on principles of political and religious liberty. The Clarkes did not believe in campaigning for any concessions from Westminster, whether home rule or votes for women. By 1913, Tom was deeply involved in setting up the military arm of Irish nationalists, the Irish Volunteers, and using such new techniques as film to galvanise public support. Kathleen was a founder member of Cumann na mBan, the women's division, whose purpose was the organisation and training of women 'to take their places by the side of those who are working for a free Ireland'.

The problem perceived by both Clarkes at this time was the Irish Parliamentary Party, led by John Redmond, which began to lobby for an effective majority on the Executive of the Volunteers. The Clarkes campaigned against Redmond in their respective organisations, believing that the earlier the split with Westminster politicians, the better the chances for unanimity on the question of a Rising. Membership of Kathleen's Central Branch of Cumann na mBan dropped from two hundred to two dozen and she began to rebuild the organisation. She organised the publishing of rousing pamphlets on Irish rebels (then mainly absent from the schoolbooks), which met with public and commercial success. She ran first-aid classes, signalling and rifle practice, along with less contentious schemes like whist drives and céilithe, valued more highly by the Volunteers.

Plans for a Rising began after the funeral of O'Donovan Rossa in 1915. The Irish Republican Brotherhood decided to entrust to Kathleen Clarke the plans for what should happen after the Rising, because they could trust her to carry on the work in the event of their own arrest and probable death. Within two weeks of the Easter Rising of 1916, Kathleen's husband Tom and brother

Ned Daly had been executed. She herself had been arrested and imprisoned at Ship Street Barracks. Kathleen had said goodbye to Tom on the night before his execution; she had refused to cry for his sake, promising him to give her life for their beliefs. Tom died not knowing that Kathleen was pregnant with their fourth child. She started her mission on the following night, establishing the first committee of the Prisoners' Dependants' Fund. Kathleen helped to regroup the nationalist forces after 1916. Her immediate objective was to channel funds to the relatives of those dead and imprisoned (she refused assistance for her own family, as did her mother and sisters in Limerick). Her longer-term objective was to canvass public opinion in support of the Irish Republic, by propaganda, by maintaining and extending the network of supporters throughout Ireland and, through John Devoy in New York, by damaging Britain's image in the US. Devoy's significance as a leader of Clann na Gael and dispenser of US funds to Ireland was most important to the Irish leaders. Kathleen was his chief liaison in Ireland and thus in a position to influence the Clann's views of all the Irish leaders.

The caring work of the Prisoners' Dependants' Fund contrasted with what were perceived as brutal actions by the British government in its treatment of the signatories and their supporters, even among people who had not supported the Rising. After negotiation, Kathleen amalgamated the Fund with one sponsored by the Irish Parliamentary Party and took full advantage of the extensive network thus created by appointing the relatively unknown Michael Collins as its secretary. Under this innocent cover, Collins was free to rally republican sympathy throughout the country. Kathleen's health suffered as a consequence of her efforts, and she lost her baby.

The tactic of creating a blameless event as an instrument of propaganda was repeated in the Mansion House rally for the return of the signatories' remains to the Irish people. Kathleen invited Éamon de Valera to address the rally. Kathleen believed that public opinion could finish the work started in 1916, unlike De Valera who believed physical force would be necessary.

Kathleen was one of four women elected to the executive of Sinn Féin at its 1917 Convention, which began the task of constructing the Irish Republic. Under pressure from Dr Kathleen Lynn (*see p. 86*) and Jennie Wyse Power (*see p. 164*), the delegates adopted unanimously the inclusion of a specific statement on the equality of men and women in its new constitution.

As a mother of three children, Kathleen found it impractical to go on the run, as Collins advised. She was arrested and deported to Holloway Prison in England, where, with Countess Markievicz and Maud Gonne MacBride, she was placed in the equivalent of an isolation unit. Her isolation brought with it the full import of Tom's death; she was grief-stricken and racked with anxiety about her sons. On her release in 1918, she fell seriously ill.

In the municipal elections of 1919, Kathleen Clarke was returned to Dublin Corporation, representing Wood Quay and Mountjoy, and was elected Alderman for both. She worked with fellow councillors to gain formal recognition of the Sinn Féin government, achieved in May 1920. She was appointed to the judiciary of Sinn Féin courts, a three-circuit system of justice whose hearings were constantly disrupted by Black and Tan raids. Sinn Féin's constitutional commitment to women required the presence of a woman judge at all hearings involving women and so Kathleen acted with the paid professional members of the Circuit Court. She also served as Chairman of the Dublin North City judiciary, whose judges included Jennie Wyse Power (*see p. 164*). Throughout those years, Kathleen's home and her mother's home in Limerick were raided repeatedly, and her mother and sister were brutally beaten. But she refused to be intimidated. Her record of efficiency in the courts led to her appointment as President of the Court of Conscience and the Children's Court in 1920. Her courthouse in South William Street is now the Dublin Civic Museum.

Kathleen voted against the Treaty because she refused to swear allegiance to the King. In her speech against the Treaty she accepted the fact that it gave 'the biggest Home Rule Bill we have ever been offered' but said that that was not freedom. It left Ireland divided and in the Empire. During and after the Civil War, Kathleen Clarke lobbied anti-Treaty members to mount a campaign for the removal of the Oath of Allegiance by force of public opinion. Her efforts redoubled in 1924, when she realised that their viewpoint was now excluded from all aspects of public administration in Ireland, given that elected TDs would not enter the Dáil, and the Free State Government had replaced elected corporations with a system of directly appointed Commissioners. De Valera invited her to work with him in establishing a new political party, Fianna Fáil, whose militarist reference was now restricted to this title alone (isolating the IRA, which began to develop outside the democratic process). Although busy with her new shop in D'Olier Street, Kathleen put her best effort into the new party.

She broke with Fianna Fáil in 1943 because of a disagreement over policies.

Ada (Adeline) English, MB, BCh, BAO

DATE/PLACE OF BIRTH: C. 1878/MULLINGAR

PARTY: SINN FÉIN

CONSTITUENCY: NATIONAL UNIVERSITY OF IRELAND

DÁIL/SEANAD: 2ND DÁIL (19 MAY 1921–15 JUNE 1922)

AGE AT ENTRY TO DÁIL: C. 43

FAMILY: YOUNGER DAUGHTER OF P.J. AND NORA ENGLISH

EDUCATION: LORETO CONVENT, MULLINGAR. ROYAL UNIVERSITY OF IRELAND, GRADUATED IN 1903, CATHOLIC UNIVERSITY SCHOOL OF MEDICINE, CECILIA STREET, DUBLIN

OCCUPATION: MEDICAL DOCTOR

CAREER:
Member, Sinn Féin. Medical Officer, Irish Volunteers, 1913. Executive Member, Founder member, Cumann na mBan branch in Ballinasloe, 1915. Lecturer, examiner on mental diseases in University College Galway, 1914.

DATE OF DEATH: 1944

DR ADA ENGLISH devoted her life's professional work to Ballinasloe and Castlerea Mental Hospitals. Upon graduation from the Royal University, she was one of the first female doctors in Ireland. She served for a period in the Mater, Richmond and Temple Street Hospitals, Dublin, before taking up duty at St Brigid's Hospital, Ballinasloe, in 1914, where she was appointed Resident Medical Superintendent (RMS) in 1941. With Dr Kirwan, then RMS, she joined in a campaign in favour of Irish manufacturing for use in Irish institutions and the substitution of the Galway Arms for Queen Victoria on the uniform buttons worn by the staff.

Ada English was to the fore in bringing about the changes which transformed the then 'Lunatic Asylum' into one of the finest mental hospitals in the country. She developed occupational therapy to a high degree, and Ballinasloe was the first mental hospital in Ireland to start electroconvulsive therapy (ECT). Dr English was lecturer and examiner on mental diseases in UCG from 1914.

An active member of Sinn Féin, Ada English became prominent in the Republican movement and was the founder member of Cumann na mBan branch in Ballinasloe in 1915, and for many years was an executive member. She was an intimate friend of Joseph McDonagh, Patrick Pearse, Arthur Griffith, and very many other national figures of the struggle for independence. She gave asylum to Éamon de Valera and Liam Mellows in the hospital on many occasions.

Ada was a Medical Officer of the Irish Volunteers from their inception and attended at Athenry during the 1916 Rising. A fluent Irish speaker, she was politically very active in the years following 1916, was arrested by the British in 1920 and sentenced to nine months' imprisonment in Galway Jail for possession of Cumann na mBan literature. She was released after six months with ptomaine poisoning. She voted against the Articles of Agreement, and was in the Hammam Hotel with Cathal Brugha in July, 1922.

In 1921, Dr English was offered promotion to be RMS of Sligo Mental Hospital, by the Minister of Local Government, Austin Stack, but she refused to be parted from her patients in Ballinasloe. In 1914 and in the Emergency she organised Red Cross lectures. She died in 1944. By her own wish, she is buried beside some of her patients in Creagh Cemetery, adjoining the Mental Hospital.

Mary MacSwiney

DATE/PLACE OF BIRTH: 27 MARCH 1872/SURREY, ENGLAND

PARTY: SINN FÉIN/REPUBLICAN

CONSTITUENCY: CORK CITY

DÁIL/SEANAD: 2ND, 3RD, 4TH DÁIL (19 MAY 1921–8 JUNE 1927)

AGE AT ENTRY TO DÁIL: 49

FAMILY: DAUGHTER OF JOHN MACSWINEY, CORK AND MARY WILKINSON,
LONDON. SISTER OF TERENCE MACSWINEY (LORD MAYOR OF CORK),
AND SEAN MACSWINEY (TD, 1921–2)

EDUCATION: ST ANGELA'S URSULINE COLLEGE, CORK. QUEEN'S COLLEGE, CORK, ROYAL UNIVERSITY,
CAMBRIDGE UNIVERSITY (TEACHING DIPLOMA)

OCCUPATION: SECONDARY SCHOOLTEACHER

CAREER:
Member, Council of State, 1922. Member, Munster Women's Franchise League. Pioneer of language revival movement in Cork. Founder member, Inghinidhe na hÉireann and Cumann na mBan, 1914-33. Vice-president Cumann na mBan. First president Cumann na mBan in Cork. Member, Sinn Féin, 1917. Member, Governing Body of University College, Cork as a graduates' representative. Member, Cork Literary Society. *Particular policy interest*: Anti-Treaty. Abstentionist in 3rd and 4th Dáil.

PUBLICATIONS:
Fallon, Charlotte H. *Soul of Fire: A Biography of Mary MacSwiney*, Cork, Mercier Press, 1986.

DATE OF DEATH: 7 MARCH 1942

ADDRESS: BELGRAVE PLACE, WELLINGTON ROAD, CORK

MARY MACSWINEY was a teacher in Farnborough, England until 1906, and later in France. She returned to teach at St Angela's Ursuline College, Cork, where she had received her education. She was dismissed after her arrest for nationalist activities in 1916 and, upon her release from prison later that year, established in her home her own school, St Ita's, modelled on St Enda's, the school founded by Patrick Pearse.

She joined the women's suffrage movement, the Munster Women's Franchise League, and was a member of the Cork committee of that movement. She was a pioneer of the language revival movement in Cork and a founder member of Inghinidhe na hÉireann and of Cumann na mBan, the women's counterpart of the Irish Volunteers. She became its first president in Cork, a position which she held until her death, and was also vice-president of the organisation as a whole. In 1917 she joined Sinn Féin, influenced by her brother Terence, a prominent officer in the Irish Volunteers. Terence MacSwiney, Lord Mayor of Cork, died on hunger strike in Brixton Prison in 1920.

In 1920 Mary went to Washington to give evidence before the American Commission on conditions in Ireland, inquiring into the activities of the

Black and Tans. While she was in the US she met Éamon de Valera who, when he was called back to Ireland, asked her to fulfil his lecturing engagements, a task which she fulfilled with success.

After the death of Terence, Mary became TD for Cork. She was one of the most vehement critics of the Treaty, which, in a three-hour Dáil speech, she described as 'the grossest act of betrayal that Ireland ever endured'. She said that if it was accepted, she would use her influence as a teacher to teach rebellion against the proposed Free State.

On 25 October 1922, when the Republican deputies met secretly in Dublin, Mary MacSwiney was appointed as one of the twelve members of Éamon de Valera's Council of State. She was the first woman to resort to a hunger strike during the Civil War, beginning immediately after her imprisonment in Mountjoy Jail on 4 November 1922. Cumann na mBan organised meetings and marched on the prison and government offices. A nightly vigil of the rosary was held at the prison gates. Free State troops fired shots over the heads of the protesters, primarily members of Cumann na mBan, and hosed and harassed them, which served to enhance the publicity surrounding their protest.

On 21 November, when Annie MacSwiney was refused permission to see her sister, she encamped at the prison gates and went on hunger strike also. In protest at the exclusion of her sister, Mary MacSwiney then refused to have nurses or doctors attend her. On the twentieth day of her hunger strike, her condition became critical. She was given the Last Rites. People from both Ireland and abroad lobbied the government for her release, and four days later she was set free. Henceforth, the strike was seen as an effective weapon against the Free State Government. She also endured twenty-one days on hunger strike in Kilmainham in 1923 along with Kate O'Callaghan (*see p. 82*) and other well-known women. Of this strike she later wrote; 'the only kind of strike' was when the striker realised 'fully the probability of death and [was] ready for it.'. Again she was released.

In 1927 De Valera, leading the Fianna Fáil party, decided to break with the Sinn Féin policy of abstention. The party entered the Dáil on 11 August. Mary MacSwiney, however, adhered to the Sinn Féin organisation and continued as a leader. She bitterly criticised the step taken by her former anti-Treaty colleagues, which she described as the 'first step down the slippery slope'.

Some years before her death, she broke with Sinn Féin on the grounds that its Ard-Fheis sanctioned the acceptance of pensions for its employees. In 1933 she resigned from Cumann na mBan because the portion of its constitution pledging allegiance to the Dáil was deleted. Up to the time of her death, Mary MacSwiney continued to espouse the Republican cause. A brilliant public speaker, possessed of a charming personality, she was held in the highest esteem even by her political opponents.

Kathleen O'Callaghan, née Murphy

DATE/PLACE OF BIRTH: 1888, CROSSMAHON/LISSARDA, COUNTY CORK
PARTY: (1) SINN FÉIN, (2) CUMANN NA POBLACHTA/REPUBLICAN ASSOCIATION
CONSTITUENCY: LIMERICK CITY. LIMERICK EAST
DÁIL/SEANAD: 2ND DÁIL (19 MAY 1921-15 JUNE, 1922), 3RD DÁIL
(16 JUNE 1922-26 AUGUST 1923)
AGE AT ENTRY TO DÁIL: 33
FAMILY: MARRIED CLLR MICHAEL O'CALLAGHAN (MAYOR OF LIMERICK, 1920)
EDUCATION: DOMINICAN CONVENT, ECCLES STREET, DUBLIN. ROYAL UNIVERSITY, CAMBRIDGE
UNIVERSITY (MA IN LANGUAGES)
OCCUPATION: PROFESSOR, MARY IMMACULATE TEACHER TRAINING COLLEGE, LIMERICK
CAREER:
Treaty Speeches – 2nd Dáil. As an Anti-Treaty Cumann na Poblachta candidate, refused to take her seat in the 3rd Dáil. Founder member, Féile Luimní. Founder member, Cumann na mBan and the Gaelic League in Limerick. Trustee, Green Cross Fund (established to help the dependants of IRA soldiers lost in the fight for freedom).
DATE OF DEATH: 1961
ADDRESS: ST MARGARET'S, O'CALLAGHAN STRAND, LIMERICK (NAMED AFTER HER HUSBAND)

KATHLEEN O'CALLAGHAN came from a republican family and was a lifelong friend and associate of Mary MacSwiney. In 1949, in a speech on Sarsfield Bridge, before a large crowd, she made the declaration, for Limerick, of Ireland as a Republic. On 7 March 1921, she had witnessed the murder by British forces of her husband, Councillor Michael O'Callaghan, a former Mayor of Limerick.

Kate O'Callaghan took a distinguished part in the cultural, antiquarian and charitable life of Limerick. She succeeded her late sister, Mairéad O'Donovan, on the professorial staff of the Training College of Mary Immaculate, Limerick, and was herself succeeded by another sister, Eilis Murphy. She is buried in Mount Saint Laurence Cemetery, Limerick.

Margaret Pearse, née Brady

DATE OF BIRTH: 1857
PARTY: SINN FÉIN
CONSTITUENCY: DUBLIN COUNTY
DÁIL/SEANAD: 2ND DÁIL (19 MAY 1921-15 JUNE, 1922)
AGE AT ENTRY TO DÁIL: 64
FAMILY: MOTHER OF PATRICK AND WILLIAM PEARSE. DAUGHTER OF PATRICK
BRADY, A COAL FACTOR, OF COUNTY MEATH BACKGROUND. SHOP ASSISTANT IN
STATIONER'S. MARRIED JAMES PEARSE, AN ENGLISH IMMIGRANT STONE CARVER
AND SCULPTOR IN 1876 OR 1877. WITHIN SIX YEARS HAD FOUR CHILDREN,
MARGARET, PATRICK, WILLIE AND MARY BRIDGET (LATER BRIGID)

OCCUPATION: MATRON AND HOUSEKEEPER AT ST ENDA'S SCHOOL

CAREER:

Committee Member, Irish Volunteers' Dependants' Fund, 1916. Honorary Member, Cumann na mBan, 1917–18. Particular policy interests – Anti-Treaty

DATE OF DEATH: 1932

ADDRESS: 27 GREAT BRUNSWICK STREET, DUBLIN (ADDRESS WHILE IN DÁIL)

Third Dáil ——————————————————————————————

General Election: 16 June 1922 (The 'Pact Election')   *128 SEATS*

Women Elected

MACSWINEY, MARY (*SEE P. 80*) (CUMANN NA POBLACHTA/REPUBLICAN ASSOCIATION, CORK CITY)
O'CALLAGHAN, KATHLEEN (*SEE P. 82*) (CUMANN NA POBLACHTA/REPUBLICAN ASSOCIATION, LIMERICK CITY AND LIMERICK EAST)

A last-minute electoral pact was agreed upon by Michael Collins and Éamon de Valera in May 1922, whereby there would be a national coalition panel for the Third Dáil, the number of candidates being determined by the existing strength of each faction. A coalition government would then be formed. Collins reneged on the electoral pact and the peace initiative disintegrated rapidly. Of the pro-Treaty panel, fifty-eight won seats and thirty-five seats were won by the anti-Treaty section. For the first time, Labour took part in an election, winning seventeen seats. Farmers and independents won seven seats each. Countess Markievicz, Margaret Pearse, Ada English and Kathleen Clarke were all defeated. The only women returned to the Third Dáil were Mary MacSwiney in Cork and Kate O'Callaghan in Limerick, both areas with strong anti-Treaty support. Anti-Treaty, or Cumann na Poblachta, deputies refused to take their seats. In any case, the Dáil, due to assemble on 30 June, was aborted by the start of military action.

Fourth Dáil ——————————————————————————————

General Election: 27 August 1923   *153 SEATS*

Women Elected

BRUGHA, CAITLÍN (REPUBLICAN, COUNTY WATERFORD)
COLLINS-O'DRISCOLL, MARGARET (CUMANN NA NGAEDHEAL, DUBLIN NORTH)
LYNN, DR KATHLEEN (DUBLIN COUNTY)
MACSWINEY, MARY (*SEE P. 80*) (REPUBLICAN, CORK CITY)
MARKIEVICZ, CONSTANCE DE (*SEE P. 71*) (REPUBLICAN, DUBLIN SOUTH)

Sinn Féin deputies refused to take their seats.

Caitlín Brugha, née Kingston

DATE/PLACE OF BIRTH: DECEMBER 1879/BIRR, COUNTY OFFALY

PARTY: REPUBLICAN (SINN FÉIN)

CONSTITUENCY: COUNTY WATERFORD

DÁIL/SEANAD: 4TH, 5TH DÁIL: 27 AUGUST 1923-14 SEPTEMBER 1927

AGE AT ENTRY TO DÁIL: 43

FAMILY: MARRIED TO CATHAL BRUGHA (MINISTER FOR DEFENCE, 1919-2). FIVE DAUGHTERS, ONE SON (RUAIDHRÍ BRUGHA, TD – DUBLIN COUNTY, SOUTH, 1973-77; SENATOR, 1969-73, 1977-81)

EDUCATION: SACRED HEART CONVENT, ROSCREA

OCCUPATION: COMPANY DIRECTOR

CAREER: Organiser, Gaelic League, Birr and Dublin. Secretary, Sinn Féin executive for several years, persuaded to continue at the Ard-Fheis of 1926. Trustee, Prisoners' National Aid Society. *Particular policy interest*: Abstentionist in Fourth Dáil. *Other interests*: Irish culture, art and industry.

DATE OF DEATH: 1 DECEMBER 1959

ADDRESS: ROS NA RIOGH, RATHDOWN CRESCENT, TERENURE, DUBLIN

CAITLÍN BRUGHA was elected at the first election after her husband's death. She took his Waterford seat, topping the poll. Born in Birr, County Offaly, where her family had been in business for over a century, in 1910 she moved with her family to Dublin where she rejoined the Gaelic League and there met Cathal Brugha whom she married on 12 February 1912. Cathal Brugha was a founder director of Lalor Ltd., candle manufacturers, IRA chief of staff 1917–18 and acting president of the meeting of the 1st Dáil in 1919.

Throughout the 1916 Rising, Caitlín Brugha actively supported the Volunteers, while her husband was second in command at the South Dublin Union.

> *Does any man contemplate with equanimity a renewal of the conditions in this country in which his wife [Caitlín Brugha]will be dragged in the dead of the night out of her house, hustled along through the garden, and put into a motor lorry, and kept there in order that she will not be present while her husband is being murdered if the English cut-throats can get him?*

CATHAL BRUGHA, TREATY DEBATE, *DÁIL ÉIREANN OFFICIAL REPORT*, 7 JANUARY, 1922, COL. 328

Caitlín Brugha was bringing up a young family when her husband was mortally wounded, emerging from a back door of the Hammam Hotel, Upper O'Connell Street, Dublin, while fighting on the Republican side in July 1922. He died two days later. Caitlín Brugha made a public request for the women of the Republican movement alone to act as chief mourners and guard of honour at her husband's funeral. Her decision was a protest, she declared, against the civil war which had been waged by the [Free State] government against Republicans.

In January 1924, Caitlín Brugha established Kingston's Ltd., a drapery business in Nassau Street. In 1928 the business was transferred to Hammam Buildings, Upper O'Connell Street, where Cathal Brugha had been shot in 1922. Later branches were established in Grafton Street and George's Street. She is buried in Glasnevin Cemetery.

Margaret Collins-O'Driscoll

DATE/PLACE OF BIRTH: 1878/WOODFIELD, CLONAKILTY, COUNTY CORK

PARTY: CUMANN NA NGAEDHEAL

CONSTITUENCY: DUBLIN NORTH

DÁIL/SEANAD: 4TH, 5TH, 6TH, 7TH DÁIL (27 AUGUST 1923-23 JANUARY 1933)

AGE AT ENTRY TO DÁIL: 45

FAMILY: MARRIED PATRICK O'DRISCOLL, 1901; FIVE SONS, NINE DAUGHTERS, ELEVEN SURVIVING. SISTER OF GENERAL MICHAEL COLLINS (MINISTER OF HOME AFFAIRS, AND MINISTER OF FINANCE, 1919-1922. COMMANDER-IN-CHIEF OF THE GOVERNMENT FORCES IN THE CIVIL WAR); GRANDAUNT OF NORA OWEN, TD (*SEE P. 122*) AND MARY BANOTTI, MEP (*SEE P. 216*)

EDUCATION: BAGGOT STREET TRAINING COLLEGE

OCCUPATION: PRIMARY SCHOOLTEACHER. PRINCIPAL OF LISAVARD GIRLS' SCHOOL, CLONAKILTY, COUNTY CORK, 1896-1922; TEACHER IN WEST DUBLIN MODEL SCHOOLS UNTIL 1928

CAREER:

Vice-president, Cumann na nGaedheal, May 1926-7. *Other interests*: Antique collecting, whist drives.

DATE OF DEATH: 17 JUNE 1945

ADDRESS: 147 NORTH CIRCULAR ROAD, DUBLIN

MARGARET COLLINS-O'DRISCOLL was elected at the first election after her brother, Michael Collins, had been shot dead at Béal na Bláth (22 August 1922). During her Dáil term she held the record among private members for attendance at divisions, even though she held a teaching job also until 1928. She also addressed hundreds of public meetings. In her Dáil speeches, she drew on her professional background, especially on the *School Attendance Act, 1926*.

As a government backbencher Margaret was expected to vote for government legislation and defend government policy. She explained her support for the *Civil Service Regulation (Amendment) Bill*, which made women ineligible for certain jobs, as follows:

> *There is no one in this Dáil more interested in this Bill than I am, and for that reason I do not propose to give a silent vote on the Second Reading. During the*

past few days I have been canvassed by very influential members of my sex to vote against this Bill ... I cannot see that it infringes our rights under the Constitution in any respect. I am not enamoured of this Bill. I am by no means in love with it, and I must admit it limits to a certain extent the appointments for which women are eligible.... When I was elected to the Dáil I was not elected on the question of sex. I gave a pledge to my constituents that I would do the best I can for the interests of the community at large. The more I study this Bill the more I see that I would be injuring my sex by voting against it. The number of appointments women would be excluded from would be very small and the Minister has given us a good explanation.... All I can say to those people who canvassed me to vote against this Bill is that women, when the next election will come on, will have an opportunity to return women on the Government ticket to this Dáil who will have the power to amend this Bill if it is passed. I think I have given a sufficient explanation ... and I ask the Minister and Government to limit the number of appointments as far as possible for which women would be ineligible under this Bill.

DÁIL ÉIREANN OFFICIAL REPORT, VOL. 13, 18 NOVEMBER 1924, COLS. 514–5

Margaret Collins-O'Driscoll was committed to equal opportunities and ensured that her daughters were enabled to enter professional careers. She opposed corporal punishment and never slapped a child.

Her husband was editor of the *Skibbereen Eagle* and a parliamentary reporter. She was the only woman Member of the 6th Dáil (1927–32).

Kathleen Lynn

DATE/PLACE OF BIRTH: 1874/CONG, COUNTY MAYO
PARTY: SINN FÉIN
CONSTITUENCY: DUBLIN COUNTY
DÁIL/SEANAD: 4TH DÁIL (27 AUGUST 1923-8 JUNE 1927)
AGE AT ENTRY TO DÁIL: 49
FAMILY: DAUGHTER OF REVEREND ROBERT LYNN, RECTOR OF CONG, COUNTY MAYO
EDUCATION: ALEXANDRA COLLEGE, DUBLIN; ENGLAND, GERMANY. ROYAL UNIVERSITY OF IRELAND, GRADUATED 1899. FRCSI, 1909
OCCUPATION: MEDICAL DOCTOR
CAREER:
Vice-president, Irish Women's Workers' Union. *Particular policy interests*: Anti-Treaty. Abstentionist.
PUBLICATION:
Ruane, Medb, 'Kathleen Lynn' in *Ten Dublin Women*, Dublin: Women's Commemoration and Celebration Committee, 1991.
DATE OF DEATH: 14 SEPTEMBER 1955
ADDRESS: BELGRAVE ROAD, RATHMINES

KATHLEEN LYNN was born when the Mayo harvests began to fail again after the Famine. Her father was the Church of Ireland rector. The people of Mayo had worked with Fanny and Anna Parnell's Ladies' Land League in the pioneering campaign of resistance that led to the Land Act of 1881. Kathleen was familiar with the stories of the people's defence of their homes and desperate struggle to survive. She noticed that the local doctor was a source of help and hope, and decided to study medicine.

In 1899, she was one of the first women to obtain a medical degree from the Royal University. She was elected as a house surgeon at the Adelaide Hospital but objections from other doctors to having a female colleague prevented her appointment from being ratified. She finally managed to join the staff of Sir Patrick Dun's Hospital, and then worked at the Rotunda before starting her own practice at 9 Belgrave Road in Rathmines. Her experience as an unemployed woman doctor, and her sense of injustice, led her to become involved in the Women's Suffrage Movement with other women graduates like Hanna Sheehy-Skeffington. She was an activist with the suffragettes and a medical attendant to them during their militant campaign, which led to imprisonment and hunger strikes from 1912. Through this involvement, Kathleen was drawn to national-ism and especially to the beliefs of James Connolly, Ulster organiser for the Irish Transport and General Workers' Union; Connolly was a committed feminist.

Kathleen Lynn joined the Citizen Army at Connolly's invitation during the 1913 Lockout and organised first-aid instruction and ambulances at Liberty Hall. She also worked in the soup kitchen with Constance Markievicz (*see p. 71*) and other women whose differing interpretations of the paths of labour or feminism or nationalism had been temporarily put aside in face of the life-threatening situation of Dublin workers. Connolly's appointment as Commandant of the Citizen Army led to Kathleen's appointment as Chief Medical Officer, in which capacity she gained first-hand knowledge of the appalling living and working conditions of the Dublin working class.

Apart from its socialist concerns, the Citizen Army was unique among nationalist organisations in providing its women members with arms and arms training. Women had been excluded from membership of the Volunteers, estab-lished in November 1913 in response to the formation of the Ulster Volunteers in 1912, and the growing move towards militarism across Europe. Pressure from women had led eventually to a women's auxiliary organisation, Cumann na mBan, in April 1914. Although Cumann na mBan began rifle practice, its mem-bers were not allowed to use arms; their role was seen as non-combatant and supportive of their male colleagues. By contrast, James Connolly made clear his decision that, whatever the reservation of the men, women in the Citizen Army would play an equal part in the imminent confrontation.

As a newly promoted captain, Kathleen was assigned to the St Stephen's Green unit in the Easter Rising of 1916 — a Citizen Army post headed by Michael Mallin and Constance Markievicz (*see p. 71*). As Chief Medical Officer, she was responsible for medical planning and supplies to all the Citizen Army stations but, en route to the Green, decided to inspect the City Hall station which was expected to incur heavy casualties from the Dublin Castle garrison. She set up a surgery with Jenny Shanahan, and treated both military and civilian casualties, including the fatal injury to the station's captain, Sean Connolly, an Abbey actor whose fiancée and Abbey colleague Helena Moloney of the Irish Women Workers' Union was under Kathleen's command. On receiving instructions to surrender, Kathleen presented herself as Senior Officer, and was immediately arrested and imprisoned, first at Ship Street Barracks and then at Kilmainham and Mountjoy Jails until her deportation to England in June.

Released in 1917, Kathleen was elected to the 24-person executive at the Sinn Féin Convention in October 1917, along with Kathleen Clarke (*see p. 75*), Grace Gifford Plunkett and Constance Markievicz. With Jennie Wyse Power (*see p. 164*) she reacted instantly to suggestions for re-interpreting the 1916 proclamation, which had promised equal rights and opportunities to all citizens of the Republic as well as a commitment to cherish equally all the nation's children. They succeeded in winning unanimous support for the motion that Sinn Féin emphasise the equality of men and women in all speeches and pamphlets, the first such specific commitment by a nationalist organisation. The women executive members then formed Cumann na dTeachtaire to promote matters of particular concern to women, ranging from employment issues to increased provisions of ladies' toilets in Dublin. Dr Lynn served as Surgeon-General to Sinn Féin.

Kathleen Lynn's house was repeatedly raided and she carried out her medical calls disguised as a well-dressed lady with a flowing feather boa. After the round-up of Sinn Féin leaders in 1918, Kathleen, who had been on the run, appeared at a Sinn Féin Convention, and inserted a notice in the press indicating that she had retired to her residence in Rathmines. She was arrested and awaited deportation to prison in England. However, following a massive petition organised by the Lord Mayor of Dublin 'with a view to having her professional services made available during the influenza epidemic', she was released and went to work among the dying; thousands died during the flu epidemic of 1918.

In 1919, 164 of every 1,000 Dublin infants died from preventable diseases (a rate higher than that of modern-day Malawi). Kathleen decided to start her own hospital. With her Citizen Army colleague, Madeleine ffrench-Mullen, Kathleen bought a run-down house at 37 Charlemont Street and, on Ascension Thursday 1919, launched Teach Ultan, a hospital 'for the medical treatment of infants under one year of age'. Her resources consisted of two cots and £70. The hospital was staffed entirely by women doctors in its early years. Cleaners included Maud Gonne and Constance Markievicz. Former first-aid pupils from the Citizen Army and Irish Women Workers' Union were among the first nurses. Kathleen was responsible for medical provision and planning. The hospital was named after the Gaelic leader who, as Bishop of Meath, cared for children orphaned by the Buí Conall or Yellow Plague which had swept through Europe. Kathleen and Madeleine made a pilgrimage to St Ultan's Well in Ardbraccan near Navan each year on Ultan's feast-day, 4 September.

Dr Kathleen Lynn's political involvement continued with committee work for prisoners' political status and conditions, through the League of Women Delegates. From 1917, she served as vice-president of the Irish Women's Workers' Union and campaigned for Constance Markievicz in the December 1918 elections to Westminster, when Irish propertied women over the age of thirty voted for the first time. Kathleen stood on an anti-Treaty ticket in the 1923 election to Dáil Éireann and was one of five women elected in a franchise open to all citizens over the age of twenty-one. She was abstentionist and did not take her seat. Thereafter, politics took a back seat to medicine, though Dr Lynn continued to be an active member of Rathmines Urban District Council.

At St Ultan's, Kathleen Lynn introduced a series of pioneering programmes ranging from the training of local women as auxiliary nurses, to classes for mothers on the diet, hygiene and development of their children. By 1936, her public statements addressed the epidemic rate of tuberculosis among the patients, many of whom developed the disease at no more than two months old. She was impressed by the work of paediatrician Dorothy Stopford-Price (niece of Alice Stopford Green — *see p. 162*), who was studying the new bacillus known as BCG, and invited her to carry out a sample programme at St Ultan's. At the end of 1936, Dorothy, had vaccinated thirty-five children at St Ultan's; it was the first hospital in Ireland to use the BCG vaccine and the model for the Dublin Corporation scheme. The St Ultan's-based National BCG Committee had virtually eradicated TB in Ireland by 1970.

Constant fundraising and brilliant administration were necessary to keep St Ultan's going. Garden parties were hosted in the grounds of the Ely O'Carroll mansion at Peter's Place off Adelaide Road, and subscribers were enlisted by such fundraisers as the 'St Ultan's Book', which included contributions from artists John and Jack Yeats and Harry Kernoff. Kathleen made a number of fundraising tours of the United States. These efforts, combined with income from the newly formed Irish Hospitals Trust, allowed St Ultan's to operate without charge to its patients. The hospital contained one of the world's first Montessori wards, Kathleen Lynn having begun a correspondence with Maria Montessori, who visited St Ultan's in 1934. Both doctors shared a profound belief in the essential human and civil rights of the child.

Dr Lynn aimed to build a modern children's hospital. St Ultan's gradually acquired an area of neighbouring slum property and drew up architectural and financial plans. Difficulties in fundraising arose from the low status of St Ultan's in the hospital hierarchy of the time, combined with the stated opposition of Catholic Archbishop, John Charles McQuaid, to a hospital which did not give him a veto over staff appointments and allowed Catholic and Protestant staff to work side by side. Shortly afterwards, the National Children's Hospital was built in Crumlin, with approval of staff appointments assigned to the Archbishop. He raised objections to the work of the National BCG Committee at St Ultan's, but public opinion in favour of the hospital was such that his objections were overcome. Kathleen succeeded in building a special BCG wing.

Dr Kathleen Lynn attended her last clinic at St Ultan's hospital in April 1955. She died on 14 September of that year and was buried with full military honours.

Fifth Dáil ————————————————————————

General Election: 9 June 1927 *153 SEATS*

Women Elected

BRUGHA, CAITLÍN (*SEE P. 84*) (SINN FÉIN, COUNTY WATERFORD)
CLARKE, KATHLEEN (*SEE P. 75*) (FF, DUBLIN CITY, NORTH)
COLLINS-O'DRISCOLL, MARGARET (*SEE P. 85*) (CUMANN NA NGAEDHEAL, DUBLIN NORTH)
MARKIEVICZ, CONSTANCE DE (*SEE P. 71*) (FF, DUBLIN CITY, SOUTH) (DIED 15 JULY 1927)

Sixth Dáil ————————————————————————

General Election: 15 September 1927 *153 SEATS*

Women Elected

COLLINS-O'DRISCOLL, MARGARET (*SEE P. 85*) (CUMANN NA NGAEDHEAL, DUBLIN NORTH)

Seventh Dáil ————————————————————————

General Election: 16 February 1932 *153 SEATS*

Women Elected

COLLINS-O'DRISCOLL, MARGARET (*SEE P. 85*) (CUMANN NA NGAEDHEAL, DUBLIN CITY NORTH)
REYNOLDS, MARY (CUMANN NA NGAEDHEAL, SLIGO/LEITRIM)

Mary Reynolds

DATE/PLACE OF BIRTH: C. 1890/DRUMCOWRA, BALLINAMORE, COUNTY LEITRIM

PARTY: CUMANN NA NGAEDHEAL/FINE GAEL

CONSTITUENCY: SLIGO/LEITRIM

DÁIL/SEANAD: 7TH DÁIL (16 FEBRUARY 1932-23 JANUARY 1933), 9TH, 10TH, 11TH, 12TH, 13TH, 14TH, 15TH, 16TH DÁIL (JULY 1937-3 OCTOBER 1961). DID NOT STAND IN 1961

AGE AT ENTRY TO DÁIL: C. 42

FAMILY: WIDOW OF PATRICK REYNOLDS (FINE GAEL TD, SLIGO); SEVEN CHILDREN INCLUDING PATRICK JOSEPH REYNOLDS (TD, ROSCOMMON AND ROSCOMMON/LEITRIM, 1961-77, LATER A SENATOR). GRANDMOTHER OF GERRY REYNOLDS (TD, SLIGO/LEITRIM, 1989-92, 1997)

OCCUPATION: FARMER, GROCER, SPIRIT MERCHANT

EDUCATION: LOCAL NATIONAL SCHOOL

DATE OF DEATH: 29 AUGUST 1974

ADDRESS: MAIN STREET, BALLINAMORE, COUNTY LEITRIM

MARY REYNOLDS was first returned to the Dáil in the 1932 election, following the death of her husband Deputy Paddy Reynolds who was fatally shot, together with Detective Officer McGeehan, during the election campaign. As a result of the tragedy, the election in the constituency was postponed. Mary was returned in nine of the ten subsequent elections which she contested, and holds the record for the woman winning most elections. She was not elected in 1933, and she did not contest the 1961 election as Leitrim was divided between Sligo and Roscommon.

Mary Reynolds saw her role primarily as a constituency worker, asking parliamentary questions, as opposed to speaking in debates. Her closest parliamentary associates were Donough O'Malley and Dan Spring. She attended daily mass.

Eighth Dáil ————————————————————————

General Election: 24 January 1933   *153 SEATS*

Women Elected

HELENA CONCANNON (FF, NATIONAL UNIVERSITY)

MARGARET MARY PEARSE (FF, DUBLIN COUNTY)

BRIDGET MARY REDMOND (CUMANN NA NGAEDHEAL, WATERFORD)

Helena Concannon, née Walsh

DATE/PLACE OF BIRTH: 1878/MAGHERA, COUNTY DERRY

PARTY: FIANNA FÁIL

CONSTITUENCY: DÁIL: NATIONAL UNIVERSITY. SEANAD: NATIONAL UNIVERSITY

DÁIL/SEANAD: 8TH DÁIL: 24 JANUARY 1933-30 JUNE, 1937

SEANAD: 28 MARCH 1938-28 FEBRUARY 1952

AGE AT ENTRY TO DÁIL: 54

FAMILY: MARRIED THOMAS CONCANNON OF THE ARAN ISLANDS, 1906

EDUCATION: LORETO COLLEGES, BALBRIGGAN AND ST STEPHEN'S GREEN, ROYAL UNIVERSITY (BA, MA)
STUDIED LANGUAGES AT THE SORBONNE AND THE COLLEGE DE FRANCE IN PARIS, BERLIN UNIVERSITY,
ROME. D.LITT. (1929), SENATE OF THE NATIONAL UNIVERSITY OF IRELAND

OCCUPATION: HISTORIAN, LANGUAGE SCHOLAR, AUTHOR

CAREER:

Member, Gaelic League. Member, Senate of the National University; Governing Body of
University College, Galway.

PUBLICATIONS:

Women of Ninety Eight (1919), *Makers of Irish History* (1920), *Irish History for Junior Classes*
(1921), *Daughters of Banba* (1922), *Defenders of the Ford* (1925), *A Garden of Girls* (1928),
The Poor Clares in Ireland (1929), *White Horsemen* (1930), *Irish Nuns in Penal Days* (1931),
St Patrick (1931), *St Columban* (n.d.), *The Blessed Eucharist in Irish History* (1932), *Blessed
Oliver Plunket* (1935), *The Queen of Ireland* (1938), *The Irish Sisters of Mercy in the
Crimean War* (1950), and *Poems* (1953). Contributed to influential nationalist periodicals and
journals and wrote religious articles for the *Irish Messenger.*

DATE OF DEATH: 27 FEBRUARY 1952

HELENA CONCANNON was the National University representative in the Dáil until
university representation was abolished under the 1937 Constitution. She was
the only woman in the Dáil to make a substantial speech in the debate on the
draft Constitution. Regarding the controversial Article 41 ('The state shall ...
endeavour to ensure that mothers shall not be obliged by economic necessity to
engage in labour to neglect of their duties in the home'), she pointed out that
the government, in one of its earliest social reforms, had accepted the principle
in the *Widows and Orphans Pensions Act, 1932.* She said:

> *Deputies are aware that many women's societies are perturbed by certain
> Articles in the Draft Constitution, and we have been told should this measure
> go through the House unamended the status of women in the State will defi-
> nitely be lowered.... It is to Irish mothers and Irish homes that we owe the fact
> that we have won, to the extent that we have won it, success for the long fight
> we have had for our faith and nationality, and I am very glad that Article 41
> has recognised the services of women in the home. It does not mean — and I for
> one would protest most actively against it if it did mean — to close the door to
> work for women in any other sphere. That is not the intention at all. It will be
> found that women will work better in the homes if they have been educated
> and if they have had contact with outside life. Therefore, I hope that this
> Article will stand and that women will avail of it....*

OFFICIAL REPORT DÁIL ÉIREANN, VOL. 67, 12 MAY 1937. BUNREACHT NA HÉIREANN (DRÉACHT),
COL. 241–242

The following year, she became a member of the Seanad for the National Universities of Ireland, and remained a Senator until her death. She took an active part in the Senate, and was particularly interested in all forms of legislation relating to women.

> *I recall especially all the fear entertained regarding Article 41 and its supposed threat to women, who would henceforth be confined to their kitchens.... Fortunately, all these fears have been set at rest, and if there is any grouse at all about Article 41 it will come from me.... If those words mean anything, it is that there should be something in the nature of family allowances, and that a woman, through the unemployment of her husband, the normal breadwinner, should not find it necessary to go out to work, or that her family should be unable to exist without the fruits of her labour.*
>
> OFFICIAL REPORT SEANAD ÉIREANN, VOL. 25, 27 MAY 1941. SECOND AMENDMENT OF THE CONSTITUTION BILL, 1940, COLS. 1336–7

Helena Concannon brought a Christian line of thought into her parliamentary work, and in her capacity as University representative she addressed herself particularly to the welfare of women students and graduates.

Thomas Concannon, her husband, was one of the pioneers of the Gaelic League movement who had returned to Ireland from America for the 1798 centenary and remained as organiser for the League. During the 1798 centenary, gestures were made to incorporate the women of 1798 in the rash of literature and ballads which marked the celebrations. The temper of the time and the Catholic nationalism which dominated the commemorations stressed their femininity and confined women to a supporting role. The process of including women reached its climax with the publication of Helena's *Women of Ninety Eight* (1919), written in the context of the Anglo–Irish war, which dealt with the mothers of 1798, the wives of 1798 and similar topics as likely to have been intended as an inspiration to her contemporaries as a history of the rebellion. Concannon's book remained the unique study of the subject until 1998.

Best known of Helena Concannon's work was *The Daughters of Banba*, a history of Ireland centred on the part women played in Irish history; it won her the Tailteann Medal in 1924. Her *Life of St Patrick* won the Tailteann Medal in 1932, and she received the Bishop Shanahan (Rector of the Catholic University of Washington) prize for her *The Poor Clares in Ireland* as the best work of the year by one of its graduates. She was a frequent contributor to the *Irish Independent* and other periodicals. In the Eucharistic Congress Year of 1932, she published *The Blessed Eucharist in Irish History*, acclaimed the 'Golden Book' of the Congress. In 1933 she was honoured by Pope Pius XI who sent her the Apostolic Benediction and accepted a copy of the book. Six years later she completed a companion volume to it entitled *The Blessed Virgin in Irish History*.

The life of Blessed Oliver Plunket was written at the special request of the Oliver Plunket Union. For her outstanding contribution to historical knowledge, the National University, in 1929, conferred on her the honorary degree of D.Litt.

Helena Concannon's Galway home, Lios na Mara, was christened by Patrick Pearse. It was visited by many Irish leaders during the War of Independence, and Éamon de Valera frequently stayed there when in the west on business. She is buried in Bothar Mór Cemetery, Galway.

Margaret Mary Pearse

DATE/PLACE OF BIRTH: 1878/GREAT BRUNSWICK STREET (LATER PEARSE STREET), DUBLIN

PARTY: FIANNA FÁIL

CONSTITUENCY: COUNTY DUBLIN (DÁIL)

DÁIL/SEANAD: 8TH DÁIL (24 JANUARY 1933-30 JUNE 1937)

SEANAD (28 MARCH 1938-7 NOVEMBER, 1968 (DEATH))

AGE AT ENTRY TO DÁIL: 55

FAMILY: SISTER OF PATRICK AND WILLIE PEARSE (EXECUTED AFTER 1916 RISING). DAUGHTER OF MARGARET PEARSE (SEE P. 82)

EDUCATION: CONVENT OF THE HOLY FAITH, GLASNEVIN, DUBLIN

OCCUPATION: TEACHER

CAREER: Founder with her brothers of St Enda's College, Rathfarnham; Member, Catholic Women's Federation

DATE OF DEATH: 7 NOVEMBER 1968

ADDRESS: ST ENDA'S, RATHFARNHAM, COUNTY DUBLIN

MARGARET MARY PEARSE, having helped her brothers in the establishment of St Enda's College, was one of the group that carried it on for seventeen years after the execution of Patrick and Willie Pearse. In 1926 she made a lecture tour of America to raise funds for the school. St Enda's and the land with it were bequeathed by Margaret Pearse to the nation, to be maintained as a memorial to her brothers and to their endeavours for the freedom of Ireland and for the Irish language.

She was accorded a state funeral, and the following tribute was paid to her:

The Senator was the last of a famous family whose members gave their lives in the cause of Irish freedom and whose name will be forever cherished by the Irish people. She first came into prominence as a public representative when she was elected to Dáil Éireann in 1933 as a Member for County Dublin. On the re-establishment of Seanad Éireann in 1938, she was elected from the

Administrative Panel and from that date until the time of her death she was continuously a Member of the House. For many years she served on the Joint Restaurant Committee and was a member of the Executive Committee of the Irish Parliamentary Association of which she was joint honorary treasurer. She kept up her insatiable interest in public affairs which she was willing to discuss on all occasions.

Senator Nic Phiarais was a women of outstanding personality and firm convictions which, when occasion demanded, she had no hesitation in expressing in a forceful and compelling way. Her great love was the Irish language and she never lost an opportunity to encourage people, particularly young people, to study and to speak it. Of a quiet disposition, she never sought publicity and the immense amount of work of a charitable nature which she carried out was known only to a few.

SEANAD ÉIREANN OFFICIAL REPORT, 11 DECEMBER 1968, COL. 2–3

Bridget Mary Redmond, née Mallick

DATE OF BIRTH: 1905

PARTY: CUMANN NA NGAEDHEAL

CONSTITUENCY: WATERFORD

DÁIL/SEANAD: 8TH, 9TH, 10TH, 11TH, 12TH, 13TH, AND 14TH DÁIL: (24 JANUARY 1933–
3 MAY 1952 (DEATH))

AGE AT ENTRY TO DÁIL: 28

FAMILY: DAUGHTER OF MR AND MRS JOHN MALLICK, THE CURRAGH. MARRIED TO CAPTAIN WILLIAM
ARCHER REDMOND (DSO, TD, ONLY SON OF MR JOHN REDMOND, MP, CHAIRMAN OF THE IRISH
PARLIAMENTARY PARTY)

EDUCATION: URSULINE CONVENT, WATERFORD

OCCUPATION: LANDOWNER

CAREER:
Elected in first general election following the death of her husband. *Particular policy interests*:
housing and social conditions. *Other interests*: sports, riding to hounds.

DATE OF DEATH: 3 MAY 1952

BRIDGET MARY REDMOND succeeded her husband, William, and retained the Waterford seat at each subsequent election until her own death. Her father was a noted judge of horses and the Mallick colours were familiar at meetings in England as well as in Ireland.

Bridget's election to the Dáil as Cumann na nGaedheal representative added a link to the Parliamentary tradition of the Redmond family in Waterford — a member of the family had represented Waterford in Parliament continuously since 1891, when John Redmond MP had begun to represent the county in the

British House of Commons. On John Redmond's death in 1918, his son, Captain William Redmond, left Tyrone to sit for Waterford, first in Westminster and afterwards in the Dáil, where he served until his death in April 1932.

His widow was punctilious in her attendance to her Dáil duties and was a frequent contributor to debates, as the following excerpts from her speeches show:

> *I just wish to say that I do not agree with the teaching absolutely through Irish of every subject which children in the schools are taught. The teaching of Irish as a subject is very desirable, and we would all agree with it. I think when it comes to teaching subjects that have absolutely no relation whatever to Irish, through the medium of Irish, it is absolutely foolish to think that we can ever impart to the children the knowledge which we want to impart to them. I think it is all part of the wave of insanity that has swept over this country for some years past in trying to force Irish on children and on the people when it is not necessary and when it is not advisable.*

OFFICIAL REPORT DÁIL ÉIREANN, VOL. 61, 25 MARCH 1936. IN COMMITTEE ON FINANCE — VOTE 45 — OFFICE OF THE MINISTER FOR EDUCATION, COLS. 232–3

> *... it is unfortunately the case in this country that when one speaks the truth it is often misinterpreted, and one is ballyragged around the country for being opposed to everything national. For a long number of years this country has heard a great deal about national culture in connection with this Irish teaching in schools. I have no objection whatever to the teaching of Irish as a subject, but I am absolutely opposed to the teaching of every other subject in Irish.*

OFFICIAL REPORT DÁIL ÉIREANN, VOL. 74, 23 MARCH 1939, COMMITTEE ON FINANCE — VOTE 45 — OFFICE OF THE MINISTER FOR EDUCATION, COL. 2404

> *I should like to voice my protest in the strongest possible terms against this Bill.... There is a far greater evil in the Bill and, to my mind, it is one that ought to receive attention. The Bill does away with competition. The pig dealer, no matter what anybody may say in this House, has always been regarded as a decent and honourable man.... Why should we hand over their business to people who will have a complete monopoly of the bacon trade?*

OFFICIAL REPORT DÁIL ÉIREANN, VOL. 67, 14 MAY 1937, COMMITTEE ON FINANCE, PIGS AND BACON BILL, 1937 — FINANCIAL RESOLUTION, COLS. 518–9

Ninth Dáil

General Election: 1 July 1937

153 SEATS

Women Elected
BRIDGET MARY REDMOND (*SEE P. 95*) (FG, WATERFORD)
MARY REYNOLDS (*SEE P. 91*) (FG, LEITRIM)

Tenth Dáil

General Election: 17 June 1938

153 SEATS

Women Elected
BRIDGET MARY REDMOND (*SEE P. 95*) (FG, WATERFORD)
MARY REYNOLDS (*SEE P. 91*) (FG, LEITRIM)
BRIDGET MARY RICE (FF, MONAGHAN)

Bridget Mary Rice, née Henaghan

DATE/PLACE OF BIRTH: 1885/LOUISBURGH, COUNTY MAYO
PARTY: FIANNA FÁIL
CONSTITUENCY: MONAGHAN
DÁIL/SEANAD: 10TH, 11TH, 12TH, 13TH, 14TH DÁIL (17 JUNE 1938-17 MAY 1954)
AGE AT ENTRY TO DÁIL: 53
FAMILY: WIDOW OF EAMONN RICE (FIANNA FÁIL TD, MONAGHAN, 1932-3, 1937-8),
    TWO DAUGHTERS, TWO SONS
EDUCATION: PRESENTATION CONVENT, TUAM, COUNTY GALWAY
OCCUPATION: POSTMISTRESS, LOUISBURGH POST OFFICE, COUNTY MAYO
CAREER:
Elected at next general election after the death of her husband. Member, Monaghan County Council, Vocational Education Committee, Old Age Pensions Committee. Monaghan representative, General Council of County Councils.
DATE OF DEATH: 7 DECEMBER 1967
ADDRESS: KNOCKNAGARMON, INNISKEEN, DUNDALK, COUNTY LOUTH. CLOUGHVALLEY, CARRICKMACROSS,
    COUNTY MONAGHAN (1938-)

BRIDGET HENAGHAN married Eamonn Rice, son of James Blayney Rice of Tyholland, Monaghan, a noted Fenian leader. For Eamonn's part in the struggle for independence, he was interned on the prison ship *Argenta* and deported from County Tyrone. The couple settled in Inniskeen, County Monaghan, where Eamonn was elected as a Fianna Fáil deputy in 1932, and served until his death. Bridget helped her husband in his political work, attending to correspondence, meeting callers, deputising for him when constituents came for advice and help, accompanying him to Dublin during Dáil sittings. On her election, she was the only woman member on the government benches until 1944. She was also the first woman TD for Monaghan.

Bridget Rice took up the case of some young men from County Monaghan who went to the United States and were conscripted to fight in the Korean War. She referred to Article 3 of the Treaty of Friendship between Ireland and the United States, ratified by the Government on 14 September 1950, which stated that 'Irish nationals shall be exempt from compulsory service in the armed forces of the United States of America'; she was condemned in the state of Nevada in the US for 'interference'. Her Dáil contributions focused primarily on agricultural, educational, tourism and cultural matters, discussing shortcomings in government policy and suggesting improvements. She became concerned about reports of American movie stars' adoption of children, and pressed for legislation until the introduction of the Adoption Act.

> *Who could better understand children than a married woman teacher who is rearing a family of her own? Before this [marriage bar] rule was introduced we had many married teachers in this country, and it is universally agreed that they not only reared excellent families themselves but that they did the two jobs equally well. I hope the Minister will reconsider the operation of that rule and cancel it if at all possible.*
>
> *OFFICIAL REPORT, DÁIL ÉIREANN*, VOL. 131, 13 MAY 1952, COL. 1080

> *Mrs. Rice evidently does not share the views about women drivers expressed by male Deputies last week. Obviously she thinks women are better drivers than men and had a question down for the Minister for Justice seeking figures for the number of prosecutions of women and men drivers. Mr. Boland replied that the figures were not available whereupon Mrs. Rice thought it a pity for they would have disproved the allegations of those Deputies who thought women were careless drivers. 'They are not really a menace to public safety'. Said Mrs. Rice outside the House afterwards: 'You rarely find a woman driver in the courts for a driving offence. Women are so careful, that is why they are considered an obstruction on the roads. It's always the men who want to do all the speeding'*
>
> *IRISH PRESS*, 14 MAY 1952

> *Mrs. Rice:* Was there not a Bill introduced by the previous Minister to that effect?
>
> *Mr. Dillon:* I do not like to contradict the lady but she is talking through her most becoming hat.
>
> *OFFICIAL REPORT*, DÁIL ÉIREANN, 18 FEBRUARY 1953, COL. 1141

Eleventh Dáil

General Election: 22 June 1943   *138 SEATS*

Women Elected
BRIDGET MARY REDMOND (*SEE P. 95*) (FG, WATERFORD)
MARY REYNOLDS (*SEE P. 91*) (FG, LEITRIM)
BRIDGET MARY RICE (*SEE P. 97*) (FF, MONAGHAN)

Twelfth Dáil

General Election: 30 May 1944   *138 SEATS*

Women Elected
BRIDGET MARY REDMOND (*SEE P. 95*) (FG, WATERFORD)
MARY REYNOLDS (*SEE P. 91*) (FG, LEITRIM)
BRIDGET MARY RICE (*SEE P. 97*) (FF, MONAGHAN)
MARY BRIDGET RYAN (FF, TIPPERARY)

By-election: 4 December 1945

HONOR MARY CROWLEY (FF, SOUTH KERRY)

Mary Bridget Ryan, née Carey

DATE/PLACE OF BIRTH: 1898/COONMORE, REAR CROSS, COUNTY TIPPERARY
PARTY: FIANNA FÁIL
CONSTITUENCY: 12TH DÁIL: TIPPERARY, 13TH: NORTH TIPPERARY, 14TH: SOUTH TIPPERARY, 15TH AND
    16TH: NORTH TIPPERARY
DÁIL/SEANAD: 12TH 13TH, 14TH, 15TH, 16TH DÁIL (30 MAY 1944–3 OCTOBER 1961)
AGE AT ENTRY TO DÁIL: 46
FAMILY: MARRIED TO MARTIN RYAN (TD TIPPERARY, 1933–43 (DEATH)), FOUR DAUGHTERS, FIVE SONS
EDUCATION: REAR CROSS, COUNTY TIPPERARY. PRESENTATION CONVENT, THURLES
OCCUPATION: FARMER
CAREER:
Member, despatch rider, Cumann na mBan, after the Easter Rising 1916. Attended Gaelic
League classes. Founder Member of Fianna Fáil, 1926. Member, Tipperary County Council.
DATE OF DEATH: 8 FEBRUARY 1981
ADDRESS: KNOCKVIEW HOUSE, NEWPORT, COUNTY TIPPERARY (ADDRESS WHILE IN DÁIL)

MARY BRIDGET CAREY married Martin Ryan in 1923. He had been active in the
War of Independence, and they both opposed the Treaty and supported Éamon
de Valera. After the death of her husband, at the age of 43, Mary Ryan won his
seat in 1944.

    In 1926 Martin and Mary Ryan attended a meeting outside the Church at
Rear Cross to set up a new opposition party under de Valera. They immediately

joined, taking on the responsibility of holding meetings, getting support and raising funds.

When Martin died, Mary was left to bring up nine children aged from three to nineteen and to look after a 200-acre farm. It was the Emergency in Ireland, and goods and services were scarce. Nevertheless, she became the first woman deputy for Tipperary, and was punctual in her attendance at the Dáil. According to the *Irish Press*:

> *For several years she used to hire a car or be driven by trap from Newport to catch the Dublin train from Birdhill, a turf burning train with unheated carriages and no refreshments. 'I don't think I missed a single vote in the House in seventeen years and I was never absent except on the few occasions when I was sick,' she says. 'The party men from near home were very helpful. Dan Breen was great, so was Tom Moylan, Gerry Boland and Tom Derrig....*
>
> *Home again on Thursday night or Friday morning, she would be met at Birdhill. With shopping for the children's clothes done in Dublin she would slip back again into the role of parent and farmer. She ... believes it helped [her children] to be self-reliant and responsible. Even at week-ends they had to share her time with the local people who called on Sundays to have her put their case before this Department or that for extra oil for incubators or tractors, for grants for a water scheme or a new shed.*
>
> *Hers was a crowded, demanding life, yet she considers that today's woman deputy in similar circumstances to hers would find it much harder for the reason that politics have become more complex and the electorate more exacting. She also has to figure more in the public eye and has even less time for family life.*
>
> IRISH PRESS, 26 MAY 1976, FIANNA FÁIL ANNIVERSARY SUPPLEMENT

Mary lost the general election in 1961 but continued as a Fianna Fáil Councillor until 1969, when she retired from active politics. At the close of her Dáil career the North Tipperary Fianna Fáil organisation planned a presentation to mark her service. She declined, saying that she should make them a presentation in recognition of their support.

Honor Mary Crowley, née Boland

DATE/PLACE OF BIRTH: 19 OCTOBER 1903/LONDON

PARTY: FIANNA FÁIL

CONSTITUENCY: SOUTH KERRY

DÁIL/SEANAD: 12TH, 13TH, 14TH, 15TH, 16TH, 17TH, 18TH DÁIL (4 DECEMBER 1945–18 OCTOBER 1966)

AGE AT ENTRY TO DÁIL: 42

FAMILY: DAUGHTER OF JOHN PIUS BOLAND (MP FOR SOUTH KERRY 1900–18, CHIEF WHIP OF IRISH PARTY AT WESTMINSTER). MARRIED TO FREDERICK H. CROWLEY (TD, SOUTH KERRY 1927–45)

OCCUPATION: SOCIAL WORKER, LONDON

CAREER:

Member, Council of State. First woman to represent Ireland on a delegation to the Council of Europe in Strasbourg 1954–7, nominated by Inter-Party Government (Fine Gael, Labour, Clann na Talmhain and Clann na Poblachta). Member, later Vice-chair, Kerry County Council, 1948. Member, Kerry Vocational Education Committee where she helped in revival of home crafts throughout South Kerry. Member, Kerry Health Authority; Kerry County Library Committee. Honorary Secretary, Killarney Horticultural Society. Member, Irish Countrywomen's Association; Killarney Tourist Association. Patron, Kerry Drama Festival; Killarney Rowing Club. Member, Derrynane Trust; Irish Tourist Association; Kerry Tourist Association. *Particular policy interests*: social welfare problems, particularly housing.

DATE OF DEATH: 18 OCTOBER 1966

ADDRESS: DROMHALL, KILLARNEY, COUNTY KERRY

HONOR MARY CROWLEY won her seat in a by-election caused by the death of her husband, Fred H. Crowley. She was the first woman TD to represent Kerry. Her father, John Pius Boland, had been Chief Whip of the Irish Party and had represented South Kerry at Westminster from 1900 to 1918. He took part in the drawing up of the Statutes of the National University of Ireland and negotiated the registration of the Irish trade mark. Her great-grandfather established Boland's Bakery in Dublin in 1823, and her grandfather purchased in 1873 the flour mill which became known as Boland's Mills, where Easter 1916 fighting took place.

Thirteenth Dáil ——————————————————————————————

General Election: 4 February 1948   *147 SEATS*

Women Elected

HONOR MARY CROWLEY (*SEE P. 100*) (FF, SOUTH KERRY)
BRIDGET MARY REDMOND (*SEE P. 95*) (FG, WATERFORD)
MARY REYNOLDS (*SEE P. 91*) (FG, SLIGO/LEITRIM)
BRIDGET MARY RICE (*SEE P. 97*) (FF, MONAGHAN)
MARY BRIDGET RYAN (*SEE P. 99*) (FF, NORTH TIPPERARY)

Fourteenth Dáil ——————————————————————————————

General Election: 30 May 1951   *147 SEATS*

Women Elected

HONOR MARY CROWLEY (*SEE P. 100*) (FF, SOUTH KERRY)
BRIDGET MARY REDMOND (*SEE P. 95*) (FG, WATERFORD)
MARY REYNOLDS (*SEE P. 91*) (FG, SLIGO/LEITRIM)
BRIDGET MARY RICE (*SEE P. 97*) (FF, MONAGHAN)
MARY BRIDGET RYAN (*SEE P. 99*) (FF, SOUTH TIPPERARY)

Fifteenth Dáil ————————————————————————————

General Election: 18 May 1954   *147 SEATS*

Women Elected

HONOR MARY CROWLEY (*SEE P. 100*) (FF, SOUTH KERRY)
CELIA LYNCH (FF, DUBLIN SOUTH CENTRAL)
MAUREEN O'CARROLL (LAB, DUBLIN NORTH CENTRAL)
MARY REYNOLDS (*SEE P. 91*) (FG, SLIGO/LEITRIM)
MARY BRIDGET RYAN (*SEE P. 99*) (FF, NORTH TIPPERARY)

By-election: 29 February 1956

KATHLEEN O'CONNOR (CLANN NA POBLACHTA, NORTH KERRY)

Celia Lynch, née Quinn

DATE/PLACE OF BIRTH: 1908/KINVARA, COUNTY GALWAY
PARTY: FIANNA FÁIL
CONSTITUENCY: DUBLIN SOUTH CENTRAL (15TH, 16TH); DUBLIN NORTH
CENTRAL (17TH, 18TH, 19TH, 20TH)
DÁIL/SEANAD: 15TH DÁIL, 16TH, 17TH, 18TH, 19TH, 20TH (18 MAY 1954–
15 JUNE 1977). RETIRED AT END OF 20TH DÁIL
AGE AT ENTRY TO DÁIL: 46
FAMILY: MARRIED TO DR JAMES B. LYNCH (TD, DUBLIN SOUTH, 1932-1948,
SENATOR, 1951-4 (DEATH)); TWO DAUGHTERS, FIVE SONS
EDUCATION: LORETO CONVENT, ST STEPHEN'S GREEN, DUBLIN. UNIVERSITY COLLEGE GALWAY,
UNIVERSITY COLLEGE DUBLIN (BA, BCOMM, H.DIP.ED)
OCCUPATION: TEACHER IN DUBLIN VOCATIONAL SCHOOLS
CAREER:
Member, Committee of Selection, 1969. Member, Special Committee on Company Law, 1962. Member, Oireachtas Joint Library Committee; Joint Restaurant Committee. Assistant Government whip, 1957-73; Assistant Fianna Fáil whip in opposition, 1973-77. Member, Consultative Assembly of Council of Europe, 1967-9. Member, Dublin Corporation and several of its committees, 1957-67; Dublin Vocational Education Committee, 1960-69. Member, Rotunda Hospital Board, 1971-7, St Laurence Hospital Board, 1963-74. Member, Governing Body of University College, Dublin, 1969; Senate of the National University of Ireland, 1972. President, Nurses' Convalescent Home, Kilrock, Howth. Member, Widows' Association of Ireland, 1970. Represented Ireland at several meetings of Inter-Parliamentary Union.
DATE OF DEATH: 16 JUNE 1989
ADDRESS: 156 BOTANIC ROAD, GLASNEVIN, DUBLIN 9 (ADDRESS WHILE IN DÁIL)

CELIA LYNCH was born in Duras House, Kinvara, County Galway, where the Abbey Theatre was founded. She is buried in Glasnevin Cemetery.

Maureen O'Carroll, née McHugh

DATE/PLACE OF BIRTH: 29 MARCH 1913/GALWAY
PARTY: LABOUR
CONSTITUENCY: DUBLIN NORTH CENTRAL
DÁIL/SEANAD: 15TH DÁIL (18 MAY 1954–4 MARCH, 1957).
  DEFEATED IN 1957 ELECTION
AGE AT ENTRY TO DÁIL: 41
FAMILY: DAUGHTER OF MICHEÁL MCHUGH (REPUBLICAN PRISONER IN UK,
  IRISH LANGUAGE TEACHER, EDITOR OF THE *TUAM HERALD*, MEMBER OF STAFF OF *FREEMAN'S
  JOURNAL*). MARRIED TO GERARD O'CARROLL, CABINET-MAKER; FIVE DAUGHTERS, FIVE SONS
EDUCATION: JESUS AND MARY CONVENT, GORTNOR ABBEY, CROSSMOLINA, COUNTY MAYO, WHICH SHE
  ENTERED AS A NOVICE, UNIVERSITY COLLEGE, GALWAY (BA, 1935)
OCCUPATION: SECONDARY SCHOOLTEACHER. ALSO FOREIGN OFFICE OF IRISH HOSPITALS TRUST
CAREER:
First female Labour Deputy and first woman Labour Party Chief Whip, May 1954. Secretary,
Lower Prices Council Member, Housing Consultative Council. Particular policy interests: Raised
on the adjournment the issue of transfer of children to the USA for adoption.
DATE OF DEATH: 9 MAY 1984
ADDRESS: 21 KIRWAN STREET, DUBLIN (ADDRESS WHILE IN DÁIL)

MAUREEN O'CARROLL, nicknamed 'Little Mo' by the satirical magazine *Dublin
Opinion*, was a founder member of the Lower Prices Council in 1947 and served
on it, as secretary and spokeswoman, until 1954. Prices had more than doubled
during the War, and anger at high prices, scarce goods and black-marketeering led
to demands for government-sponsored price controls. The Lower Prices Council,
formed by the Dublin Trades Union Council, succeeded in mobilising huge numbers of people outside the framework of formal political activity as recognised by
the political parties. Over 100,000 people turned up for some of their public meetings, including large numbers of women. The Council was described by the secret
police as an organisation 'which has been so active throughout '47 in fomenting
discontent in Dublin City'. As well as mobilising public opinion to agitate against
the increases in the cost of living, the Lower Prices Council recognised the need
to highlight women's 'right to participate in the national housekeeping'. Thus, the
Lower Prices Council, with the Irish Housewives' Association, convened the
Women's National Council of Action, which became known as the 'Women's
Parliament'. As any organisation questioning government policy was seen as a
threat by the Local Government minister, Seán MacEntee, and monitored by
police, there is a secret police file on the Irish Housewives' Association (See Mac
Dermott, Eithne, *Clann na Poblachta*, Cork: Cork University Press, 1998).
    Maureen O'Carroll was selected to run in the Dublin North Central con-
stituency in 1954 to boost the party's overall vote; she surprised everybody by

being elected. On the day of the count she made a First Communion dress for a neighbour's child, cooked dinner for her children and then went to see the results. Her youngest child, Brendan, was born in 1955 while she was a TD, and was named after Brendan Corish, then Labour Minister for Social Welfare. Maureen O'Carroll was believed by her son to be the only TD living in a Corporation house (O'Carroll, Brendan, *The Mammy*, 1994), although she moved to it after her Dáil career had ended and the family fortunes had declined.

During her service in the Dáil Maureen was instrumental in having the Ban Gardaí formed, and she campaigned to have the word 'bastard' eliminated from birth certificates of children born to unmarried parents. She appeared before Inquiries by the Prices Advisory Body and succeeded in having food prices lowered. Her maiden speech on the *Supplies and Services (Temporary Provisions) Act, 1946 (Continuance and Amendment) Bill, 1954* opened as follows:

> *I had hoped when making my maiden speech on this Bill to be able to make a reasoned and possibly constructive contribution. I have been so incensed by the utter nonsense and poppycock which has come from the opposite benches that I can only hope I shall not be too much diverted from the points I wish to make....*
>
> OFFICIAL REPORT, DÁIL ÉIREANN, VOL. 148, 23 FEBRUARY 1955

She spoke on the *City and County Management (Amendment) Bill, 1954*, the *Finance Bill, 1956*, the *Greyhound Industry Bill, 1955*, the *Rates on Agricultural Land (Relief) Bill, 1956*, and on a motion concerning a Bureau of Standards for consumers' goods, cost of living increases and rural electrification charges.

In 1954, she instigated proceedings in the Dublin District Court against Batchelor and Co. (Ireland) Ltd., for fraudulent trading. Packets of peas described as marrowfat were found to contain a mixture of marrowfat and blue peas. This broke the company's monopoly, but had unfortunate political consequences for Maureen O'Carroll because of the loss of jobs. She was defeated in the 1957 election but remained in politics until 1970. Ban Gardaí formed a guard of honour at her funeral in 1984. O'Carroll Villas (off Kevin Street, Dublin) is named after her.

Kathleen O'Connor

DATE OF BIRTH: 1935

PARTY: CLANN NA POBLACHTA

CONSTITUENCY: NORTH KERRY

DÁIL/SEANAD: 15TH DÁIL (29 FEBRUARY 1956 (BY-ELECTION)–4 MARCH 1957)

AGE AT ENTRY TO DÁIL: 21

FAMILY: DAUGHTER OF MR JOHN O'CONNOR (TD, CLANN NA POBLACHTA), WHOSE DEATH CAUSED THE VACANCY

EDUCATION: BALLYSEEDY NATIONAL SCHOOL; MOYDERWELL CONVENT, TRALEE; CARYSFORT TEACHER TRAINING COLLEGE

OCCUPATION: PRIMARY SCHOOLTEACHER, ST AGNES'S NATIONAL SCHOOL, CRUMLIN, AND
  MAIN NATIONAL SCHOOL, KNOCKNAGOSHEL, COUNTY KERRY
CAREER:
First single woman returned since 1922 and the youngest member of the Dáil

KATHLEEN O'CONNOR's name was not yet on the electoral register when she was elected in 1956; she had just turned 21, and she was unable to vote for herself. All the parties forming the Inter-Party Government supported the Clann na Poblachta candidate, and her victory was seen as an endorsement of the efforts of the Inter-Party Government.

Sixteenth Dáil

General Election: 5 March 1957   *147 SEATS*

Women Elected

HONOR MARY CROWLEY (*SEE P. 100*) (FF, SOUTH KERRY)
BRIGID HOGAN (FG, SOUTH GALWAY)
CELIA LYNCH (*SEE P. 102*) (FF, DUBLIN SOUTH CENTRAL)
MARY REYNOLDS (*SEE P. 91*) (FG, SLIGO/LEITRIM)
MARY BRIDGET RYAN (*SEE P. 99*) (FF, NORTH TIPPERARY)

Brigid Hogan, later Hogan-O'Higgins

DATE/PLACE OF BIRTH: MARCH 1932/DUBLIN
PARTY: FINE GAEL
CONSTITUENCY: SOUTH GALWAY (16TH DÁIL, 1957-61), EAST GALWAY
  (17TH, 18TH DÁIL, 1961-9) CLARE/SOUTH GALWAY
  (19TH, 20TH DÁIL, 1969-77)
DÁIL/SEANAD: 16TH DÁIL, 17TH, 18TH, 19TH, AND 20TH
  (5 MARCH 1957-1 JUNE 1977). DEFEATED IN 1977 IN NEWLY FORMED
  CONSTITUENCY OF GALWAY EAST
AGE AT ENTRY TO DÁIL: 25
FAMILY: DAUGHTER OF PATRICK HOGAN (TD FOR GALWAY, 1921-36, MINISTER FOR AGRICULTURE,
  1922-32). MARRIED TO MICHAEL O'HIGGINS (FINE GAEL TD FOR DUBLIN SOUTH
  WEST/WICKLOW, 1948-69, LATER A SENATOR); FOUR DAUGHTERS AND FOUR SONS
EDUCATION: DOMINICAN CONVENTS, TAYLOR'S HILL, GALWAY AND WICKLOW
OCCUPATION: FARMER
ADDRESS: CLONBULLOGUE, COUNTY OFFALY. KILRICKLE, LOUGHREA, COUNTY GALWAY
  (ADDRESS WHILE IN DÁIL)

BRIGID HOGAN was the first woman to represent Galway in the Dáil. In 1958 she married Michael J. O'Higgins, then a deputy for Dublin South West, later a leader of the Seanad. They were the only husband and wife to sit in the Dáil at the same time. From 1969 to 1972 she was the Fine Gael front-bench spokesperson on Posts and Telegraphs.

Seventeenth Dáil _____

General Election: 4 October 1961   *144 SEATS*

Women Elected
HONOR MARY CROWLEY (*SEE P. 100*) (FF, SOUTH KERRY)
BRIGID HOGAN-O'HIGGINS (*SEE P. 105*) (FG, EAST GALWAY)
CELIA LYNCH (*SEE P. 102*) (FF, DUBLIN NORTH CENTRAL)

By-election: 19 February 1964
SHEILA GALVIN (FF, CORK)

By-election: 8 July 1964
JOAN T. BURKE (FG, ROSCOMMON)

By-election: 10 March 1965
EILEEN DESMOND (LAB, MID CORK)

Sheila Galvin
DATE/PLACE OF BIRTH: 23 FEBRUARY 1914/CORK CITY
PARTY: FIANNA FÁIL
CONSTITUENCY: CORK CITY
DÁIL/SEANAD: 17TH DÁIL (19 FEBRUARY 1964–6 APRIL 1965) ELECTED IN
BY-ELECTION OF 19 FEBRUARY 1964
AGE AT ENTRY TO DÁIL: 49
FAMILY: WIDOW OF ALDERMAN JOHN GALVIN (FIANNA FÁIL TD, 1956–11 OCTOBER
1963); TWO DAUGHTERS, CAROL (COTTER), MARY (BUCKLEY) (AGED 18
AND 14 AT ELECTION), ONE SON, BARRY GALVIN (AGED 16 AT ELECTION)
OCCUPATION: LICENSED VINTNER
CAREER:
Particular policy interests: social and community issues, health/family.
DATE OF DEATH: 20 MARCH 1983
ADDRESS: 37 BANDON ROAD, CORK

SHEILA GALVIN was the second woman to represent Cork city, after Mary MacSwiney, Her election showed, according to the Taoiseach, Seán Lemass, 'emphatic evidence of public support for Fianna Fáil', who were in Government at the time of her election.

According to the *Irish Press* of 21 February 1964:

At 50 Mrs Galvin is still a very pretty woman.... She neither drinks nor smokes. Since the sudden death of her husband four months ago she has been under great strain, but does not show it except when asked sudden and unexpected questions. Speeches do not as yet come easily to her, but she has the reputation in her district of having been an excellent worker for her husband and having a well-developed sense of politics....

A few minutes later she went out in the glare of flashing bulbs to face the public.... In her first official speech as deputy she said 'We are living at a time when the country must either go forward or fall behind.... Fianna Fáil are the only party which has put forward a definite practical policy for expansion, and I am glad and proud that the people of Cork realised the importance of this election and showed their confidence in the Government by returning me. I will do everything in my power to live up to the trust they have placed in me'.

Eileen Desmond, née Harrington

DATE/PLACE OF BIRTH: DECEMBER 1932/OLD HEAD, KINSALE, COUNTY CORK
PARTY: LABOUR
CONSTITUENCY: MID-CORK, CORK SOUTH CENTRAL. SEANAD: INDUSTRIAL AND
    COMMERCIAL PANEL
DÁIL/SEANAD: 17TH DÁIL (10 MARCH 1965 (BY-ELECTION)–18 MARCH 1965),
    18TH DÁIL (7APRIL 1965-17 JUNE 1969). 20TH, 21ST, 22ND, 23RD,
    24TH (28 FEBRUARY 1973-16 FEBRUARY 1987). SEANAD: 12 AUGUST
    1969-30 APRIL 1973. DID NOT SEEK RE-ELECTION TO THE 25TH DÁIL
AGE AT ENTRY TO DÁIL: 32
FAMILY: WIDOW OF DAN DESMOND (TD FOR CORK SOUTH, 1948-61, MID-CORK 1961-4);
    TWO DAUGHTERS
EDUCATION: CONVENT OF MERCY, KINSALE
OCCUPATION: CIVIL SERVANT, DEPARTMENT OF POSTS & TELEGRAPHS
CAREER:
Minister for Health and Minister for Social Welfare, June 1981-March 1982. Labour Party opposition front-bench spokesperson on Education 1965-9. Chairperson, Women's Representative Committee, 1975. Member, Committee on Procedure and Privileges 1965-9; Dáil and Seanad Standing Joint Committee on Consolidation Bills, 1973. Member, Joint Committee on Marriage Breakdown, 1983; Member, Joint Committee on Women's Rights, 1983; Dáil and Seanad Joint Library Committee 1973; Member, European Parliament, 1979-81, elected in the first direct elections for Munster constituency. Member, Cork County Council, 1965; Cork County Vocational Education Committee, 1965; Cork Health Authority, 1965-71.
ADDRESS: MAIN STREET, CARRIGALINE, COUNTY CORK (ADDRESS WHILE IN DÁIL)

EILEEN DESMOND was elected to the Dáil in 1965 at a by-election in Mid-Cork caused by the death of her husband. Her victory in that by-election forced the dissolution of the 17th Dáil; she did not have the opportunity to take her seat, but was elected in the ensuing general election. The Dáil was dissolved because Seán Lemass, leader of Fianna Fáil, had declared during the campaign that if Fianna Fáil did not win the seat, he would call a general election. She was defeated in the general election in 1969 and in a by-election in 1972. She was again elected in Mid-Cork in the general election of 1973.

An influential figure in the Labour Party from the time of her election in 1965, Eileen Desmond could have been a contender for the leadership of the party after the 1981 election but decided to support Michael O'Leary, having opposed him in the 1977 Labour Party leadership election against Frank Cluskey.

As Minister for Health and Social Welfare in the 1981 coalition government, Eileen Desmond was the first woman to have held a senior cabinet portfolio since the foundation of the State. However, her career as Minister was hampered by poor health.

Joan T. Burke, née Crowley

DATE/PLACE OF BIRTH: FEBRUARY 1929/BANDON, COUNTY CORK

PARTY: FINE GAEL

CONSTITUENCY: ROSCOMMON, ROSCOMMON/LEITRIM

DÁIL/SEANAD: 17TH DÁIL (BY-ELECTION), 18TH, 19TH, 20TH, 21ST (8 JULY 1964–10 JUNE 1981)

AGE AT ENTRY TO DÁIL: 35

FAMILY: WIDOW OF JAMES BURKE (TD FOR ROSCOMMON, 1954–64); ONE SON, ONE DAUGHTER

EDUCATION: LORETO CONVENT, KILLARNEY, COUNTY KERRY; GALWAY REGIONAL HOSPITAL

OCCUPATION: NURSE/FARMER

CAREER:

Member of the Dáil and Seanad Joint Restaurant Committee, 1969

Member, Select Committee on the Health Services, 1977.

ADDRESS: CARGINS, TULSK, CASTLEREA, COUNTY ROSCOMMON (ADDRESS WHILE IN DÁIL)

JOAN BURKE was elected for Roscommon in 1964 in a by-election caused by the death of her husband, and was returned in the same constituency in the general election of 1965, and for Roscommon/Leitrim in the 1969 and 1973 general elections. The first woman to represent Roscommon, she was the only woman to head the poll in any constituency in the 1973 general election. A State-registered nurse, Joan Burke was later a ward sister in Cherry Orchard Fever Hospital, Dublin.

Eighteenth Dáil ——————————————————————

General Election: 7 April 1965   *144 SEATS*

Women Elected
JOAN T. BURKE (*SEE P. 108*) (FG, ROSCOMMON)
HONOR MARY CROWLEY (*SEE P. 100*) (FF, SOUTH KERRY)
EILEEN DESMOND (*SEE P. 107*) (LAB, MID-CORK)
BRIGID HOGAN-O'HIGGINS (*SEE P. 105*) (FG, EAST GALWAY)
CELIA LYNCH (*SEE P. 102*) (FF, DUBLIN NORTH CENTRAL)

Nineteenth Dáil ——————————————————————

General Election: 18 June 1969   *144 SEATS*

Women Elected
JOAN T. BURKE (*SEE P. 108*) (FG, ROSCOMMON/LEITRIM)
BRIGID HOGAN-O'HIGGINS (*SEE P. 105*) (FG, CLARE/SOUTH GALWAY)
CELIA LYNCH (*SEE P. 102*) (FF, DUBLIN NORTH CENTRAL)

Twentieth Dáil ——————————————————————

General Election: 28 February 1973   *144 SEATS*

Women Elected
JOAN T. BURKE (*SEE P. 108*) (FG, ROSCOMMON/LEITRIM)
EILEEN DESMOND (*SEE P. 107*) (LAB, MID-CORK)
BRIGID HOGAN-O'HIGGINS (*SEE P. 105*) (FG, CLARE/SOUTH GALWAY)
CELIA LYNCH (*SEE P. 102*) (FF, DUBLIN NORTH CENTRAL)

By-election: 4 March 1975
MÁIRE GEOGHEGAN-QUINN (FF, GALWAY WEST)

Máire Geoghegan-Quinn

DATE/PLACE OF BIRTH: 5 SEPTEMBER 1950/CARNA, COUNTY GALWAY
PARTY: FIANNA FÁIL
CONSTITUENCY: GALWAY WEST
DÁIL/SEANAD: 20TH-27TH DÁIL (4 MARCH 1975-5 JUNE 1997)
AGE AT ENTRY TO DÁIL: 24
FAMILY: DAUGHTER OF JOHN GEOGHEGAN (TD, GALWAY WEST 1954-75).
    MARRIED TO JOHN V. QUINN; TWO SONS
EDUCATION: COLÁISTE MHUIRE, TRÁ MHIC ÉADAIGH, COUNTY MAYO, CARYSFORT TEACHERS' TRAINING
    COLLEGE, BLACKROCK, COUNTY DUBLIN
OCCUPATION: PRIMARY SCHOOLTEACHER

CAREER:
Minister for Justice, 4 January 1993 (first woman Minister for Justice). Minister for Equality and Law Reform, 18 November 1994-15 December 1994 (government changed without dissolution of Dáil). Minister for Tourism, Transport & Communications, February 1992-January 1993; Minister of State at the Department of the Taoiseach with special responsibility as co-ordinator of Government Policy and EC matters, March 1987-November 1991; Minister of State at the Department of Education with special responsibility for Youth & Sport, March-December 1982. Minister for the Gaeltacht, 1979-1981 (first woman cabinet minister since Constance Markievicz). Parliamentary Secretary to the Minister for Industry, Commerce & Energy, 1977-18, Minister of State at the Department 1978-9, with special responsibility for Consumer Affairs. Chairperson, first Joint Committee on Women's Rights, 1983. Member, Joint Committee on Marriage Breakdown, 1983. Member, Special Committee on the Judicial Separation and Family Law Reform Bill, 1987, Member, Select Committee on Social Affairs, 10 March 1995. Member of Galway City Council 1985; Member of Galway Cheshire Home Committee; Chair, Wanting Older Women Well; Chair, Saffron Initiative; Chair of Fianna Fáil. Columnist *The Irish Times,* 1997; Consultant to several companies; non-executive director, the Ryan Hotel Group; TV broadcaster. *Other interests*: Reading, writing and travel.

PUBLICATIONS:
The Green Diamond (a novel), Marino, 1996.
ADDRESS: TEARMANN, 5 WOODFIELD, CAPPAGH, BARNA, GALWAY

MÁIRE GEOGHEGAN-QUINN was first elected to the Dáil in March 1975, in a by-election in Galway West caused by the death of her father. On social issues she was on the liberal wing of Fianna Fáil, supporting family planning. As Minister for Justice she undertook substantial law reform legislation, notably in the *Criminal Law (Sexual Offences) Act, 1993*, which decriminalised homosexuality.

In November 1991 she resigned her post of Minister of State at the Department of the Taoiseach in opposition to Charles Haughey's leadership. When Albert Reynolds succeeded Charles Haughey early the following year she was appointed Minister for Tourism, Transport and Communications and in January 1993 she became Minister for Justice, losing office in December 1994 on the collapse of the Fianna Fáil/Labour government. After the resignation of Reynolds as party leader, she announced that she would challenge Bertie Ahern for the leadership post, but withdrew on the day of the planned ballot. She was appointed to his new front bench.

The main character in Máire Geoghegan-Quinn's novel, *The Green Diamond*, is the student teacher daughter of a Galway politician who wants her mother to become the first woman Taoiseach.

On 25 January 1997, Máire Geoghegan-Quinn informed the Taoiseach, Bertie Ahern, of her decision to step down from politics, citing media intrusion into her family life. In *The Irish Times* of 29 January 1997, Vincent Browne paid tribute to her:

Máire Geoghegan-Quinn is a huge loss to Irish politics. She is perhaps the finest public representative in Dáil Éireann. She has courage, clarity of expression, a fine intellect, integrity and decisiveness. She may be the greatest Taoiseach we never had.

On 29 July 1999, Máire Geoghegan-Quinn was nominated by Taoiseach Bertie Ahern to the EU Court of Auditors, the body responsible for auditing the legality of EU spending and sound financial management of EU resources, and which highlights inefficiency and waste.

Twenty-First Dáil ——————————————————————

General Election: 16 June 1977 148 SEATS

Women Elected
KIT AHERN (FF, KERRY NORTH)
JOAN T. BURKE (*SEE P. 108*) (FG, ROSCOMMON/LEITRIM)
EILEEN DESMOND (*SEE P. 107*) (LAB, MID-CORK)
SÍLE DE VALERA (FF, DUBLIN MID-COUNTY)
MÁIRE GEOGHEGAN-QUINN (*SEE P. 109*) (FF, GALWAY WEST)
EILEEN LEMASS (FF, DUBLIN-BALLYFERMOT)

By-election: 7 November 1979
MYRA BARRY (FG, CORK NORTH EAST)

Catherine Ita (Kit) Ahern, née Liston

DATE OF BIRTH: 13 JANUARY 1915/ATHEA, COUNTY LIMERICK
PARTY: FIANNA FÁIL
CONSTITUENCY: KERRY NORTH (DÁIL). SEANAD: TAOISEACH'S NOMINEE
  (SEAN LEMASS) 1964-5 (CASUAL VACANCY), 1965-9; CULTURAL &
  EDUCATIONAL PANEL, 1969-77
DÁIL/SEANAD: 21ST DÁIL (16 JUNE 1977-10 JUNE, 1981); SEANAD, 2
  DECEMBER 1964-7 JUNE 1965 (CASUAL VACANCY), 8 JUNE 1965-
  16 AUGUST 1977
AGE AT ENTRY TO SEANAD: 50
AGE AT ENTRY TO DÁIL: 62
FAMILY: MARRIED DAN AHERN, APRIL 1941
EDUCATION: CONVENT OF MERCY, TUAM; CONVENT OF MERCY, NEWCASTLE WEST; COLLEGE OF ART,
  DUBLIN
OCCUPATION: SECONDARY SCHOOLTEACHER, COLÁISTE MHUIRE, ABBEYFEALE, COUNTY LIMERICK
CAREER:
Member, Dáil and Senate Joint Restaurant Committee; Joint Library Committee, 1973-7.
Member, Committee on Procedure and Privileges, 1977. Member, Consultative Assembly of the

Council of Europe, 1970-73. Member, Kerry County Council, 1967. First woman councillor for Listowel area, 1967, 1974, 1979, heading the poll. First woman Cathaoirleach of Kerry County Council, 1977-8. National President, Irish Countrywomen's Association, 1961-4, first president of the Association in Kerry, founder of new guilds in Kerry, teacher of crafts (specialising in lace-making) at An Grianán (ICA college) and representative of the Association at many international conferences. Buan Cara na Gaedhilge. En route from Associated Countrywomen of the World conference in Melbourne in 1962, addressed women's associations in New Zealand, Honolulu, San Diego, Battlecreek and Atlanta. Brought conference of Associated Countrywomen of the World to Ireland in 1965 and chaired the conference committee, 1963-4. Member, Comhar Cultúra Éireann (Cultural Relations Committee), nominated by Frank Aiken, 1964; Comhdháil Náisiúnta na Gaeilge, Macra na Tuaithe, Credit Union Movement, Folk School Movement. Founder member, Ballybunion Development Association. Director of Bord Fáilte, appointed by Erskine Childers, 1964. President, Kerry Historical and Archaeological Society. Member, Red Cross and V.A.D., in Abbeyfeale during Emergency. Particular policy interests: education, promotion of Irish language, health, community development.

ADDRESS: LARTIGUE BUNGALOW, BALLYBUNION, COUNTY KERRY

KIT AHERN contested the general elections of 1965, 1969, and 1973 as a Fianna Fáil candidate in Kerry North. She recalls that Senators were obliged to wear a hat in the Seanad, and she was once reprimanded by the Cathaoirleach, Liam Ó Buachalla, for being hatless.

Síle de Valera

DATE/PLACE OF BIRTH: DECEMBER 1954/DUBLIN

PARTY: FIANNA FÁIL

CONSTITUENCY: DUBLIN MID-COUNTY (1977-81), CLARE (1987 TO DATE)

DÁIL/SEANAD: 21ST DÁIL (16 JUNE 1977-11 JUNE 1981), 25TH-28TH DÁIL (17 FEBRUARY 1987 TO DATE)

AGE AT ENTRY TO DÁIL: 22

FAMILY: GRANDDAUGHTER OF ÉAMON DE VALERA (PRESIDENT OF IRELAND, 1959-73; TAOISEACH, 1937-48, 1951-4, 1957-9; PRESIDENT OF THE EXECUTIVE OF THE IRISH FREE STATE 1932-7; PRESIDENT, 1ST DÁIL, 1919-21. TD FOR CLARE, 1918-61. PRESIDENT, 2ND DÁIL, 21 JANUARY 1922). COUSIN OF ÉAMON Ó CUÍV (TD, GALWAY WEST, 1992 TO DATE, MINISTER OF STATE FOR GAELTACHT AND THE ISLANDS, JULY 1997 TO DATE)

EDUCATION: LORETO CONVENT, FOXROCK, COUNTY DUBLIN, UNIVERSITY COLLEGE DUBLIN (BA, H.DIP.ED., DIP IN CAREER GUIDANCE, D PSYCH.SCI.)

OCCUPATION: CAREER GUIDANCE TEACHER

CAREER:

Minister for Arts, Heritage & Gaeltacht and the Islands, June 1997 to date. Fianna Fáil frontbench spokesperson on Arts, Culture & Heritage, 1995-7. Member, Committee on Procedure and Privileges, 1977; Joint Committee on the Secondary Legislation of the European Communities, 1977; Joint Committee on Women's Rights, 1987-9, 1989-92; Joint Committee on Employment, 1992; Select Committee on Social Affairs, April 1993; Select Committee on Legislation and Security, 1993-7. Member of European Parliament, 1979-84, and of its Committees for Social Affairs and Employment, Youth, Education and Sport and the Ad Hoc Women's Committees. *Other interests*: reading, history, music, dance, theatre.

ADDRESS: 6 RIVERDALE, TULLA ROAD, ENNIS, COUNTY CLARE

SÍLE DE VALERA was, at election, the youngest member of the Dáil. She contested the constituency of Dublin South in 1981 and February 1982, and the constituency of Clare in November 1982. In her early career she called for a British withdrawal from Northern Ireland and a government demonstration of republicanism. She visited Bobby Sands in prison and criticised Margaret Thatcher's handling of the H-Block hunger strikes.

> *If our political leaders are not seen to be furthering our republican aspirations through constitutional means, the idealistic young members of our community will become disillusioned ... and turn to violence to achieve their aims.*

> SPEECH AT LIAM LYNCH COMMEMORATION AT FERMOY, COUNTY CORK, SEEN AS CHALLENGE TO
> LEADERSHIP OF JACK LYNCH. *THE IRISH TIMES*, 10 SEPTEMBER 1979

Síle de Valera resigned the Fianna Fáil party whip in July 1993 in protest against the government's removal of the obligatory stopover at Shannon Airport, County Clare, for transatlantic flights to and from Ireland; she rejoined the party in 1994. In December 1994, Bertie Ahern appointed her to the front bench as spokesperson on Arts & Culture. Her brief as Minister for Arts and Heritage includes Ireland's unique regime for writers and composers, a growing film industry, and the music industry. She introduced the *Broadcasting Bill, 1999* — the first major piece of legislation in the area for more than a decade — to introduce the world of digital television, provide for thirty-five channels, define public service broadcasting, and aid the Irish film industry. The Minister sought to address issues raised by the market, by social and cultural demands, and by viewers.

> *Other countries in Europe are standing back and saying 'Let's see how it develops.' I don't think we have the luxury of that.... Obviously digitalisation brings on a completely new era of technology — it is a very exciting one and it means great change and great choice. But we have to ensure that our own cultural identity isn't lost in this morass.*

> *THE IRISH TIMES*, 11 JUNE 1999

She introduced the *Broadcasting (Major Events Television Coverage) Act, 1991*, which aims to ensure that the public can continue to watch the most important sporting contests on ordinary television. The GAA expressed concern that the proposed law could deny it the right to get the best price for the television rights to its games, but she believed that the citizens' rights must be safeguarded.

She extended the Section 35 tax break for the film industry from 1999 to 2000, and set up the Film Industry Strategic Review Group which reported in 1999, to consider how to develop the audio-visual sector.

Eileen Lemass, née Delaney

DATE/PLACE OF BIRTH: JULY 1932/CORK CITY

PARTY: FIANNA FÁIL

CONSTITUENCY: DUBLIN BALLYFERMOT, DUBLIN WEST

DÁIL/SEANAD: 21ST–22ND DÁIL (16 JUNE 1977–FEBRUARY 1982), 24TH DÁIL (24 NOVEMBER 1982–16 FEBRUARY 1987)

AGE AT ENTRY TO DÁIL: 44

FAMILY: DAUGHTER-IN-LAW OF SEÁN LEMASS (TD, DUBLIN SOUTH CENTRAL, 1924–69, TAOISEACH 1959–66); WIDOW OF NOEL LEMASS (TD, DUBLIN SOUTH WEST, 1956–76 (DEATH), PARLIAMENTARY SECRETARY TO THE MINISTER FOR FINANCE, 1969–73), THREE DAUGHTERS, ONE SON

EDUCATION: ST KEVIN'S SCHOOL, HARRINGTON STREET, DUBLIN; NATIONAL COLLEGE OF ART; GRAFTON ACADEMY OF DRESS DESIGNING; ABBEY SCHOOL OF ACTING

OCCUPATION: FULL-TIME PUBLIC REPRESENTATIVE

CAREER: Member, Committee on Procedure and Privileges, 1977; Member, Joint Committee on Women's Rights, 1983–84. Member of Dublin City Council, 1974; Member, Eastern Health Board, 1974. Member of the European Parliament, 1984–9; Member, European Parliament Committees on Regional Policy, Regional Planning, and Women's Rights; Substitute member, Committee on Youth Culture, Education, Information and Sport.

ADDRESS: 34 GROSVENOR COURT, TEMPLEVILLE ROAD, DUBLIN 6

EILEEN LEMASS was a Dáil deputy from 1977 to February 1982, representing the Dublin-Ballyfermot constituency, and later Dublin West. In June 1976, in the old constituency of Dublin South West, she contested a Dáil by-election caused by the death of her husband. She was also a candidate in Dublin West in the February 1982 general election, and in the May 1982 by-election caused by the resignation of Deputy Dick Burke (Fine Gael), following his appointment as a European Commissioner.

Myra Barry

DATE/PLACE OF BIRTH: JUNE 1957/FERMOY, COUNTY CORK

PARTY: FINE GAEL

CONSTITUENCY: CORK NORTH EAST, CORK EAST

DÁIL/SEANAD: 21ST–24TH DÁIL (7 NOVEMBER 1979–
    16 NOVEMBER 1987)

OCCUPATION: PRIMARY SCHOOL TEACHER

AGE AT ENTRY TO DÁIL: 22

FAMILY: DAUGHTER OF DICK BARRY (TD FOR CORK NORTH EAST, 1953–81, PARLIAMENTARY
    SECRETARY TO THE MINISTER FOR HEALTH, 1973–7)

EDUCATION: PRESENTATION CONVENT AND LORETO CONVENT, FERMOY, ST PATRICK'S TEACHER
    TRAINING COLLEGE, DUBLIN (BA, NT)

OCCUPATION: PRIMARY SCHOOLTEACHER

CAREER:
Member, Joint Committee on Women's Rights, 1983. Joint Committee on Marriage Breakdown, 1983. Fine Gael spokesperson on Youth Affairs, 1980-82. Member, Irish National Teachers Organisation; Friends of the Mentally Handicapped, Fermoy; Fermoy Squash Club; Toastmasters International.

ADDRESS: PATRICK STREET, FERMOY, COUNTY CORK

MYRA BARRY was first elected to the Dáil in a by-election in Cork North East in November 1979.

Twenty-Second Dáil ——————————————————

General Election: 11 June 1981   *166 SEATS*

Women Elected

CARRIE ACHESON (FF, TIPPERARY SOUTH)
MYRA BARRY (*SEE P. 115*) (FG, CORK EAST)
EILEEN DESMOND (*SEE P. 107*) (LAB, MID-CORK)
NUALA FENNELL (FG, DUBLIN SOUTH)
MARY FLAHERTY (FG, DUBLIN NORTH WEST)
MÁIRE GEOGHEGAN-QUINN (*SEE P. 109*) (FF, GALWAY WEST)
ALICE GLENN (FG, DUBLIN CENTRAL)
MARY HARNEY (FF, DUBLIN SOUTH WEST)
EILEEN LEMASS (*SEE P. 114*) (FF, DUBLIN WEST)
NORA OWEN (FG, DUBLIN NORTH)
MADELEINE TAYLOR-QUINN (FG, CLARE)

Carrie Acheson, née Barlow

DATE/PLACE OF BIRTH: SEPTEMBER 1934/TIPPERARY

PARTY: FIANNA FÁIL

CONSTITUENCY: TIPPERARY SOUTH

DÁIL/SEANAD: 22ND DÁIL (11 JUNE 1981–18 FEBRUARY 1982)

AGE AT ENTRY TO DÁIL: 46

FAMILY: MARRIED TO HUGH ACHESON; ONE SON. SISTER OF
SENATOR TRAS HONAN (*SEE P. 190*)

EDUCATION: PRESENTATION CONVENT, CLONMEL; MERCY CONVENT CARLOW; LONDON SCHOOL OF
BUSINESS STUDIES

OCCUPATION: COMPANY DIRECTOR

CAREER:
Alderman, Clonmel Borough Council and Mayor of Clonmel 1981/1982. Member, Tipperary South Riding County Council, 1974. President, Clonmel Chamber of Commerce, 1980-82. Member, Tipperary South Riding Committee on Agriculture, Chairperson, 1981-2. Member, Waterford Harbour Board; Tipperary South Riding Museum and Arts Committee. Chair, County Ploughing Association, 1977-81. Member, Public Services Advisory Council, 1978-81. Member, Irish Management Institute; Life Member, Clonmel Gaelic Athletic Association Social Centre. Director, Irish Shipping Ltd. 1980-81.

ADDRESS: WESTERN LODGE, CLONMEL, COUNTY TIPPERARY

CARRIE ACHESON contested a Dáil seat for the first time in the 1981 General Election, and was elected to the Dáil to represent Tipperary South.

Nuala Fennell, née Campbell

DATE/PLACE OF BIRTH: NOVEMBER 1935/DUBLIN

PARTY: FINE GAEL

CONSTITUENCY: DUBLIN SOUTH

DÁIL/SEANAD: 22ND, 23RD, 24TH DÁIL (11 JUNE 1981–16 FEBRUARY 1987),
26TH DÁIL (15 JUNE 1989–24 NOVEMBER 1992).
SENATOR (CASUAL VACANCY), 20 FEBRUARY–13 APRIL 1987.
SENATOR, LABOUR PANEL, 14 APRIL 1987–15 AUGUST 1989

AGE AT ENTRY TO DÁIL: 45

FAMILY: MARRIED TO BRIAN FENNELL; TWO DAUGHTERS, ONE SON

EDUCATION: DOMINICAN COLLEGE, ECCLES STREET, DUBLIN

OCCUPATION: JOURNALIST, AUTHOR

CAREER:
Minister of State at the Department of the Taoiseach and the Department of Justice with responsibility for Women's Affairs and Family Law Reform, 16 December 1982-February 1987. Member, Joint Committee on Women's Rights, 1987-9, 1989-92. Fine Gael opposition spokesperson on Health, October 1989-92. Founder Member, AIM, 1972. Founder Member,

ADAPT, 1974. First Chair, Irish Women's Aid, 1975. Member, Council for the Status of Women. Executive, Marriage Counselling Service, 1986-9: Member, Women's Political Association, National Union of Journalists.

PUBLICATIONS:
Irish Marriage: How Are You?, Dublin: Mercier, 1974; co-author *Can You Stay Married?*, Kinvara, 1980.

ADDRESS: 20 CRAIGLANDS, ARDEEVIN ROAD, DALKEY, COUNTY DUBLIN

NUALA FENNELL, a columnist with the *Evening Herald*, contested the 1977 general election as an Independent candidate in Dublin South County constituency. She joined Fine Gael in 1978 and contested the 1979 European Parliament elections as a Fine Gael candidate in the Dublin constituency. She was the first avowed feminist from the second wave of feminism to be elected to the Dáil, having been a founder member of the Irish Women's Liberation Movement in 1971, founded the highly effective family law reform organisation, Action Information Motivation (AIM) in 1972, ADAPT, the organisation for deserted wives, in 1973, and Women's Aid, a refuge for fugitives from domestic violence, in 1974. AIM opened a Women's Centre in 1975 to provide support and advice on legal and marital problems.

The Office of Women's Affairs was a response by Fine Gael to pressure from the women's movement. Its task was to compile a programme aimed at eliminating discrimination against women, and to recommend administrative structures to implement it. While Nuala Fennell was Minister of State, the department published *Irish Women: Agenda for Practical Action* (Dublin: Stationery Office, 1985), and initiated a Women in Business project, publishing *Women Mean Business: An Introduction to Setting up Your Own Small Business* (Office of the Minister of State for Women's Affairs, 1986)

She introduced the *Domicile and Recognition of Foreign Divorces Act, 1986*, the *Irish Nationality and Citizenship Act, 1986* and the *Status of Children Act, 1987*, which abolished the concept of illegitimacy. She amended the law in the *Health (Family Planning) Act, 1985*, to empower family planning centres to sell contraceptive sheaths. She started the country's first free cancer-screening clinic for women in Hume Street Hospital, Dublin, and opened the Sexual Assault unit in the Rotunda Hospital. Her attempt to have legislative language changed to include 'him' and 'her' met with the response that for legislative purposes 'him' was deemed to include 'her'.

Nuala Fennell felt herself to be hampered by the meagre budget — £175, 000 for 1986 — allocated to the Office of Women's Affairs. Her hope for a second Dáil term to complete her programme of anti-discrimination legislation was dashed when Fianna Fáil won the 1987 election and decided not to have an Office for Women's Affairs.

In 1992, in the lead-up to the abortion referenda on 26 November 26, Nuala Fennell's home was picketed by Youth Defence, an anti-abortion group.

Mary Flaherty

DATE/PLACE OF BIRTH: MAY 1953/DUBLIN

PARTY: FINE GAEL

CONSTITUENCY: DUBLIN NORTH WEST

DÁIL/SEANAD: 22ND–27TH DÁIL (11 JUNE 1981–5 JUNE 1997)

AGE AT ENTRY TO DÁIL: 28

FAMILY: MARRIED TO ALEXIS FITZGERALD (LORD MAYOR OF DUBLIN AT TIME OF MARRIAGE); FOUR SONS

EDUCATION: HOLY FAITH CONVENT, GLASNEVIN, DUBLIN; UNIVERSITY COLLEGE, DUBLIN (BA, HDE)

OCCUPATION: SECONDARY SCHOOLTEACHER

CAREER:

Minister of State at the Department of Social Welfare; Minister of State at the Department of Health, with special responsibility for Poverty and Family Affairs, June 1981–March 1982. Member, Joint Committee on Legislation, 1983. Member, Select Committee on Crime, Lawlessness and Vandalism, 1983. Member, Select Committee on Social Affairs, April 1993; Joint Committee on Sustainable Development, 1995-7. Spokesperson on Labour Affairs, 1993. Front-bench spokesperson on Energy, 1990-93. Front-bench spokesperson on Social Welfare, 1989-90. Front-bench spokesperson on Overseas Development Aid, 1988. Front-bench spokesperson on Health 1987. Member, Association for Western European Parliamentarians Against Apartheid (AWEPAA). Member, Institute for European Affairs (IEA) Social Affairs Group. Head of Young Fine Gael national campaign to abolish illegitimacy. Secretary, Fine Gael parliamentary party, June 1989. Member, Dublin City Council, 1979, and Leader of the Fine Gael Group, 1991. Member, City of Dublin Vocational Educational Committee 1979-85; Eastern Health Board, 1979-85. Director, Dublin Tourism 1979-83. Chairperson, Finglas Vocational Schools Advisory Board. Member, Boards of Whitehall House, Plunkett School, Ballsbridge College of Business Studies, Kevin Street College of Technology and Mount Temple Comprehensive School.

ADDRESS: 2, RICHMOND PLACE, DUBLIN 6

MARY FLAHERTY was elected to Dublin Corporation in 1979, at the expense of the former Lord Mayor, Paddy Belton. She impressed Garret FitzGerald, who, on her first day in the Dáil, appointed her Minister of State at the Department of Social Welfare with responsibility for Poverty. Under John Bruton her fortunes declined. She disagreed with the party hierarchy on a number of issues, including a Fine Gael amendment to the Homosexuality Bill increasing the minimum age from 17 to 18 (which she opposed), and Tony Gregory's hare coursing bill (which she supported). Since then she has concerned herself with the welfare of Irish prisoners in Britain, and visited some of them.

Alice Glenn

DATE/PLACE OF BIRTH: 17 DECEMBER 1927/DUBLIN

PARTY: FINE GAEL

CONSTITUENCY: DUBLIN CENTRAL

DÁIL/SEANAD: 22ND DÁIL (11 JUNE 1981–17 FEBRUARY 1982), 24TH DÁIL (24 NOVEMBER 1982–16 FEBRUARY 1987)

AGE AT ENTRY TO DÁIL: 58

FAMILY: MARRIED TO BRIGADIER-GENERAL WILLIAM GLENN (FORMER GENERAL OFFICER COMMANDING THE AIR CORPS); TWO SONS

EDUCATION: SISTERS OF CHARITY, STANHOPE ST, DUBLIN; HASLEM SCHOOL OF DRESS DESIGNING, DUBLIN

OCCUPATION: DRESS DESIGNER

CAREER:

First woman elected to FG national executive. Member, Dublin City Council, 1974. Chairperson, Dublin Corporation Housing Committee, 1977–8, 1978–9, and 1980–81. Vice-chairperson, Eastern Health Board 1979–80, 1980–81. First woman Chairperson, Eastern Health Board, 1982. First woman Member (in 270 years), Dublin Port & Docks Board, 1979. Chairperson, Dublin Committee on children sleeping rough. Member, Irish Housewives' Association; Pro-Life Movement. Member, Joint Committee on Co-operation with Developing Countries, 1983–7.

PUBLICATION:

The Alice Glenn Report, bi-monthly periodical (c. 1986–7).

ADDRESS: 23 IONA VILLAS, GLASNEVIN, DUBLIN 9 (WHILE IN THE DÁIL)

ALICE GLENN had to receive special clearance from army authorities in 1973 to contest the general election, as her husband was an army officer. She stood again in 1977. After her defeat in February 1982, she stood for a Seanad seat.

Alice Glenn exemplified the conservative strand of Fine Gael and is remembered for her speeches on the abortion and divorce referenda. She declared that the presence of abortion worldwide 'must cry out to heaven for vengeance'. On the divorce referendum, her comment was, 'Any woman voting for divorce would be like a turkey voting for Christmas' (*The Irish Times*, 15 May 1986). On legislation to make contraception available to people over 18, she said: 'What man wants anything to do with a girl who has been used and abused by any man who comes along with condoms?' (*The Irish Times*, 9 November 1984).

In 1986 she criticised alleged supporters of divorce:

> *We are now in a position to identify those who can clearly be classified as enemies of the people ... these would be most of the political parties, the media, spokesmen for the trade unions ... the Council for the Status of Women, all of the radical feminist organisations, the leadership of most of the Churches, apart from the Catholic Church....*
>
> (*THE ALICE GLENN REPORT/THE IRISH TIMES*, 29 NOVEMBER 1986)

These remarks did not reflect Fine Gael thinking, and led to her resignation.

Mary Harney

DATE/PLACE OF BIRTH: 11 MARCH 1953/BALLINASLOE, COUNTY GALWAY
PARTIES: FIANNA FÁIL. PROGRESSIVE DEMOCRATS
CONSTITUENCY: DUBLIN SOUTH WEST
DÁIL/SEANAD: 22ND–28TH DÁIL (11 JUNE 1981 TO DATE); TAOISEACH'S
NOMINEE TO THE SEANAD (25 AUGUST 1977-10 JUNE 1981)
AGE AT ENTRY TO SEANAD: 24
AGE AT ENTRY TO DÁIL: 28
FAMILY: SINGLE
EDUCATION: CONVENT OF MERCY, GOLDENBRIDGE, INCHICORE, DUBLIN; COLÁISTE BHRÍDE,
CLONDALKIN, COUNTY DUBLIN; TRINITY COLLEGE, DUBLIN (BA (MOD))
OCCUPATION: RESEARCH WORKER, FINANCIAL INSTITUTION
CAREER:
Tánaiste and Minister for Enterprise, Employment and Trade, June 1997 to date – first woman
Tánaiste in the history of the State. Leader of the Progressive Democrats, October 1993 to date
– first woman leader of a national party. Minister for State at the Department of the
Environment, with special responsibility for Environmental Protection, 1989-92. Member, Joint
Committee on the Secondary Legislation of the European Communities, 1977. Member, Public
Accounts Committee, 1982, May 1988. Member, Joint Committee on Marriage Breakdown,
1983. Member, Committee on Selection, 1987. Member, Special Committee on the *Judicial
Separation and Family Law Reform Bill, 1987*, March 1988. Member, Select Committee for
Legislation and Security, 1993-7. Member, Forum for Peace and Reconciliation, 1997.
Progressive Democrat spokesperson on Justice and Social Policy, Health and Social Welfare,
and party chief whip. Member, Dublin County Council 1979-91. Vice-chairperson, County
Dublin Vocational Education Committee 1985. *Particular policy interests*: industrial/ economic
affairs, justice, social policy.

ADDRESS: SERPENTINE TERRACE, BALLSBRIDGE, DUBLIN 4

MARY HARNEY was the first woman to become auditor of the Historical Society
in Trinity College, where she was active in student politics and joined Fianna
Fáil. In that role she came to the attention of Fianna Fáil leader, Jack Lynch,
who secured her a party nomination in the Dublin South East constituency at
the 1977 election. She was unsuccessful but was nominated to the Seanad by
Taoiseach Jack Lynch on 25 August 1977, becoming the youngest member of the
that house. She was elected to Dublin County Council in 1979. In June 1981,
Mary Harney was elected to the Dáil for Dublin South West, as a Fianna Fáil
candidate.

Mary Harney had difficulties with Fianna Fáil following the election of
Charles Haughey as leader. She was one of Desmond O'Malley's most ardent
supporters in the October 1982 leadership challenge. This stand almost cost her
her seat, as she polled barely enough votes for a nomination the following
month. She opposed Haughey again in the February 1983 crisis but announced

afterwards that she accepted the majority decision. During these challenges attempts were made to intimidate her, including a threat on her life. She quit Fianna Fáil, having lost the party whip after voting in favour of the Anglo-Irish Agreement of 1985. She was instrumental in the establishment of the Progressive Democrat (PD) party on 21 December 1985.

On the formation of the Fianna Fáil/Progressive Democrat coalition government in 1989, Mary Harney was appointed Minister of State with responsibility for the Office of the Protection of the Environment. She introduced legislation outlawing the sale and use of bituminous fuel in the Dublin area, and legislation establishing an independent Environment Protection Agency. She was appointed Deputy Leader of the Progressive Democrats and Spokesperson on Justice, Equality and Law Reform in February 1993.

Following Desmond O'Malley's resignation in October 1993, she became leader of the PDs — the first woman to lead a party in Dáil Éireann. She espouses self-reliance and minimum state intervention in business. She has been quoted as saying:

Politics is not just about winning a seat, but what you do when you have a seat. I do not want a seat in the Dáil at any cost. Principle must come first....

EVENING HERALD, 23 MAY 2000

As party leader, Mary Harney's approval ratings in opinion polls have always been high, but they have not translated into support for the party, which has declined electorally. Controversies arose on foot of her 1999 holiday in France, which was at the expense of a businessman lobbying to build a new terminal at Dublin Airport, and, in May 2000, on her approval of the nomination of a resigned Supreme Court judge as Vice-president of the European Investment Bank.

As Minister for Enterprise, Trade and Employment, Mary Harney used her powers to initiate thirteen investigations into companies, including Ansbacher Bank, National Irish Bank, Garuda, Bula, Celtic Helicopters and Dunnes Stores, which tribunals had suggested might have breached company law. The authorised officers appointed by her uncovered 'an enormous amount of apparent wrongdoing'. She appointed three inspectors in 1999 to uncover details of the secret Ansbacher accounts and report to the High Court. Her role was delicate as she had also to maintain the Coalition contract with Fianna Fáil. Two years earlier, when Fianna Fáil had refused to include the Ansbacher accounts within the terms of reference of the Moriarty Tribunal, many people had thought that the details would never come out. 'But they reckoned without the quiet determination of the Tánaiste' (*The Irish Times*, 29 September 1999).

In 1993 Mary Harney was chosen as *Irish Independent* Woman of the Year.

Nora Owen, née O'Mahony

DATE/PLACE OF BIRTH: JUNE 1945/DUBLIN

PARTY: FINE GAEL

CONSTITUENCY: DUBLIN NORTH

DÁIL/SEANAD: 22ND-24TH DÁIL (11JUNE 1981-16 FEBRUARY 1987),
26TH-28TH DÁIL (15 JUNE 1989 TO DATE)

AGE AT ENTRY TO DÁIL: 36

FAMILY: MARRIED TO BRIAN OWEN, THREE SONS. GRANDNIECE OF GENERAL
MICHAEL COLLINS, AND OF MARGARET COLLINS-O'DRISCOLL (*SEE P. 85*),
NIECE OF SEAN COLLINS (TD FOR WEST CORK 1948-54, 1961-69),
SISTER OF MARY BANOTTI (*SEE P. 216*) (MEP FOR DUBLIN, 1984 TO DATE)

EDUCATION: DOMINICAN CONVENT, WICKLOW; UNIVERSITY COLLEGE, DUBLIN (BSC, DIPLOMA IN
MICROBIOLOGY)

OCCUPATION: INDUSTRIAL CHEMIST

CAREER:
Minister for Justice, 1994-1997. Deputy Leader of Fine Gael, March 1993. Front bench spokesperson on Enterprise, Trade and Employment, 1997; on Foreign Affairs, 1993-4; and European Affairs, 1994; on Health 1992-3; on Foreign Affairs 1989-92; on Overseas Development, 1982. Chairperson, Joint Committee on Co-operation with Developing Countries, October 1982-January 1987. Member, Dáil Committee on Procedure and Privileges, 1981-7, 1989. Member, British Irish Parliamentary Body, 1991-2. Member, Joint Committee on Enterprise and Small Business, 1997. Member, Dublin County Council, 1979, and its North County Committee (Chairperson 1980-81). Chairperson, Fingal Committee of Dublin County Council 1992-3. Member, Executive of Trócaire, 1987-9. Secretary and volunteer, Malahide Information Centre, 1976-80. Member, Malahide Community Council; Ard na Mara Residents Association; editorial committee of *Malahide News*.

ADDRESS: 17 ARD NA MARA, MALAHIDE, COUNTY DUBLIN

NORA OWEN worked as a chemist with Linson Ltd. from 1965–72. On joining Fine Gael in 1961, she identified herself with the social democratic wing of the party, and was invited to stand for election to Dublin County Council in 1979 because of her involvement in community work.

Her term as Minister for Justice coincided with major problems — serious crime, a divided police force, overcrowded prisons and judicial systems. Several controversies marked her time in Justice, including the failure of her Department to inform Judge Dominic Lynch that he had been delisted by Cabinet as a judge of the Special Criminal Court. A number of republican prisoners had to be released on Minister Owen's instruction, but were subsequently re-arrested. She undertook a major programme of criminal law reform. Among the major changes she implemented were the referendum on bail on 28 November 1996, leading to the *Bail Act, 1997*, which allows a court to refuse bail to a person charged with a serious offence where it is considered necessary to prevent the commission of a serious offence by that person. The *Criminal Justice (Drug Trafficking) Act, 1996* allows for detention for up to seven days of suspected drug traffickers, and restrictions on the right to silence. The *Criminal Assets Bureau Act, 1996*, the *Disclosure of Certain Information for Taxation and Other Purposes Act, 1996* and the *Proceeds of Crime Act, 1996* were designed to ensure that criminals do not benefit from their ill-gotten gains. The *Children Act, 1997* protects children against abuse and outlaws child pornography and trafficking in children. The *Sexual Offences (Jurisdiction) Act, 1996*, which deals with child sex tourism, was a Private Member's Bill which was accepted subject to extensive amendment.

Among a host of other anti-crime measures, Nora Owen commenced an unprecedented prison-building programme, designed to provide 800 prison places.

Madeleine Taylor-Quinn

DATE/PLACE OF BIRTH: MAY 1951/KILKEE, COUNTY CLARE

PARTY: FINE GAEL

CONSTITUENCY: CLARE

DÁIL/SEANAD: 22ND DÁIL (11 JUNE 1981–17 FEBRUARY 1982), 24TH–26TH
   DÁIL (24 NOVEMBER 1982–24 NOVEMBER 1992). SEANAD (CULTURAL &
   EDUCATIONAL PANEL), 21 APRIL 1982–23 NOVEMBER 1982; 1 FEBRUARY
   1993 TO DATE

AGE AT ENTRY TO DÁIL: 30

FAMILY: DAUGHTER OF FRANK TAYLOR (FINE GAEL TD FOR CLARE, 1969-81). MARRIED TO GEORGE
   QUINN; TWO SONS

EDUCATION: CONVENT OF MERCY, KILRUSH, COUNTY CLARE; UNIVERSITY COLLEGE, GALWAY (BA,
   LLB, H.DIP. ED)

OCCUPATION: SECONDARY SCHOOLTEACHER

CAREER.
Front-bench spokesperson on the Marine, 1988. Fine Gael spokesperson on Tourism, 1987.
Member, Joint Committee on Women's Rights, 1983-7, 1987-9; Joint Committee on Marriage
Breakdown, 1983. Member, Chair, Special Committee on the *Judicial Separation and Family
Law Reform Bill, 1987*, March 1988. Member, Joint Committee on Foreign Affairs, 1997.
Member, Clare County Council, 1979. Member, National Economic and Social Forum; Mid-
Western Regional Development Organisation; Arts Committee, 1979-85; West Clare Tourist
Development Association; National Health Council. Joint Honorary Secretary of Fine Gael,
1979-82. Founder member, Young Fine Gael.

ADDRESS: FRANCIS STREET, KILRUSH, COUNTY CLARE

MADELEINE TAYLOR-QUINN was the first woman to represent Clare in the Dáil, and the first woman to be elected to an officership within the Fine Gael Party (Joint Honorary Secretary, 1979). She was unsuccessful in her candidacy in the Dáil general election of February 1982, but was elected to the 24th Dáil in November of that year. The following speeches she has made to the Seanad give an insight into her experience as a female politician.

> *... it must be said that any woman who has been elected to either House of the Oireachtas has done so only by making enormous sacrifices, not just on her own part but also on the part of her husband and children ... shorter sitting hours, such as nine to five in Dublin, would not suit me who lives 180 miles from here.*

SEANAD ÉIREANN OFFICIAL REPORT, GENERAL DEBATE, REPORT OF THE SECOND COMMISSION ON THE STATUS OF WOMEN, 11 MARCH 1993, COL. 656

> *If a woman politician who delivers a child takes 14 weeks' leave the reality is that the males in her constituency will have taken every opportunity to do a hatchet job on her. I am sure the Minister will have to use all his brain power and that of his officials to try to get around that difficulty because I do not see how women politicians can be treated equally given the nature of the political game. I am speaking from experience as I gave birth to two children while a Member of Dáil Éireann and I know exactly what I am talking about. The maximum I could afford to spend out of circulation was two weeks.*

SEANAD ÉIREANN OFFICIAL REPORT, VOL. 141, (PRIVILEGE AND IMMUNITY BILL, 1994. COL. 1255) GENERAL DEBATE, SELECT COMMITTEE ON LEGISLATION AND SECURITY OF DÁIL ÉIREANN

Twenty-Third Dáil

General Election: 18 February 1982   *166 SEATS*

Women Elected

MYRA BARRY (*SEE P. 115*) (FG, EAST CORK)
EILEEN DESMOND (*SEE P. 107*) (LAB, CORK SOUTH CENTRAL)
NUALA FENNELL (*SEE P. 116*) (FG, DUBLIN SOUTH)
MARY FLAHERTY (*SEE P. 118*) (FG, DUBLIN NORTH WEST)
MÁIRE GEOGHEGAN-QUINN (*SEE P. 109*) (FF, GALWAY WEST)
MARY HARNEY (*SEE P. 120*) (FF, DUBLIN SOUTH WEST)
GEMMA HUSSEY (FG, WICKLOW)
NORA OWEN (*SEE P. 122*) (FG, DUBLIN NORTH)

Gemma Hussey, née Moran

DATE/PLACE OF BIRTH: NOVEMBER 1938/BRAY, COUNTY WICKLOW
PARTY: FINE GAEL
CONSTITUENCY: WICKLOW; SEANAD: NATIONAL UNIVERSITY OF IRELAND
DÁIL/SEANAD: 23RD–25TH DÁIL (18 FEBRUARY 1982–14 JUNE 1989). SEANAD (17 AUGUST 1977–20 APRIL 1982)
AGE AT ENTRY TO SEANAD: 38

Age at Entry to Dáil: 42

Family: Married to Dermot R. Hussey; two daughters, one son

Education: St Bridget's School, Bray; Loreto Convent, Bray; Convent of the Sacred Heart, Mount Anville, Dublin; University College Dublin (BA Economics & Politics)

Occupation: Founder director, English Language Institute, Dublin

Career:
Minister for Social Welfare, February 1986-March 1987. Minister for Labour January-March 1987. Minister for Education, December 1982-February 1986. Fine Gael spokesperson on Education, 1987; Fine Gael spokesperson on Women's Affairs, November 1980-June 1981;Fine Gael spokesperson on Arts, Culture and Broadcasting, 1982. Government Leader of the Senate 1981-82. Member, Joint Oireachtas Committee on the Secondary Legislation of the European Communities, 1977-80 and 1987; Chairperson, 1987. Member, Seanad Committee of Procedure and Privileges 1977-81. Member, Joint Committee on Building Land, 1982. Vice-chairperson, Irish-Arab Parliamentary Association, 1978-82. Committee member, British-Irish Parliamentary Association, 1978-82. Member, Commission of Enquiry into the Penal System, 1979-80. Chairperson, Women's Political Association, 1973-5 (Vice-chairperson, 1975-7), Council for the Status of Women 1973-1975. Founder member, National Women's Talent Bank. Director Abbey Theatre 1974-8. Founder director, TEAM (Children's Educational Theatre). Member, AIM Group; Bray Chamber of Commerce; Dalkey and Bray School Projects; Council for Civil Liberties; Irish Council of European Movement; Mental Health Association of Ireland; Irish Women's Aid; Association for Welfare of Children in Hospital; An Taisce; Children First. *Particular policy interests*: international democracy training, Eastern/Central European recovery, human rights/gender issues, current affairs broadcasting, political structural reform, education. *Other interests*: opera, walking, theatre, visual art, travel.

Publications:
Ireland – Status of Women (1977), *Women in broadcasting in RTE*, report (1981); *At the Cutting Edge: Cabinet Diaries, 1982-1987*, Dublin: Gill and Macmillan, 1990; *Ireland Today: Anatomy of a Changing State*, Viking Penguin/Town House, 1993; *The Ages of Learning*, discussion paper issued by the Minister of Education, 25 June 1984; *Partners in Education*, green paper, Department of Education, 1985. *Social Welfare – 4 Years of Progress*, 1987

Address: Temple Road, Dublin 6

Gemma Hussey entered the Senate in 1977 as an Independent with a background in the women's movement. She had been Chair of the Women's Political Association from 1973 to 1975, and a member of the Council for the Status of Women. She attempted as a Senator to have legislation on rape introduced, sponsoring the *Sexual Offences Bill, 1980*, which lapsed at First Stage. Although she joined Fine Gael in 1972, she did not accept the party whip in the Seanad until November 1980. She contested the Wicklow constituency during the 1981 general election, at which time she was the Fine Gael spokesperson on Women's Affairs. In this role she took a cautious approach to divorce and expressed her total opposition to abortion. She accompanied Garret FitzGerald to a meeting with a delegation from the Pro-Life Amendment Campaign, during which he committed Fine Gael to holding a referendum regarding the addition of an anti-abortion amendment to the Constitution. In 1983 she campaigned against the 'pro-life' amendment to the Constitution.

Gemma Hussey took the initiative in opposing the government's decision to close Ardmore Studios in Bray. She suggested that ministerial Mercedes cars be replaced by more modest cars to save costs.

She was appointed Minister for Education within a year of her entry into the Dáil, declining the services of the Department's Press Officer, Frank Dunlop. She began the process of modernising the education system and increasing the importance of the Department of Education. The precarious state of the public finances meant that much of her time had to be devoted to finding ways of reducing the Education budget. Within weeks of taking office, she introduced charges for the school transport system. Because it affected every townland in the country, this decision was akin to political suicide, and she was attacked from all sides. She persevered with the measure, although the government decided to exclude from the new charges the children of social welfare recipients.

Between 1980 and 1986 third-level enrolments were increasing rapidly and, in 1984, Gemma Hussey secured increased government provision for higher education. At a time of severe cutbacks in public spending, she justified this on demographic grounds, because of the rapidly expanding number of young people in the educational system. In 1984, also, as a result of her negotiation of the allocation from the European Social Fund, annual grants of £300 were provided for about a third of school-leavers who undertook employment-preparation courses.

In 1985, Gemma Hussey was embroiled in a controversy with teachers' unions, whose demands for an increase in pay had been rejected by the government. She questioned the morality of so substantial a pay claim at a time of national stringency. In 1986, another controversy erupted. Primary-school pupil numbers were set to decline and the government decided to close Carysfort teacher training college in Dublin. This information was leaked before the relevant authorities had been informed, and many accusations were made against the Minister for Education. The teachers' dispute was still in progress and, because she occupied a marginal seat, Taoiseach Garret FitzGerald decided to move Gemma Hussey in his cabinet reshuffle of early 1986. She had been the most reforming Minister for Education since Donough O'Malley, opening up the Department to new ideas and giving education a higher profile.

The Taoiseach's plan was to create a new Department of European Affairs for Gemma Hussey — a prospect which appealed to her. However, he was informed by the Secretary to the Government that his proposal would entail dividing the Department of Foreign Affairs in two and creating a separate secretariat for the new European Affairs department. Another minister, Barry Desmond (Labour), refused to be moved from Health. The result was that Gemma Hussey became Minister for Social Welfare, which she regarded as a demotion.

Late in 1986, she was active in the campaign to secure a Yes vote in the divorce referendum. From 1987 to 1989 she was front-bench spokesperson on Education. Upon her defeat in the 1989 general election, Gemma Hussey retired from politics.

Twenty-Fourth Dáil ————————————————————————————

General Election: 24 November 1982   *166 SEATS*

Women Elected
MONICA BARNES (FG, DÚN LAOGHAIRE)
MYRA BARRY (*SEE P. 115*) (FG, EAST CORK)
EILEEN DESMOND (*SEE P. 107*) (LAB, CORK SOUTH CENTRAL)
AVRIL DOYLE (FG, WEXFORD)
NUALA FENNELL (*SEE P. 116*) (FG, DUBLIN SOUTH)
MARY FLAHERTY (*SEE P. 118*) (FG, DUBLIN NORTH WEST)
MÁIRE GEOGHEGAN-QUINN (*SEE P. 109*) (FF, GALWAY WEST)
ALICE GLENN (*SEE P. 119*) (FG, DUBLIN CENTRAL)
MARY HARNEY (*SEE P. 120*) (FF, DUBLIN SOUTH WEST)
GEMMA HUSSEY (*SEE P. 124*) (FG, WICKLOW)
EILEEN LEMASS (*SEE P. 114*) (FF, DUBLIN WEST)
MARY O'ROURKE (FF, LONGFORD/WESTMEATH)
NORA OWEN (*SEE P. 122*) (FG, DUBLIN NORTH)
MADELEINE TAYLOR-QUINN (*SEE P. 123*) (FG, CLARE)

Monica Barnes, née McDermott

DATE/PLACE OF BIRTH: FEBRUARY 1936/CARRICKMACROSS, COUNTY
    MONAGHAN
PARTY: FINE GAEL
CONSTITUENCY: DÁIL – DÚN LAOGHAIRE; SEANAD – LABOUR PANEL
DÁIL/SEANAD: 24TH, 25TH, 26TH DÁIL (24 NOVEMBER 1982–
    24 NOVEMBER 1992), 28TH DÁIL (6 JUNE 1997 TO DATE)
    SEANAD: 21 APRIL 1982–NOVEMBER 1982
AGE AT ENTRY TO SEANAD: 46
AGE AT ENTRY TO DÁIL: 46
FAMILY: MARRIED BOB BARNES, 1962; TWO DAUGHTERS, ONE SON
EDUCATION: ST LOUIS CONVENT, CARRICKMACROSS; ORANGE'S ACADEMY, BELFAST
OCCUPATION: SECRETARY, COUNCIL OF THE LONDON STOCK EXCHANGE; ADMINISTRATOR; LECTURER
CAREER:
Fine Gael spokesperson on Women's Affairs in Dáil; on Law Reform and assistant whip in Seanad, April–November 1982. Vice-chairperson, Joint Committee on Women's Rights, 1983-7, 1987-9; Chair of Committee, 1989-92. Member, Special Committee on the *Judicial Separation and Family Law Reform Bill, 1987*. Vice-chairperson, Joint Committee on Justice, Equality and Women's Rights, 1997; Chair of its sub-committee on Women's Rights, July 1998. Member,

Women's Representative Committee, 1974-8; Irish Association of Civil Liberties; Irish Anti-Apartheid Movement; Campaign for Nuclear Disarmament (CND); Employment Equality Agency 1977-82. Vice-president, Women's Federation of the European People's Party, 1978; Femscan Committee; National Forum on Cancer Services. Founder member, Council for the Status of Women, 1973 (Administrator, 1978-81). Trustee, ARC Trust. Life member, Business and Professional Women's Club, Dún Laoghaire. Founder member, Vice-chairperson, Women's Political Association, 1973/4. First woman Vice-president, Fine Gael, 1980-81.

ADDRESS: 5, ARNOLD PARK, GLENAGEARY, CO. DUBLIN

MONICA BARNES bought *Women in Chains*, a pamphlet published by the Women's Liberation Movement, outside Mass one Sunday in the 1960s. It crystallised her experiences as a housebound mother of three small children and heralded her involvement in the women's movement. Her work with the Council for the Status of Women turned it into a force for change, giving it credibility, getting it funded, and opening its doors to all women. She joined Fine Gael in the early 1970s, attracted by the ideals of the Just Society document, and sought her first nomination in 1977. She contested the European elections of 1979 and 1994 in the Leinster constituency and was a Fine Gael general election candidate in 1981, February 1982 and 1992.

In 1983 Monica Barnes was one of two Fine Gael Deputies who voted in the Dáil against the Fianna Fáil wording of an abortion ban to be inserted into the Constitution, disquieted by the medical and legal implications, believing that it discriminated against minority groups and could result in medical treatment being denied to pregnant women. The wording had been accepted by the Fine Gael leader, Garret FitzGerald, and was contained in the party programme in the November 1982 election. She said:

I decided I could only compromise myself to a certain point. The referendum was a fundamental issue for women. Women were the reason I was involved at all. If I kept quiet, then as far as I was concerned, I was redundant as a politician.

SUNDAY TRIBUNE, 21 AUGUST 1983

She received hate mail, mostly from men, and was jostled and abused by pro-amendment delegations in the corridors of Leinster House, but she received a great deal of support also. She was pro-divorce in the referendum of 1995.

Reflecting on the possibility of becoming a Minister, Monica Barnes said:

If I was offered a portfolio, there would have to be a realisation on both sides that there are principles I'm committed to like women's rights and nuclear disarmament and that they go further than party political loyalty.

THE IRISH TIMES, 16 NOVEMBER 1984

Avril Doyle, née Belton

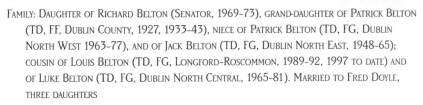

DATE/PLACE OF BIRTH: 18 APRIL 1949/DUBLIN

PARTY: FINE GAEL

CONSTITUENCY: DÁIL – WEXFORD. SEANAD – AGRICULTURAL PANEL

DÁIL/SEANAD: 24TH, 25TH DÁIL (24 NOVEMBER 1982-14 JUNE 1989), 27TH DÁIL (25 NOVEMBER 1992-5 JUNE 1997). SEANAD: 16 AUGUST 1989-23 NOVEMBER 1992; 6 AUGUST 1997 TO DATE

AGE AT ENTRY TO DÁIL: 33

FAMILY: DAUGHTER OF RICHARD BELTON (SENATOR, 1969-73), GRAND-DAUGHTER OF PATRICK BELTON (TD, FF, DUBLIN COUNTY, 1927, 1933-43), NIECE OF PATRICK BELTON (TD, FG, DUBLIN NORTH WEST 1963-77), AND OF JACK BELTON (TD, FG, DUBLIN NORTH EAST, 1948-65); COUSIN OF LOUIS BELTON (TD, FG, LONGFORD-ROSCOMMON, 1989-92, 1997 TO DATE) AND OF LUKE BELTON (TD, FG, DUBLIN NORTH CENTRAL, 1965-81). MARRIED TO FRED DOYLE, THREE DAUGHTERS

EDUCATION: HOLY CHILD CONVENT, KILLINEY, COUNTY DUBLIN; UNIVERSITY COLLEGE, DUBLIN (BSc BIOCHEMISTRY); UNIVERSITY OF GRENOBLE, FRANCE; NOTTINGHAM UNIVERSITY.

OCCUPATION: BIOCHEMIST. RETAILER. TEACHER. FARMER

CAREER:

Minister of State at the Departments of the Taoiseach, Finance and Transport, Energy and Communications, 1994-7. Minister of State at the Department of Finance with special responsibility for the Office of Public Works, and at the Department of the Environment with special responsibility for Environmental Protection, February 1986-March 1987. Front-bench spokesperson on Environment, 1993; on Agriculture, 1988-9; on Marine Affairs, 1987-8. Member, Joint Committee on Small Businesses, 1983; on Consolidation Bills, 1997. on Foreign Affairs, 1997; on Finance and the Public Service, 1997. Member, Wexford County Council, 1973; Wexford Borough Council 1973-82. First woman Mayor of Wexford 1976-7. Member of the European Parliament, 1999: Member of the Group of the European People's Party (Christian Democrats); Member, Bureau of European Democrats; Committee on the Environment, Public Health and Consumer Policy; Delegation for relations with South Africa; Substitute, Committee on Agriculture and Rural Development. *Particular policy interests*: environment, agriculture, health. Other interests: equestrian interests. Chair, Eventing Ireland (horse trials).

ADDRESS: KITESTOWN HOUSE, CROSSABEG, WEXFORD

AVRIL DOYLE has had a career of fluctuating fortunes, overcoming several setbacks to retain a high profile within Fine Gael and become a Deputy, Junior Minister, Senator and MEP. She became active in politics as a student in UCD where she dated John Bruton, later leader of Fine Gael, and Taoiseach. She was narrowly defeated by Mary Banotti for the Fine Gael nomination for the Presidency in 1997. As Junior Minister at Department of the Taoiseach during the Rainbow government she chaired the Great Famine and 1798 Commemoration Committees, organising a large EU grant for the National 1798 Centre in Enniscorthy. She also steered the Strategic Management Initiative, which is designed to ensure that the Civil Service serves the public well.

Mary O'Rourke, née Lenihan

DATE/PLACE OF BIRTH: MAY 1937/ATHLONE

PARTY: FIANNA FÁIL.

CONSTITUENCY: DÁIL – LONGFORD–WESTMEATH. WESTMEATH. SEANAD – INDUSTRIAL & COMMERCIAL PANEL, 1981–2. CULTURAL & EDUCATIONAL PANEL, APRIL–NOVEMBER 1982

DÁIL/SEANAD: 24TH, 25TH, 26TH, 27TH, 28TH DÁIL (24 NOVEMBER 1982 TO DATE). SEANAD: 12 AUGUST 1981–23 NOVEMBER 1982

AGE AT ENTRY TO SEANAD: 44

AGE AT ENTRY TO DÁIL: 45

FAMILY: DAUGHTER OF P.J. LENIHAN, (TD, LONGFORD-WESTMEATH 1965–70), SISTER OF BRIAN LENIHAN (TD, ROSCOMMON–LEITRIM, DUBLIN WEST/TÁNAISTE AND MINISTER IN MOST DEPARTMENTS, 1961–95), AUNT OF BRIAN LENIHAN (TD, DUBLIN WEST, 1996 TO DATE) AND OF CONOR LENIHAN (TD, DUBLIN SOUTH-WEST, 1997 TO DATE). MARRIED TO ENDA O'ROURKE, TWO SONS

EDUCATION: ST PETER'S, ATHLONE; LORETO CONVENT, BRAY, COUNTY WICKLOW; UNIVERSITY COLLEGE DUBLIN; MAYNOOTH COLLEGE (BA, H.DIP. ED)

OCCUPATION: SECONDARY SCHOOLTEACHER

CAREER:

Minister for Public Enterprise, 26 June 1997 to date. Front-bench spokesperson on Enterprise and Employment, 1995–7. Deputy Leader, Fianna Fáil, 1994. Minister of State at the Department of Enterprise and Employment, with special responsibilities for Labour Affairs, 1993–4. Minister of State at the Department of Industry & Commerce (Trade & Marketing) February 1992–January 1993. Minister for Health, 14 November 1991–February 1992. Minister for Education, 1987–91. Member, Joint Committee on Women's Rights, 1983; on Small Business and Services, 1995. Member, Forum for Peace and Reconciliation, 1997. Member, Westmeath County Council, 1979–87. Member, Athlone UDC, 1974–87 (chairperson 1980-81, 1984-5 and 1986-7).

ADDRESS: AISLING, ARCADIA, ATHLONE, COUNTY WESTMEATH

MARY O'ROURKE was first elected to the Dáil in November 1982 for the constituency of Longford–Westmeath and represented that constituency until the boundary revisions of 1992. She and her brother, Brian Lenihan, became the first sister and brother to serve in the same Cabinet, the twenty-first Government, appointed on 12 July 1989; they served together until 31 October 1990. In February 1992, she contested the leadership of Fianna Fáil with Albert Reynolds and Michael Woods, and won six votes. She was dropped from Cabinet when Albert Reynolds became party leader, and was appointed Minister of State at the Department of Industry & Commerce (Trade & Marketing) in February 1992. This blow was keenly felt:

> *I couldn't believe it.... That struck me right in the stomach. I talked, shouted, cried and drank that night. I wept so much, I had the duvet over my head and ranted again all night with Enda.*

IRELAND ON SUNDAY, 17 MAY 1998

She was appointed Deputy Leader of Fianna Fáil in 1994 when Bertie Ahern became leader. She was embroiled in controversy from 1987 to 1989 over the purchase of Carysfort lands by the State. As Minister for Education, she set up the Applied Leaving Certificate as an alternative qualification for less academically able students, abolished the matriculation examination as a means of selection of university students, and abolished interviews as a means of selecting students for third-level courses. She completed the process of abolishing the distinction between vocational schools and secondary schools at junior level by establishing a single junior-cycle examination, the Junior Certificate, and initiated a review of the Leaving Certificate. She also set up a group to review the primary curriculum, and equalised the pupil–teacher ratio between secondary and vocational schools. The first Minister for Education to take on the Churches, Mary O'Rourke supported the Stay Safe programme for primary schoolchildren. The programme was opposed by an array of right-wing groups, but she enlisted the aid of parents, teachers and managers to implement it. She was regarded by the teaching profession as one of the best Ministers for Education in recent decades.

As Minister for Public Enterprise, her remit covers transport, energy and communications, including telecommunications infrastructure and e-commerce and the economic effect of semi-state agencies, giving her responsibility for wiring Ireland to the superhighway and moving the country from its old telephone system into a costly high-bandwidth future. Lack of competition was stunting the development of broadband infrastructure and keeping Internet charges too high to allow the growth of e-commerce. In May 1998, she stripped Telecom Éireann of its special EU exemption, which let Ireland avoid a deregulated telecoms market until 2000. Her department published a framework document on encryption and she announced the appointment of an Advisory Committee for Telecommunications, which agreed that Ireland should establish a public/private partnership approach to encourage investment and be creative about venture capital. The first recommendation was soon public policy and the public–private partnership was launched. Her department also initiated the Joint Communiqué on Electronic Commerce with the United States, signed by the Taoiseach and President Clinton in September 1998. Full telecommunications liberalisation took place on 1 December 1998. She was quoted in the *Guardian* (10 September 1998) as follows:

There's no point in keeping pace with whatever's happening in other countries. You have to dream, think and articulate what isn't even yet believable in this country.

She introduced the Electronic Commerce Bill on 6 April 2000 to give the Republic of Ireland the strongest legal framework internationally, ahead of the US framework, protecting the use of encryption, with the intention of giving the State a competitive advantage. She also oversaw the flotation of Telecom

Éireann on the stock market in July 1999 and deregulated the electricity market with the *Electricity Regulation Act, 1999.*

Although unprecedented levels of investment in transport infrastructure have been made, including the planning of the LUAS tram system in Dublin, the transport problem has proved intractable.

Mary O'Rourke recalls an incident in her childhood:

> *One particular occasion stands out in my mind — I think it must have been the general election of 1948 — when Éamon de Valera came to Athlone to address a huge rally.... I was eleven years of age, and was allowed with my three siblings to go to hear de Valera. He came to visit our house afterwards and Brian, Paddy and Ann were allowed to join with all the Party faithful in animated discussion and chat in the 'big room'.... I was packed off to bed amid howls of anger and no cajolery would pacify me....*
>
> *Up the corridor I could hear the loud talk, the laughter, the argument growing more tense as time went on. Nothing would do me but to be part of it. I got myself a cushion and plonked myself outside the door, listening, listening, listening. If I close my eyes now, I can still see myself, the dark corridor, the soft cushion, the closed door, the gaiety, the warmth, the excitement which seemed to be beyond that door and I not part of it. Oh, how I longed to be in the middle of that mysterious grown-up world of politics! Forty-five years on, that memory is still strong and vibrant. For me, it was the start of a long love affair with politics and I'm still enraptured, enthusiastic and enthralled.*
>
> S. POWER (ED.), *THOSE WERE THE DAYS*, DUBLIN: GILL AND MACMILLAN, 1995

Twenty-Fifth Dáil ——————————————————————————

General Election: 17 November 1987   *166 SEATS*

Women Elected

MONICA BARNES (*SEE P. 127*) (FG, DÚN LAOGHAIRE)
ANNE COLLEY (PD, DUBLIN SOUTH)
MARY T. COUGHLAN (FF, DONEGAL SOUTH WEST)
SÍLE DE VALERA (*SEE P. 112*) (FF, CLARE)
AVRIL DOYLE (*SEE P. 129*) (FG, WEXFORD)
MARY FLAHERTY (*SEE P. 118*) (FG, DUBLIN NORTH WEST)
MÁIRE GEOGHEGAN-QUINN (*SEE P. 109*) (FF, GALWAY WEST)
MARY HARNEY (*SEE P. 120*) (PD, DUBLIN SOUTH WEST)
GEMMA HUSSEY (*SEE P. 124*) (FG, WICKLOW)
GERALDINE KENNEDY (PD, DÚN LAOGHAIRE)
MARY MOONEY (FF, DUBLIN SOUTH CENTRAL)
MARY O'ROURKE (*SEE P. 130*) (FF, LONGFORD/WESTMEATH)
MÁIRÍN QUILL (PD, CORK NORTH CENTRAL)
MADELEINE TAYLOR-QUINN (*SEE P. 123*) (FG, CLARE)

Anne Colley

DATE/PLACE OF BIRTH: JULY 1951/DUBLIN

PARTY: PROGRESSIVE DEMOCRATS

CONSTITUENCY: DUBLIN SOUTH

DÁIL/SEANAD: 25TH DÁIL (17 FEBRUARY 1987-14 JUNE 1989)

AGE AT ENTRY TO DÁIL: 35

FAMILY: DAUGHTER OF GEORGE COLLEY (TD, FF, FOR DUBLIN CENTRAL AND
OTHER DUBLIN CONSTITUENCIES, 1961-1983, TÁNAISTE 1977-81 AND
MINISTER IN MANY DEPARTMENTS); GRANDDAUGHTER OF HARRY COLLEY (TD, FF FOR DUBLIN
NORTH EAST, 1944-57). MARRIED TO GENERAL ORMONDE; ONE DAUGHTER, TWO SONS

EDUCATION: SACRED HEART CONVENT, LEESON STREET AND MOUNT ANVILLE, DUBLIN; UNIVERSITY
COLLEGE DUBLIN (BCL); INCORPORATED LAW SOCIETY OF IRELAND

OCCUPATION: SOLICITOR

CAREER:

Founder member of Progressive Democrats; spokesperson on Institutional Reform, Labour and
the Public Service, 1987-8, on Justice, 1988-89. Member, Committee of Public Accounts,
1987-8; Working Group on Televising Dáil Proceedings, 1988-9. Member, Special Committee
on the *Judicial Separation and Family Law Reform Bill, 1987*. Worked while a student with Free
Legal Aid Advisory Centres. Voluntary counsellor, Catholic Marriage Advisory Council.

ADDRESS: LISCANNOR, BEAUMONT AVENUE, CHURCHTOWN, DUBLIN 14

ANNE COLLEY was elected at her first attempt, topping the poll with 20.9 per cent of
the vote. She lost her seat in 1989 when the Progressive Democrat vote slumped.

Mary Coughlan

DATE/PLACE OF BIRTH: MAY 1965/CRANNY, INVER, COUNTY DONEGAL

PARTY: FIANNA FÁIL

CONSTITUENCY: DONEGAL SOUTH WEST

DÁIL/SEANAD: 25TH, 26TH, 27TH, 28TH DÁIL (17 FEBRUARY 1987 TO DATE)

AGE AT ENTRY TO DÁIL: 21

FAMILY: DAUGHTER OF CATHAL COUGHLAN (TD, DONEGAL SOUTH WEST,
1983-6); NIECE OF CLEMENT COUGHLAN (TD, DONEGAL SOUTH WEST,
1980-83). MARRIED TO DAVID CHARLTON; ONE DAUGHTER, ONE SON

EDUCATION: URSULINE CONVENT, SLIGO; UNIVERSITY COLLEGE DUBLIN, (BSOC SCI.)

OCCUPATION: SOCIAL WORKER

CAREER:

Spokesperson on Educational Reform 1995-7. Member, Special Committee on the Judicial
Separation and Family Law Reform Bill, 1987, 1988. Member, Special Committee on the
Recognition of Foreign Adoptions Bill, 1990. Member, Dáil Select Committee on Crime, 1992.
Chairperson Joint Committee on the Irish Language, 1993-5. Vice-Chairperson, Joint Committee
on Tourism, Sport and Recreation, 1997. Member, Joint Committee on Employment, 1992; on

Women's Rights, 1992; on the Irish Language, 1987. Member, Donegal County Council, 1986; Donegal County Vocational Education Committee, 1986 (chairperson 1991-2). Chairperson, Board of Management, Abbey Vocational School, Donegal. Member, Board of Management Killybegs Tourism College. Honorary Secretary, Fianna Fáil party, 1995. Member of British-Irish Parliamentary Body, 1991-2, 1997. President, Killybegs Coast and Cliff Rescue Service.

MARY COUGHLAN was the first woman to represent Donegal in the Dáil. In 1999 she gave birth to her second child while her husband, a garda, recovered from a car crash which resulted in the amputation of his leg. She was still present for most Dáil divisions.

Geraldine Kennedy

DATE/PLACE OF BIRTH: SEPTEMBER 1951/TRAMORE, COUNTY WATERFORD

PARTY: PROGRESSIVE DEMOCRATS

CONSTITUENCY: DÚN LAOGHAIRE

DÁIL/SEANAD: 25TH DÁIL (17 FEBRUARY 1987-14 JUNE 1989)

AGE AT ENTRY TO DÁIL: 35

FAMILY: MARRIED TO DAVID HEGARTY, ONE DAUGHTER

EDUCATION: PRESENTATION CONVENT, CARRICK ON SUIR, COUNTY TIPPERARY; CONVENT OF THE SACRED HEART OF MARY, FERRYBANK, WATERFORD; COLLEGE OF COMMERCE, RATHMINES, DUBLIN 6

OCCUPATION: JOURNALIST

CAREER:
Progressive Democrat spokesperson on Foreign Affairs, Northern Ireland, and chief whip (assistant whip, 1987-9). Member, Committee on Selection, May 1988. Member, Committee on Procedure and Privileges, May 1988. First woman political correspondent in Ireland. First woman Chair of the Oireachtas Press Gallery, 1975.

ADDRESS: 5 GROSVENOR TERRACE, MONKSTOWN, COUNTY DUBLIN

GERALDINE KENNEDY was elected at her first attempt in any election for public office. She was a reporter with the *Cork Examiner* and the political correspondent with the *Sunday Tribune*, *Sunday Press* and *Irish Times* newspapers.

As a journalist, she covered the front-page stories — the Herrema siege in Monasterevin, the Dublin bombings and the visit of Pope John Paul II. While covering the challenges to the Fianna Fáil leadership of Charles Haughey and the activities of the Club of 22, she was intimidated by phone calls, notes, verbal warnings and broken bottles left under her windscreen; she had to receive Garda protection. The tapping of her phone in 1982 resulted in her being awarded damages by the High Court in January 1987; the Court ruled that the injury done to her was done consciously, deliberately and without justification. In February 1992, Charles Haughey was forced from office when it was revealed by Sean Doherty, Minister for Justice in 1982, that the then Taoiseach had known about and approved of the tapping of journalists' phones in 1982.

In the mid-1970s Geraldine Kennedy was approached by Fine Gael to stand as a TD, but refused. In 1985 she was asked by Fianna Fáil to stand in the local elections, an invitation she also refused.

Mary Mooney

DATE/PLACE OF BIRTH: DECEMBER 1958/DUBLIN

PARTY: FIANNA FÁIL

CONSTITUENCY: DUBLIN SOUTH CENTRAL

DÁIL/SEANAD: 25TH DÁIL (17 FEBRUARY 1987-14 JUNE 1989)

AGE AT ENTRY TO DÁIL: 28

FAMILY: MARRIED, ONE CHILD

EDUCATION: ST THERESA'S PRESENTATION CONVENT, DUBLIN

OCCUPATION: RETAILER IN FAMILY BUSINESS, DUBLIN'S LIBERTIES

CAREER:

Member and Vice-chair of Oireachtas Joint Committee on Women's Rights, 1987-9. Alderwoman, Dublin City Council, 1985; Member of its Housing Committee, General Purposes Committee, Employment and Enterprise Committee, Youth and Community Committee, Inner City and Art Advisory Committee. Member of Dublin Port and Docks Board. Member of Executive Board, Holles Street Maternity Hospital, 1985. Other interests: Member, Clonliffe Harriers Athletic Club, Irish Amateur Boxing Association. Organiser, Liberties Around the Houses Roadrace.

ADDRESS: GLENORA, LOWER STRAWBERRY BEDS, LUCAN, COUNTY DUBLIN (ADDRESS WHILE IN DÁIL)

MARY MOONEY won her seat in the Dáil at her first attempt, standing in the Dublin South Central constituency.

Máirin Quill

DATE/PLACE OF BIRTH: 15 SEPTEMBER 1940/KILGARVAN, COUNTY KERRY

PARTY: PROGRESSIVE DEMOCRATS

CONSTITUENCY: CORK NORTH-CENTRAL. SEANAD – TAOISEACH'S NOMINEE

DÁIL/SEANAD: 25TH, 26TH, 27TH DÁIL (17 FEBRUARY 1987-5 JUNE 1997).
    SEANAD: 12 SEPTEMBER 1997 TO DATE

AGE AT ENTRY TO DÁIL: 46

FAMILY: DAUGHTER OF DANNY QUILL

EDUCATION: ST MARY'S COLLEGE, MOUNTMELLICK, COUNTY LAOIS; MARY IMMACULATE COLLEGE OF
    EDUCATION, LIMERICK; UNIVERSITY COLLEGE CORK (BA, H.DIP.ED.)

OCCUPATION: SECONDARY SCHOOLTEACHER (ST VINCENT'S CONVENT SCHOOL, SHANDON, CORK)

CAREER:

Progressive Democrat spokesperson on Education and the Arts, 1987-9; on Justice 1989-92; on Education, Arts and Culture, 1992. Member, Joint Committee on the Irish Language, 1987; on

Women's Rights, 1988-9. Member, Special Committee on the Recognition of Foreign Adoptions Bill, 1990. Chairperson, Select Dáil Committee on Crime, 1991-2. Member, Select Committee on Social Affairs, March 1995-7; Joint Committee on Sustainable Development, 1995-7. Member, Joint Committee on Education and Science, 1997. Member, Cork City Council, 1979; Alderwoman 1985-91 (first elected to Cork City Council as a Fianna Fáil candidate). Member, board of management, North Infirmary, Fota Wildlife committee. Patron of Hearth, a group working on behalf of homeless mothers and children. Chairperson, Crawford Art Gallery 1985-91. Chairperson, Progressive Democrats Parliamentary Party.

ADDRESS: 1 WELLESLEY TERRACE, WELLINGTON ROAD, CORK

MÁIRIN QUILL's parents were founder members of Fianna Fáil. Her father, Danny Quill, took the Republican side during the Civil War and was imprisoned in Tintown in the Curragh. Her aunt Mary, a teacher, was jailed in Tralee, having been caught red-handed in school with the typewriter on which she typed messages for men on the run. Her paternal grandfather was a Parnellite.

The house in which Máirin Quill was born in Kilgarvan, County Kerry, was general headquarters for the Kerry No. 2 Brigade of the Old IRA during the Civil War, and she grew up listening to reminiscences of this period.

In the mid-1960s she joined Fianna Fáil and, with the encouragement of Jack Lynch, contested Dáil elections in 1977 in Cork City, and in 1981 in Cork North-Central. In 1985 Máirin Quill was a founder member of the Progressive Democrats. Among her reasons for leaving Fianna Fáil to set up the new party were her disillusionment at the failure of the established political parties to bring about political reform, and her opposition to Charles Haughey. She was first elected to the Dáil in 1987.

Twenty-Sixth Dáil ——————————————————————

General Election: 15 June 1989   *166 SEATS*

Women Elected
THERESA AHEARN (FG, TIPPERARY SOUTH)
MONICA BARNES (*SEE P. 127*) (FG, DÚN LAOGHAIRE)
MARY T. COUGHLAN (*SEE P. 133*) (FF, DONEGAL SOUTH WEST)
SÍLE DE VALERA (*SEE P. 112*) (FF, CLARE)
NUALA FENNELL (*SEE P. 116*) (FG, DUBLIN SOUTH)
MARY FLAHERTY (*SEE P. 118*) (FG, DUBLIN NORTH WEST)
MÁIRE GEOGHEGAN-QUINN (*SEE P. 109*) (FF, GALWAY WEST)
MARY HARNEY (*SEE P. 120*) (PD, DUBLIN SOUTH WEST)
MARY O'ROURKE (*SEE P. 130*) (FF, LONGFORD/WESTMEATH)
NORA OWEN (*SEE P. 122*) (FG, DUBLIN NORTH)
MÁIRÍN QUILL (*SEE P. 135*) (PD, CORK NORTH CENTRAL)
MADELEINE TAYLOR-QUINN (*SEE P. 123*) (FG, CLARE)
MARY WALLACE, (FF, MEATH)

Theresa Ahearn

DATE/PLACE OF BIRTH: MAY 1951/GOLDEN, TIPPERARY

PARTY: FINE GAEL

CONSTITUENCY: TIPPERARY SOUTH

DÁIL/SEANAD: 26TH, 27TH, 28TH DÁIL (15 JUNE 1989-20 SEPTEMBER 2000)

AGE AT ENTRY TO DÁIL: 38

FAMILY: MARRIED TO LIAM AHEARN, FOUR SONS

EDUCATION: PRESENTATION CONVENT, CASHEL; UNIVERSITY COLLEGE DUBLIN;
    ST PATRICK'S COLLEGE, MAYNOOTH (BA, H.DIP.ED.)

OCCUPATION: MATHEMATICS TEACHER, CENTRAL TECHNICAL INSTITUTE, CLONMEL

CAREER:
Fine Gael spokesperson on Equality and Disabilities 1997; front-bench spokesperson on Energy, 1992-3, and on Labour, 1992. Member, Special Committee on the *Recognition of Foreign Adoptions Bill, 1990.* Member, Dáil Select Committee on Crime, 1991. Spokesperson on Women's Affairs; Chairperson, Joint Committee on Women's Affairs 1993-5. Member, Select Committee on Social Affairs, April, 1993. Member, Joint Committee on Foreign Affairs, 1997; on Justice, Equality and Women's Rights, 1998. During the 27th Dáil she served on the Joint Committees of Foreign Affairs, Enterprise and Economic Strategy, Social Affairs and Small Business and Services, May 1996. Member, Fine Gael national executive. First woman Fine Gael Member of Tipperary (SR) County Council, 1983 (chairperson 1994-5); Tipperary (SR) County Committee of Agriculture 1983-5; South Tipperary Vocational Education Committee, 1985; Local Health Committee 1983-7; Alderman, Clonmel Corporation since 1994. Former member, Macra na Feirme. Member, Teachers' Union of Ireland, 1972. Member of Irish Farmers' Association.

DATE OF DEATH: 20 SEPTEMBER 2000

ADDRESS: BALLINDONEY, GRANGE, CLONMEL, COUNTY TIPPERARY

THERESA AHEARN made a major contribution to Equal Status and Employment Equality legislation. In March 2000 she criticised the Government for inaction on violence against women. She promoted rural development and hospital upgrading.

Mary Wallace

DATE/PLACE OF BIRTH: JUNE 1959/DUBLIN

PARTY: FIANNA FÁIL

CONSTITUENCY: MEATH. SEANAD – ADMINISTRATIVE PANEL

DÁIL/SEANAD: 26TH, 27TH, 28TH DÁIL (15 JUNE 1989 TO DATE).
    SEANAD: 14 APRIL 1987-14 JUNE 1989

AGE AT ENTRY TO SEANAD: 28

AGE AT ENTRY TO DÁIL: 30

FAMILY: DAUGHTER OF COUNCILLOR TOM WALLACE. MARRIED TO DECLAN GANNON, ONE SON

EDUCATION: LORETO CONVENT, BALBRIGGAN; LORETO CONVENT, NORTH GREAT GEORGE'S STREET;
    RATHMINES COLLEGE OF COMMERCE (DIP. HOSPITAL AND HEALTH SERVICES ADMIN.)

OCCUPATION: PERSONNEL EXECUTIVE

CAREER:
Minister of State at the Department of Justice, Equality and Law Reform, with special responsibility for Equality and Disabilities, July 1997. Fianna Fáil spokesperson for people with disabilities and carers, 1995-7. Member, Dáil Select Committee on Crime, 1991-2. Chairperson, Oireachtas Joint Committee on Women's Rights, 1995-7; Vice-chairperson 1989-92. Member, Select Committee on Social Affairs, April 1993. Chairperson, Fianna Fáil National Women's Committee, 1992-4. Member, Meath County Council 1982-97; North Eastern Health Board 1985-9; Member, Meath Vocational Education Committee, 1991-5; Meath County Committee on Agriculture 1982-7 (Chairperson 1986-7); Blanchardstown Hospital 1977-87.

PUBLICATIONS
Co-author, with Bertie Ahern, of *Meeting the Challenge of Disability: Policy Document on Disability*, Dublin: Fianna Fáil, 1996.

ADDRESS: NEWTOWN, FAIRYHOUSE ROAD, RATHOATH, COUNTY MEATH

MARY WALLACE began her career in politics in 1982, when she was co-opted to the seat of her father, Tom Wallace, on Meath County Council. She served on the Council until 1997.

Twenty-Seventh Dáil ─────────────────────────────

General Election: 25 November 1992   *166 SEATS*

Women Elected
THERESA AHEARN (*SEE P. 137*) (FG, TIPPERARY SOUTH)
NIAMH BHREATHNACH (LAB, DÚN LAOGHAIRE)
JOAN BURTON (LAB, DUBLIN WEST)
MARY COUGHLAN (*SEE P. 133*) (FF, DONEGAL SOUTH WEST)
SÍLE DE VALERA (*SEE P. 112*) (FF, CLARE)
AVRIL DOYLE (*SEE P. 129*) (FG, WEXFORD)
EITHNE FITZGERALD (LAB, DUBLIN SOUTH)
FRANCES FITZGERALD (FG, DUBLIN SOUTH EAST)
MARY FLAHERTY (*SEE P. 118*) (FG, DUBLIN NORTH WEST)
MÁIRE GEOGHEGAN-QUINN (*SEE P. 109*) (FF, GALWAY WEST)
MARY HARNEY (*SEE P. 120*) (PD, DUBLIN SOUTH WEST)
HELEN KEOGH (PD, DÚN LAOGHAIRE)
LIZ MCMANUS (DL, WICKLOW)
BREEDA MOYNIHAN-CRONIN (LAB, KERRY SOUTH)
LIZ O'DONNELL (PD, DUBLIN SOUTH)
MARY O'ROURKE (*SEE P. 130*) (FF, WESTMEATH)
NORA OWEN (*SEE P. 122*) (FG, DUBLIN NORTH)
MÁIRÍN QUILL (*SEE P. 135*) (PD, CORK NORTH CENTRAL)
RÓISÍN SHORTALL (LAB, DUBLIN NORTH WEST)
MARY WALLACE (*SEE P. 137*) (FF, MEATH)

By-election: 10 November 1994
KATHLEEN LYNCH (DL, CORK NORTH CENTRAL)

By-election: 29 June 1995
MILDRED FOX (NON-PARTY, WICKLOW)

By-election: 2 April 1996
CECILIA KEAVENEY (FF, DONEGAL NORTH EAST)

Niamh Bhreathnach

DATE/PLACE OF BIRTH: JUNE 1945/DUBLIN

PARTY: LABOUR

CONSTITUENCY: DÚN LAOGHAIRE

DÁIL/SEANAD: 27TH DÁIL (25 NOVEMBER 1992-5 JUNE 1997); SEANAD: 13
    JUNE-5 AUGUST 1997 (CASUAL VACANCY)

AGE AT ENTRY TO DÁIL: 47

FAMILY: MARRIED TO TOM FERRIS; ONE DAUGHTER, ONE SON

EDUCATION: SION HILL SCHOOL, BLACKROCK, COUNTY DUBLIN; FROEBEL TEACHER TRAINING
    COLLEGE, BLACKROCK

OCCUPATION: REMEDIAL TEACHER

CAREER:
Minister for Education, 12 December 1993-26 June 1997 (resigned on 17 November 1994 on
change of government, portfolio reassigned on 18 November 1994). Member, Dublin County
Council 1991-January 1993; Dún Laoghaire Borough Council 1991-1 January 1993; Dún
Laoghaire-Rathdown County Council, 1999. Vice-chairperson Labour Party, 1989-90.
Chairperson Labour Party 1990-January 1993. Chairwoman, Labour Women's National
Council. Founder member and Chairperson, Carysfort Area Residents' Association; Blackrock
Combined Residents' Association; Booterstown Community Council. Executive member, Dún
Laoghaire An Taisce. Member, SIPTU; Maritime Museum Friends; Uniferm (Ireland). Patron,
Blackrock Athletic Club. Served two terms on Women's Political Association. Member, Board
for the Employment of the Blind.

ADDRESS: 12 ANGLESEA AVENUE, BLACKROCK, COUNTY DUBLIN

NIAMH BHREATHNACH was appointed Minister for Education in January 1993. She
was the first woman (and one of only five people) to be appointed a Cabinet
Minister immediately after election to Dáil. This was the first occasion on
which she contested a Dáil seat. She had twice contested Seanad elections.

As Minister for Education, Niamh Bhreathnach published the first White
Paper on Education, *Charting our Education Future* (1995), introduced the
Leaving Certificate Applied programme, and made the Transition year available
to all second-level schools. She abolished third-level undergraduate tuition fees
and achieved significant increases in education spending. She also initiated the
Breaking the Cycle programme, targeted at rural and urban schools in disad-
vantaged areas — an initiative regarded by the teaching profession as a
significant achievement.

She introduced the *Education Bill, 1997* — the first major legislative break-through since the Stanley Letter of 1831 — and the *University Act, 1997*, which makes universities accountable for the public money they receive. Trinity College resisted this move and further legislation was required in 2000 to enable Trinity College to comply with it.

Joan Burton

DATE/PLACE OF BIRTH: FEBRUARY 1949/DUBLIN

PARTY: LABOUR

CONSTITUENCY: DUBLIN WEST

DÁIL/SEANAD: 27TH DÁIL (25 NOVEMBER 1992-5 JUNE 1997)

AGE AT ENTRY TO THE DÁIL: 43

FAMILY: MARRIED TO PAT CARROLL (MEMBER OF DUBLIN COUNTY COUNCIL);
ONE DAUGHTER

EDUCATION: SISTERS OF CHARITY, STANHOPE STREET, DUBLIN; UNIVERSITY COLLEGE, DUBLIN
(BCOMM, FCA)

OCCUPATION: LECTURER AND CHARTERED ACCOUNTANT

CAREER:
Minister of State at the Department of Social Welfare with special responsibility for poverty, including EU Poverty Plans, and integration of the tax and social welfare codes, 1992. Member, Dublin County Council, 1991-3. Delegate, Council for the Status of Women 1988-93. Fellow of the Institute of Chartered Accountants. Member, Teachers' Union of Ireland. Lecturer, College of Commerce, Rathmines 1987-93. Lecturer, University of Dar es Salaam, Tanzania 1983-6, where she worked as part of the Irish Development Corporation Programme.

ADDRESS: 81 OLD CABRA ROAD, DUBLIN 7

JOAN BURTON was first elected to the Dáil in 1992, to represent Dublin West. She had been a candidate in Dublin Central in the 1989 general election.

As a member of Dublin County Council, Joan Burton was a strong opponent of land rezonings. In 1993, she was quoted in the newspapers as having said that events in the Dublin County Council Chamber provided proof of the need for reform and the disclosure of financial interests by public representatives. The following is an excerpt from her speech, made in County Westmeath:

> *I think the public is entitled to know from each and every councillor what campaign contributions, what hospitality, and what assistance, direct or indirect in recent elections or at any other time they or their parties received from the developers, land owners, associated builders and their agents.*

> IRISH INDEPENDENT, 22 FEBRUARY 1993

She was accused of libel by forty-two of her former colleagues and threatened with legal action. However, an agent for developers, Frank Dunlop, revealed to the Flood Tribunal on 19 April 2000 that he had made payments to certain members of Dublin County Council.

Joan Burton took responsibility for piloting the *Refugee Act, 1996* through the Dáil.

Eithne FitzGerald, née Ingoldsby

DATE/PLACE OF BIRTH: NOVEMBER 1950/DUBLIN

PARTY: LABOUR

CONSTITUENCY: DUBLIN SOUTH

DÁIL/SEANAD: 27TH DÁIL (25 NOVEMBER 1992–5 JUNE 1997)

AGE AT ENTRY TO DÁIL: 42

FAMILY: MARRIED TO JOHN FITZGERALD, THREE DAUGHTERS. DAUGHTER-IN-LAW
  OF DR GARRET FITZGERALD (TAOISEACH 1981-2, AND 1982-7, MINISTER
  IN A NUMBER OF DEPARTMENTS; TD 1969-87; LEADER OF FINE GAEL 1977-87)

EDUCATION: SCOIL CHAITRÍONA; UNIVERSITY COLLEGE DUBLIN (MA IN ECONOMICS)

OCCUPATION: ECONOMIST

CAREER:
Minister of State at the Office of the Tánaiste and at the Department of Finance with special responsibility for the National Development Plan, 14 January 1993. Member, Dublin County Council 1979-93 (chairperson 1992-3); Member, Eastern Health Board, 1982-6. Member, Commission on Social Welfare, 1984-6. Consumer representative, Dental Council 1986-91. Research Officer, Threshold 1988-90. Former Executive member, National Campaign for the Homeless. Worked on social policy with the Department of Finance and National Economic and Social Council.

PUBLICATIONS:
Several reports for the National Economic and Social Council on Irish Social Services, Family Income Supports and Women's Rights.

ADDRESS: 9 CLONARD AVENUE, DUBLIN 16

EITHNE FITZGERALD was forced to resign from her post as an official in the Department of Finance by the marriage bar then in existence. This experience influenced her feminist views. She was first elected to the Dáil in 1992 in a surge of support that swept Labour to power. She polled 17,000 votes — the highest first-preference vote in the country. She had previously stood as a candidate in the Dublin South constituency in the general elections of 1981, 1982, 1987 and 1989, but had been unsuccessful.

Her political legacy includes the *Ethics in Public Office Act, 1995*, enacted in the face of derision by Fianna Fáil and Fine Gael opponents; and the *Freedom of Information Act, 1997*. She was also responsible for handling £8 billion in funding from the European Union. She supported the merger of Labour and Democratic Left.

Frances Fitzgerald

DATE/PLACE OF BIRTH: AUGUST 1950/CROOM, COUNTY LIMERICK
PARTY: FINE GAEL
CONSTITUENCY: DUBLIN SOUTH EAST
DÁIL/SEANAD: 27TH, 28TH DÁIL (25 NOVEMBER 1992 TO DATE)
AGE AT ENTRY TO DÁIL: 42
FAMILY: MARRIED TO MICHAEL FITZGERALD, THREE SONS
EDUCATION: SION HILL CONVENT, BLACKROCK, COUNTY DUBLIN; UNIVERSITY
COLLEGE DUBLIN; LONDON SCHOOL OF ECONOMICS
OCCUPATION: SOCIAL WORKER
CAREER:
Front-bench spokesperson on Defence, 1997. Front-bench spokesperson on Arts, Culture and the Gaeltacht, 1993-94. Member, Select Committee on Social Affairs, April 1993; Member, Joint Committee on Justice, Equality and Law Reform, 1997; and of its Sub-Committee on Women's Rights, 1998. Chairwoman, Council for the Status of Women, 1988-92. Member, Second Commission on the Status of Women, 1990-93. Vice President, Irish Council of the European Movement, 1991-3. Member, All-Party Constitutional Committee, 1997; Forum for Peace and Reconciliation, 1995-6, 1997. Board member of the Employment Equality Agency, 1987-91. Irish Representative to European Women's Lobby, 1988-92 (Vice-president, 1992). Chairwoman, Women's Political Association 1987-9 (formerly Vice-chairwoman and public relations officer). Board member, Dublin Institute of Adult Education since 1987. Executive Committee member, Institute of European Affairs, 1993.

PUBLICATIONS:
Co-author, with Maureen Gaffney, Andy Conway and Fr Paul Andrews, of *Parenting: A Handbook for Parents.*

ADDRESS: 116 GEORGIAN VILLAGE, CASTLEKNOCK, DUBLIN 15

FRANCES FITZGERALD was courted by several political parties before the 1992 election. The parties believed that, as a high-profile Chair of the Council for the Status of Women, she would attract a woman's vote. Fianna Fáil appointed her to the Health Promotion Council shortly before she agreed to run for Fine Gael.

Helen Keogh

DATE/PLACE OF BIRTH: JUNE 1951/DUBLIN
PARTY: PROGRESSIVE DEMOCRATS. FINE GAEL
CONSTITUENCY: DÚN LAOGHAIRE. SEANAD — TAOISEACH'S NOMINEE
DÁIL/SEANAD: 27TH DÁIL (25 NOVEMBER 1992-5 JUNE 1997). SEANAD: 27
OCTOBER 1989-24 NOVEMBER 1992, 12 SEPTEMBER 1997 TO DATE
AGE AT ENTRY TO SEANAD: 38
AGE AT ENTRY TO DÁIL: 41
FAMILY: MARRIED TO PADDY HAYES; TWO DAUGHTERS

EDUCATION: LORETO CONVENT, BEAUFORT, RATHFARNHAM, DUBLIN. UNIVERSITY COLLEGE DUBLIN
(BA, H.DIP.ED. DIP. CAREER GUIDANCE COUNSELLING)

OCCUPATION: COMPANY DIRECTOR. SECONDARY SCHOOLTEACHER; GUIDANCE COUNSELLOR

CAREER:
Progressive Democrat spokesperson on Education and Northern Ireland in the Seanad,
1989-92. Party spokesperson on the Environment and party chief whip, 1993. Member,
Committee on Finance and General Affairs 1993. Member, Third Joint Committee on Women's
Rights, 1989-92. Member, Joint Committee on European Affairs, 1997. Member, Select
Committee on Social Affairs, 10 March 1995. Associate Member, British-Irish Parliamentary
Body, 1991-2. Member, Dún Laoghaire Borough Corporation, 1991; Dublin County Council,
1991; Dún Laoghaire/Rathdown Area Committee of Dublin County Council, 1991. Director,
Dublin Tourism, 1990. President, Women's Political Association 1985-6. Council member,
Institute of European Affairs, 1992.

ADDRESS: 12 BEECH COURT, KILLINEY, COUNTY DUBLIN

HELEN KEOGH was a candidate in the Dún Laoghaire constituency in the general
election of 1987. In 1992 she was elected to the Dáil, having served in the Seanad
from 1989 to 1992. She lost her Dáil seat in the 1997 general election but was one
of the Taoiseach's nominees to the Seanad, where she has served since 1997. In
June 2000 she left the Progressive Democrats to join Fine Gael. Her move
followed the controversy surrounding the nomination of former Supreme Court
Judge Hugh O'Flaherty to the European Investment Bank.

Liz McManus, née O'Driscoll

DATE/PLACE OF BIRTH: MARCH 1947/MONTREAL, CANADA

PARTY: DEMOCRATIC LEFT; LABOUR

CONSTITUENCY: WICKLOW

DÁIL/SEANAD: 27TH, 28TH DÁIL (25 NOVEMBER 1992 TO DATE)

AGE AT ENTRY TO DÁIL: 45

FAMILY: DAUGHTER OF TIM O'DRISCOLL, HEAD OF BORD FÁILTE. MARRIED TO
JOHN MCMANUS; ONE DAUGHTER, THREE SONS

EDUCATION: HOLY CHILD CONVENT, KILLINEY, COUNTY DUBLIN/UNIVERSITY COLLEGE DUBLIN
(B.ARCH.)

OCCUPATION: ARCHITECT, WRITER

CAREER:
Minister of State at the Department of the Environment, with special responsibility for Housing
and Urban Renewal, 1994-7. Democratic Left spokesperson on Health and Children, Justice,
Equality and Law Reform, Arts, Heritage, Gaeltacht and the Islands. Spokesperson in the Dáil
on Agriculture and Food, Equality and Law Reform and Health, 1993-4. Labour spokesperson
on Health. Member, Select Committee on Social Affairs, April 1993. Member, Joint Committee
on Justice, Equality and Women's Rights, 1997; Member of its Sub-Committee on Women's
Rights, 1998. Member, All-Party Oireachtas Committee on the Constitution. Member, Joint
Committee on the Constitution, May 2000, which conducted the public hearings on abortion.

Chairperson, Task Force on the Needs of the Travelling Community, 1993. Member, Sinn Féin the Workers' Party, 1971. Member, Wicklow County Council; County Wicklow Library Committee; County Wicklow National Monuments Advisory Committee. Member, Bray Urban District Council, Chairperson 1984–5. Director, Wicklow Tourism. Founder Member, Bray Women's Group and Refuge. Founder Member, Bray Economic Action Committee. Joint Founder, Group of 84, the cross-party association of women deputies. Columnist with the *Sunday Tribune*.

PUBLICATIONS:
Liz McManus won the Hennessy/New Irish Writing Award, the Listowel Award, and the Irish PEN Award for her fiction. In 1990 her first novel, *Acts of Subversion*, was nominated for the Aer Lingus/*Irish Times* Award for new writing.

ADDRESS: 1 MARTELLO TERRACE, BRAY, COUNTY WICKLOW

LIZ McMANUS was the first woman TD to be elected for Democratic Left. As Minister with responsibility for Housing, she achieved the highest number of housing completions ever. She introduced legislation to assist local authorities in dealing with anti-social behaviour and drug-dealing in local authority estates, the *Housing (Miscellaneous Provisions) Act, 1996*. She made the *Housing (Registration of Rented Houses) Regulations, 1996*, requiring landlords to regis-ter with local authorities their properties for rent, and pay a £40 fee for annual inspection.

In 1998 she sponsored Private Members Bills on Asylum Seekers, which were withdrawn or defeated, and also the *Criminal Law (Rape) (Sexual Experience of Complainant) Bill* and a *Censorship of Publications (Amendment) Bill*, which are at First Stage at the time of going to press (Autumn 2000). She also sponsored the *Protection of Patients and Doctors in Training Bill, 1999*.

Liz McManus came second to Proinnsías De Rossa in a leadership contest at the 1997 Democratic Left annual general conference. She is believed to have helped Democratic Left make the transition from the extreme left to the Cabinet.

Breeda Moynihan-Cronin

DATE/PLACE OF BIRTH: MARCH 1953/KILLARNEY, COUNTY KERRY
PARTY: LABOUR
CONSTITUENCY: KERRY SOUTH
DÁIL/SEANAD: 27TH, 28TH DÁIL (25 NOVEMBER 1992 TO DATE)
AGE AT ENTRY TO DÁIL: 39
FAMILY: DAUGHTER OF MICHAEL MOYNIHAN (TD FOR KERRY SOUTH, 1981-7
AND MINISTER FOR STATE FOR TOURISM, 1989-92);
MARRIED TO DANIEL C. CRONIN
EDUCATION: ST BRIDGET'S SECONDARY SCHOOL, KILLARNEY; SION HILL COLLEGE, DUBLIN;
SKERRY'S COLLEGE, CORK
OCCUPATION: BANK OFFICIAL

CAREER:
Currently (2000) Labour Party spokesperson on Tourism and Recreation. Chairwoman, Joint Committee on Tourism, Sport and Recreation, 13 April 2000; Member, Joint Oireachtas Committee on Tourism, Sport and Recreation, 1997. Joint Committee on Family, Community and Social Affairs, 1997. During the 27th Dáil she served on Joint Oireachtas Committee on Women's Rights, Joint Oireachtas Committee on the Family, 1993-7 and Select Committee on Social Affairs, April 1993. Party spokesperson on Equality and Law Reform, 1997. Member, Council of Europe, 1991-2. Member of Kerry County Council, 1991, re-elected 1999; County Kerry Vocational Education Committee 1991; Kerry Historical Monuments Committee, 1991; Kerry County Enterprise Board. Member, Labour Party General Council (nominated by parliamentary party). Former Member, Labour Party Women's National Council. *Other interests*: amateur drama.
ADDRESS: 10 MUCKROSS GROVE, KILLARNEY, COUNTY KERRY

BREEDA MOYNIHAN-CRONIN contested and won her first general election in 1992, replacing her father who had retired. When appointed Chair of the Oireachtas Committee on Tourism, Sport and Recreation, she announced that she intended to address the regional imbalance in the industry by bringing the Committee out of the confines of Kildare House and into the regions, to hear submissions from the people operating businesses on the ground.

She has won many awards for amateur drama. While working with the Bank of Ireland in Castleisland, she helped form the Ivy Leaf Theatre Company in Castleisland, and was instrumental in setting up the Ivy Leaf Centre in the town.

Liz O'Donnell

DATE/PLACE OF BIRTH: JULY 1956/DUBLIN
PARTY: PROGRESSIVE DEMOCRATS
CONSTITUENCY: DUBLIN SOUTH
DÁIL/SEANAD: 27TH, 28TH DÁIL (25 NOVEMBER 1992 TO DATE)
AGE AT ENTRY TO DÁIL: 36
FAMILY: MARRIED TO MICHAEL T. CARSON; ONE DAUGHTER, ONE SON
EDUCATION: SALESIAN CONVENT, FERRYBANK, LIMERICK, TRINITY COLLEGE
    DUBLIN (BA (MOD), LEGAL SCIENCE)

OCCUPATION: SOLICITOR
CAREER:
Minister of State at the Department of Foreign Affairs, with special responsibility for Overseas Development Assistance and Human Rights, June 1997. Member, Select Committee on Social Affairs, April, 1993; Member, Forum for Peace and Reconciliation, 1997. Progressive Democrats spokesperson on Health and Social Welfare, Justice, and party chief whip, 1993-7. Chairperson, Progressive Democrats Policy Development Committee. Member, Dublin City Council, 1991-4, and several subsidiary bodies. Member, Local Authority Committee of Dublin Transportation Initiative. Member, Executive Committee of the Women's Political Association 1989-91 (Vice-chairwoman and delegate to Council for the Status of Women 1990-91).
ADDRESS: 23 TEMPLE GARDENS, DUBLIN 6

LIZ O'DONNELL made a notable contribution in Belfast as part of the Government's Northern peace process team surrounding the Belfast/Good Friday Agreement.

She threatened to resign in November 1998 unless Third World aid was increased dramatically, and on 14 November 1999, she described Ireland's treatment of refugees as a 'shambles', which encouraged the Opposition to table a vote of no confidence in the government. Although she supported the government in this vote, she was credited with forcing the Department to begin seriously to address the immigration problem and put workable structures in place to do so. Shortly before this, she had called on John Ellis to consider his position as Chair of the Agriculture Committee, in the wake of unfavourable revelations on his financial dealings. She has been labelled a 'conviction' politician.

Róisín Shortall

DATE/PLACE OF BIRTH: 25 APRIL 1954/DUBLIN

PARTY: LABOUR

CONSTITUENCY: DUBLIN NORTH WEST

DÁIL/SEANAD: 27TH, 28TH DÁIL (25 NOVEMBER 1992 TO DATE)

AGE AT ENTRY TO DÁIL: 38

FAMILY: MARRIED TO SEAMUS O'BYRNE; THREE DAUGHTERS

EDUCATION: DOMINICAN COLLEGE, ECCLES STREET, DUBLIN; UNIVERSITY COLLEGE DUBLIN (BA; LATER DIPLOMA TEACHER OF THE DEAF); ST MARY'S COLLEGE OF EDUCATION, MARINO, DUBLIN (DIPLOMA IN EDUCATION)

OCCUPATION: PRIMARY SCHOOLTEACHER OF THE DEAF, ST JOSEPH'S SCHOOL, CABRA, DUBLIN

CAREER: LABOUR PARTY spokesperson on Health and Children, on Justice, 1997. Member, Joint Committee on Community, Family and Social Affairs, 1999 to date; Select Committee on Legislation and Security, 1993-7; Select Committee on Health and Children, 1997-8; Select Committee on Social Affairs, April 1993. Member, Dublin City Council, 1991 to date. Member, Eastern Health Board, 1991-9; Chairperson 1996-8. Member, Ballymun Housing Task Force, 1991-9; Ballymun Local Drugs Task Force, 1991-9; North Dublin National School Project, 1985-9. Board Member, Finglas Vocational Education Committee schools, 1991-9. *Particular policy interests*: poverty, drugs and crime, taxation, education, health, public transport, child welfare.

ADDRESS: 12 IVERAGH ROAD, GAELTACHT PARK, DUBLIN 9

RÓISÍN SHORTALL contested her first general election in 1992. She was elected to represent the Dublin North West constituency.

Kathleen Lynch

DATE/PLACE OF BIRTH: 1953/CORK

PARTY: DEMOCRATIC LEFT

CONSTITUENCY: CORK NORTH CENTRAL

DÁIL/SEANAD: 27TH DÁIL (10 NOVEMBER 1994 [BY-ELECTION]–5 JUNE 1997)

AGE AT ENTRY TO DÁIL: 41

FAMILY: MARRIED TO BERNARD LYNCH; FOUR CHILDREN

EDUCATION: BLACKROCK NATIONAL SCHOOL, CORK. HOSPITALISATION FOLLOWING
   AN ACCIDENT PREVENTED HER ATTENDANCE AT SECONDARY SCHOOL

OCCUPATION: CLOTHING INDUSTRY WORKER

CAREER:
Member, Select Committee on Social Affairs, 10 March 1995. Member, Cork County Borough Council, 1985. Member of several community groups. Member, Southern Health Board. Board Member, Cork Opera House. Member, Married Women for Equality, which campaigned for equal social-welfare treatment.

ADDRESS: FARRANCLEARY PLACE, CORK

KATHLEEN LYNCH became involved in politics in 1983 through the National Association of Tenants Organisation, and campaigned actively against local-authority service charges, which she saw as a form of double taxation. She joined the Workers Party in 1984, and was first elected to Cork Corporation in 1985. As a City Councillor, she was a member of the group which prepared the Cork City Development Plan, and the sub-committee which drew up the regional submission for structural funds from the European Union.

Kathleen Lynch was a founding member of Democratic Left following a split in the Worker's Party. Although her political base was in the neighbouring constituency of Cork South Central, it was felt that she had a better chance of taking a seat in North Central in 1994. In the 1992 general election, Democratic Left secured 4 per cent of the vote in North Central, but Kathleen Lynch increased this to 22 per cent when she stood in the European Elections in June 1994. Her European campaign yielded some 15,570 first preferences in the Munster Constituency.

The 1994 by-election was Kathleen Lynch's fourth time standing for the Dáil — she had run in the general elections of 1987, 1989 and 1992. The day her election victory was announced, Labour walked out of Cabinet and the Fianna Fáil government fell shortly afterwards. For a time it looked as if she might be the shortest serving TD ever. However, the Rainbow Coalition of Fine Gael, Labour and Democratic Left took over on 15 December 1994, without a dissolution of the Dáil, and she became a government backbencher.

Kathleen Lynch protested vigorously against the government's Employment Equality Bill, which was later found by the Supreme Court to be unconstitutional.

Mildred Fox

DATE AND PLACE OF BIRTH: JUNE 1971/DUBLIN

PARTY: INDEPENDENT

CONSTITUENCY: WICKLOW

DÁIL/SEANAD: 27TH, 28TH DÁIL (29 JUNE 1995 [BY-ELECTION] TO PRESENT)

AGE AT ENTRY TO DÁIL: 24

FAMILY: DAUGHTER OF JOHNNY FOX (TD FOR WICKLOW, 1992-5).

MARRIED TO DARYL TIGHE

EDUCATION: ST KILIAN'S COMMUNITY SCHOOL, BALLYWALTRIM, BRAY, COUNTY WICKLOW;

UNIVERSITY COLLEGE DUBLIN (BA)

OCCUPATION: HOTEL FRONT-OFFICE MANAGER

CAREER:
Member, Select Committee on Enterprise and Economic Strategy, 1995-7. Member, Wicklow County Council, May, 1995. Secretary, Wicklow County Board of Ladies' GAA and playing member of local football and camogie clubs. Member, Macra na Feirme.

ADDRESS: LOWER CALARY, KILMACANOGUE, COUNTY WICKLOW

MILDRED FOX was elected to the Dáil in June 1995, in a by-election caused by the death of her father, Johnny Fox, who had been elected as an Independent deputy in Wicklow, in the general election of 1992. She was the youngest member of the 27th Dáil, and the only Independent woman deputy in the 27th and 28th Dálaí.

In the vote for Taoiseach in June 1997, Mildred Fox supported Bertie Ahern, having outlined to the Dáil projects that she had secured for her Wicklow (and east Carlow) constituency. She was one of three Independent deputies on whom the minority Fianna Fáil/Progressive Democrats government depended to remain in power. Her influence was exercised in weekly meetings with the Government whip and she was instrumental in delivering a number of schemes.

She voted against the government on the motion approving participation in Partnership for Peace in November 1999, and in May 2000 abstained on a motion supporting the nomination of former Supreme Court Judge Hugh O'Flaherty to the European Investment Bank.

Mildred Fox is anti-abortion and indicated that her continued support for the government depended on its commitment to hold a referendum aimed at overturning the X case (a Supreme Court case which permitted limited abortion) and outlawing abortion.

Cecilia Keaveney

DATE/PLACE OF BIRTH: NOVEMBER 1968/DERRY

PARTY: FIANNA FÁIL

CONSTITUENCY: DONEGAL NORTH EAST

DÁIL/SEANAD: 27TH, 28TH DÁIL (2 APRIL 1996 [BY-ELECTION] TO DATE)

AGE AT ENTRY TO DÁIL: 27

FAMILY: DAUGHTER OF PADDY KEAVENEY (TD, 1976-7)

EDUCATION: CARNDONAGH COMMUNITY SCHOOL, COUNTY DONEGAL;
    UNIVERSITY OF ULSTER AT JORDANSTOWN (BMus, MPHIL), LTCL PGCE

OCCUPATION: MUSIC TEACHER

CAREER:

Member, Joint Committees on Health and Children; Education and Science. Member, Committee on Procedure and Privileges, 1997. Alternate Member, Forum for Peace and Reconciliation, 1997. Member, North-West Region Cross Border Group; Fisheries and Coastal Protection; Coiste; Magilligan Car Ferry. Member of Donegal County Council since July 1995 and many of its subsidiary committees. Chairperson, Arts Committee 1995-6. Member, UUJ All-Ireland Intervarsities Equestrian winning team and Ulster Camogie Championship Team. She reached Grade 8 on clarinet, violin, piano and singing, through the Royal Irish Academy of Music, and obtained a Performer's diploma on clarinet through Trinity College, London. As a music teacher, she worked in Nigeria, England and Northern Ireland.

ADDRESS: LORETO, MOVILLE, COUNTY DONEGAL

CECILIA KEAVENEY was first elected to the Dáil in April 1996, at a by-election in Donegal North East, caused by the death of Neil T. Blaney.

Twenty-Eighth Dáil ——————————————————————————

General Election: 6 June 1997   *166 SEATS*

Women Elected

THERESA AHEARN (*SEE P. 137*) (FG, TIPPERARY SOUTH)
MONICA BARNES (*SEE P. 127*) (FG, DÚN LAOGHAIRE)
DEIRDRE CLUNE (FG, CORK SOUTH CENTRAL)
BEVERLEY COOPER-FLYNN (FF, MAYO)
MARY COUGHLAN (*SEE P. 133*) (FF, DONEGAL SOUTH WEST)
SÍLE DE VALERA (*SEE P. 112*) (FF, CLARE)
FRANCES FITZGERALD (*SEE P. 142*) (FG, DUBLIN SOUTH EAST)
MILDRED FOX (*SEE P. 148*) (IND, WICKLOW)
MARY HANAFIN (FF, DÚN LAOGHAIRE)
MARY HARNEY (*SEE P. 120*) (PD, DUBLIN SOUTH WEST)
CECILIA KEAVENEY (*SEE P. 149*) (FF, DONEGAL NORTH EAST)
MARIAN MCGENNIS (FF, DUBLIN CENTRAL)
LIZ MCMANUS (*SEE P. 143*) (DL, WICKLOW)
OLIVIA MITCHELL (FG, DUBLIN SOUTH)

Breeda Moynihan-Cronin (*SEE P. 144*) (Lab, Kerry South)
Liz O'Donnell (*SEE P. 145*) (PD, Dublin South)
Mary O'Rourke (*SEE P. 130*) (FF, Westmeath)
Nora Owen (*SEE P. 122*) (FG, Dublin North)
Róisín Shortall (*SEE P. 146*) (Lab, Dublin North West)
Mary Wallace (*SEE P. 137*) (FF, Meath)

By-election: 12 March 1998
Jan O'Sullivan (Lab, Limerick East)

By-election: 27 October 1999
Mary Upton, (Lab, Dublin South Central)

Deirdre Clune, née Barry
Date/Place of Birth: June 1959/Cork
Party: Fine Gael
Constituency: Cork South Central
Dáil/Seanad: 28th Dáil (6 June 1997 to date)
Age at Entry to Dáil: 38
Family: Daughter of Peter Barry, (TD for Cork constituencies, 1969-97; Tánaiste 1987; Minister for Foreign Affairs, 1982-7; Minister for the Environment, 1981-2; Minister for Transport and Power, 1973-6; Minister for Education, 1976-7; and Deputy Leader of Fine Gael, 1979-1987, 1989-93); granddaughter of Anthony Barry, (TD, 1954-7, 1961-5). Married to Conor Clune, four sons
Education: Ursuline Convent, Blackrock, Cork; University College Cork; Trinity College Dublin (BE, Diploma in Management for Engineers, Higher Diploma in Environmental Engineering)
Occupation: Civil engineer/mother working in the home
Career:
Fine Gael junior spokesperson on Environmental Information and Protection, September 1997. Member, Joint Committees on Environment and Local Government; Health and Children, 1997. Member, Women's Political Association. Member, European Movement.
Address: Adare, Rochestown, Cork

Deirdre Clune was elected to the Dáil in 1997 in the first general election in which she stood as a candidate.

Beverley Cooper-Flynn

DATE/PLACE OF BIRTH: JUNE 1966/TUAM, COUNTY GALWAY

PARTY: FIANNA FÁIL

CONSTITUENCY: MAYO

DÁIL/SEANAD: 28TH DÁIL (6 JUNE 1997 TO DATE)

AGE AT ENTRY TO DÁIL: 31

FAMILY: DAUGHTER OF PADRAIG FLYNN, (FIANNA FÁIL DÁIL TD FOR
MAYO WEST, 1977-93; MINISTER FOR JUSTICE, FOR INDUSTRY AND
COMMERCE, FOR THE ENVIRONMENT, FOR TRADE, COMMERCE AND TOURISM AND FOR THE
GAELTACHT; EUROPEAN COMMISSIONER, JANUARY 1993-9). MARRIED TO JOHN COOPER

EDUCATION: ST JOSEPH'S SECONDARY SCHOOL, CASTLEBAR; UNIVERSITY COLLEGE, DUBLIN (BCOMM),
PM, AC11

OCCUPATION: FINANCIAL SERVICE MANAGER, NATIONAL IRISH BANK

CAREER:
Member, Joint Committees on Justice, Equality and Women's Rights; Health and Children.
Member, Committee on Public Accounts. Member, Mayo County Council, 1996.

ADDRESS: 2 THE MANOR VILLAGE, WESTPORT ROAD, CASTLEBAR, COUNTY MAYO

BEVERLEY COOPER-FLYNN is the first woman to represent Mayo in the Dáil. She was a candidate in the Mayo West by-election in June 1994, and rebounded from a defeat to top the poll in the next general election.

In an interview with the *Sunday Business Post* in March 1994, she agreed with her father that politicians who say they are not interested in becoming Taoiseach are either lying or should not be in politics. She was quoted as saying:

Would I like to become Taoiseach? I wouldn't rule it out.... I'm certainly very ambitious and I want to succeed and maximise my potential at every level.

In June 1998, a client of National Irish Bank alleged on RTÉ that Beverley Cooper-Flynn had advised him to buy products which allowed him to evade tax. She denied these claims and took him and RTÉ to court. Though she had worked in National Irish Bank, which was being investigated as part of the DIRT inquiry, she participated in the questioning of Allied Irish Bank, in the early stages of the Public Accounts Committee hearings.

In a radio interview with Marion Finucane, she recounted that, as a child, she once attended her father's political clinic to request a new tennis racquet.

Beverley Cooper-Flynn voted against a government motion in February 1999 calling on her father to clarify his position about an alleged donation; she lost the Fianna Fáil whip in the Dáil but remained a member of the party until the whip was reinstated in November 1999.

Mary Hanafin

DATE/PLACE OF BIRTH: JUNE 1959/THURLES, COUNTY TIPPERARY

PARTY: FIANNA FÁIL

CONSTITUENCY: DÚN LAOGHAIRE

DÁIL/SEANAD: 28TH DÁIL (6 JUNE 1997 TO DATE)

AGE AT ENTRY TO DÁIL: 38

FAMILY: DAUGHTER OF DES HANAFIN (SENATOR, 1969-93, 1997 TO DATE);
GRANDDAUGHTER OF JOHN HANAFIN (SINN FÉIN COUNCILLOR, LONGFORD
URBAN DISTRICT COUNCIL, TIPPERARY NORTH RIDING COUNCIL;
FOUNDER MEMBER OF FIANNA FÁIL). MARRIED TO EAMON LEAHY

EDUCATION: PRESENTATION CONVENT, THURLES; ST PATRICK'S COLLEGE, MAYNOOTH; DUBLIN
INSTITUTE OF TECHNOLOGY (BA, H. DIP. ED; DIPLOMA IN LEGAL STUDIES)

OCCUPATION: SECONDARY SCHOOLTEACHER

CAREER:
Minister of State at the Department of Health and Children, 2000. Member, Joint Committees,
Heritage and the Irish language; Justice, Equality and Women's Rights; Education and Science,
1997. Member, Dublin City Council, 1985-91; City of Dublin Vocational Education Committee,
1985-91. Member, Senate of the National University of Ireland, 1988. Member, National
Executive, Fianna Fáil, 1980. Joint Honorary Treasurer of Fianna Fáil, 1993. Board Member,
Dublin Institute of Technology; City of Dublin Youth Services Board. Chairperson, College of
Catering. Vice-president CENYC – European Youth Council. Organiser, Co-operation North
youth exchanges. Stagiaire scholarship to European Parliament. Robert Schuman silver medal
for services towards European unity. Member, Blackrock Historical Society. Secretary, Board of
Visitors of the National Museum. Ball de Bhord Gael Linn. Member, Board for the Employment
of the Blind. Director, National Building Agency.

ADDRESS: 7 OAKLANDS DRIVE, RATHGAR, DUBLIN 6

MARY HANAFIN was appointed Minister of State at the Department of Health and
Children in the government reshuffle of 27 January 2000. She had made her
mark as a backbencher by defending tough government decisions, such as the
2000 Budget which introduced the concept of individualisation. She had been a
candidate in the Dublin South East constituency in the 1989 general election.

Marian McGennis

DATE/PLACE OF BIRTH: NOVEMBER 1953/DUBLIN

PARTY: FIANNA FÁIL

CONSTITUENCY: DÁIL – DUBLIN CENTRAL. SEANAD – TAOISEACH'S NOMINEE

DÁIL/SEANAD: 28TH DÁIL (6 JUNE 1997 TO DATE). SEANAD: 10 FEBRUARY
1993-5 JUNE 1997

AGE AT ENTRY TO SEANAD: 39

AGE AT ENTRY TO DÁIL: 43

FAMILY: MARRIED TO BRYAN MCGENNIS; TWO SONS, ONE DAUGHTER

OCCUPATION: CIVIL SERVANT

CAREER:
Fianna Fáil spokesperson in Seanad on Equality and Law Reform and Women's Affairs 1996-7. Member, All-Party Oireachtas Committee on the Constitution, 1997. Member, Joint Committee on the Constitution, May 2000. Member, British-Irish Interparliamentary Body, 1997. Member, Dublin County Council, 1985-93; Fingal County Council, 1993-8. Member, Dublin Corporation, 1999.

ADDRESS: 44 BRAMLEY WALK, DUBLIN 15

MARIAN McGENNIS contested the general election of 1992, but was unsuccessful in her bid to win a seat in the Dublin North constituency. The following year she was nominated to the Seanad, where she served until her election to the Dáil. The Joint Committee on the Constitution, of which she was a member, conducted public hearings on abortion in May 2000.

Olivia Mitchell

DATE/PLACE OF BIRTH: JULY 1947/BIRR, COUNTY OFFALY

PARTY: FINE GAEL.

CONSTITUENCY: DUBLIN SOUTH

DÁIL/SEANAD: 28TH DÁIL (6 JUNE 1997 TO DATE)

AGE AT ENTRY TO DÁIL: 49

FAMILY: MARRIED TO JAMES MITCHELL; ONE DAUGHTER, TWO SONS

EDUCATION: DOMINICAN CONVENT, ECCLES STREET, DUBLIN; TRINITY COLLEGE, DUBLIN (BA, H.DIP.ED.)

OCCUPATION: SECONDARY SCHOOLTEACHER

CAREER:
Fine Gael spokesperson on Local Development, National Drugs Strategy, and Dublin Traffic, 1997. Member, Joint Committee on Environment and Local Government, 1997. Member, Dublin County Council, 1985-93; Dún Laoghaire-Rathdown County Council 1994 (Cathaoirleach 1995-6). Member, Eastern Health Board; Dublin Regional Authority; Dublin Transport Office Local Advisory Committee. Member, Fine Gael delegation to the Forum for Peace and Reconciliation. Member, Co-ordinating Committee of the European Sustainable Cities and Towns Campaign.

ADDRESS: 18 BALLAWLEY COURT, DUNDRUM, DUBLIN 16

OLIVIA MITCHELL was a candidate in Dublin South in the 1989 and 1992 general elections. She was elected to the Dáil on her third attempt, in 1997.

Jan O'Sullivan, née Gale

DATE/PLACE OF BIRTH: 6 DECEMBER 1950/CLONLARA, COUNTY CLARE
PARTY: DEMOCRATIC SOCIALIST PARTY, 1982-90; LABOUR, 1990 TO DATE
CONSTITUENCY: LIMERICK EAST
DÁIL/SEANAD: 28TH DÁIL (12 MARCH 1998 [BY-ELECTION] TO DATE).
SEANAD: 1 FEBRUARY 1993-6 AUGUST 1997
AGE AT ENTRY TO SEANAD: 42
AGE AT ENTRY TO DÁIL: 47
FAMILY: DAUGHTER OF JOURNALIST ON THE *LIMERICK ECHO* AND *LIMERICK LEADER*. MARRIED TO PAUL
O'SULLIVAN; ONE DAUGHTER, ONE SON
EDUCATION: ST MICHAEL'S PRIMARY SCHOOL, PERY SQUARE, LIMERICK. VILLIERS SCHOOL, LIMERICK.
TRINITY COLLEGE DUBLIN (BA (MOD)); UNIVERSITY COLLEGE CORK (H.DIP.ED.);
MONTESSORI DIP. ED.
OCCUPATION: SECONDARY SCHOOLTEACHER; MONTESSORI SCHOOLTEACHER
CAREER:
Member, Joint Committee on Justice, Equality and Women's Rights, 1999 to date. Member,
Limerick City Council 1985 to date; Limerick VEC, 1985-91; Mid-western Health Board, 1991
to date; Mid-western Regional Authority, 1991-9; Mayor of Limerick, July 1993-4. Member,
Forum for Peace and Reconciliation; Devolution Commission, 1996-7; Member, Board of
Island Theatre Company, Limerick, Committee of Exhibition of Visual Arts. Chair, Limerick/
Quimper Twinning Committee. *Particular policy interests*: equality issues, including educational
opportunity, living conditions, poverty, women's rights, family planning. *Other interests*: Arts,
literature, jazz, swimming, hill-walking, sport. Francophile.

ADDRESS: 7 LANAHRONE AVENUE, CORBALLY, LIMERICK

JAN O'SULLIVAN was born into a Church of Ireland family, and married Dr Paul
O'Sullivan, a Catholic. Her denominational background became an issue briefly
in 1994 when, as Mayor of Limerick, she was prevented by the then bishop,
Dr Jeremiah Newman, from reading a lesson at a Mass for the city's Civic Week.
She later shook hands with Dr Newman and made only a formal protest about
the insult to the office of mayor. While mayor in 1993, she was similarly
prevented from speaking at the opening of a Christian Brothers School.
Although both controversies arose simply from her status as a non-Catholic, she
would not have endeared herself to the bishop in her role as one of 'Kemmy's
Femmies' — the name given by opponents to those who helped run Limerick's
first family-planning clinic in the 1970s.

Jan O'Sullivan lived in Canada before returning to Ireland in the late 1970s.
She entered politics because of her conviction that state intervention is needed
to redress imbalances in opportunities arising from circumstances of birth.

Having become a councillor with the Democratic Socialist Party in 1985, Jan
O'Sullivan followed Jim Kemmy into Labour in 1990, becoming mayor of
Limerick and a senator in 1993. From 1993 to 1997, she was Labour leader in the

Seanad, where she was a member of the Forum for Peace and Reconciliation. As Jim Kemmy's running mate in 1992, she came within a few hundred votes of taking a second Dáil seat for Labour, and this established her as the natural successor when he died in 1998.

In the 1999 local elections, Jan O'Sullivan became Limerick's first alderwoman.

> *'Tis Jan, says he, of womanly charm*
> *Whisht now! let there be no alarm*
> *She has great intelligence and practical wit,*
> *And on the Seanad she does her bit,*
> *The battle raged and words clashed bitter,*
> *As robes of red 'neath bright lights glitter*
> *Jan, unperturbed, did stand and ponder*
> *This mighty Gale caused all to wonder.*

EXTRACT FROM 'WELCOME, MAYOR JAN', BY MAUREEN SPARLING, FROM *RIPPLES IN THE SAND*, LIMERICK: SPARLING, 1997, BY KIND PERMISSION OF THE POET

Mary Upton

DATE/PLACE OF BIRTH: 30 MAY 1946/KILRUSH, COUNTY CLARE

PARTY: LABOUR

CONSTITUENCY: DUBLIN SOUTH CENTRAL

DÁIL/SEANAD: 28TH DÁIL (27 OCTOBER 1999 [BY-ELECTION] TO DATE)

AGE AT ENTRY TO DÁIL: 53

FAMILY: SISTER OF DR PAT UPTON (LABOUR SENATOR, 1989-92 AND TD, 1992-9)

EDUCATION: COLÁISTE MHUIRE, ENNIS (MERCY CONVENT). UNIVERSITY COLLEGE GALWAY, (MSc BACTERIOLOGY); UNIVERSITY COLLEGE, DUBLIN (PhD INDUSTRIAL MICROBIOLOGY)

OCCUPATION: LECTURER/RESEARCH SCIENTIST, UNIVERSITY COLLEGE, DUBLIN

CAREER:
Member of Labour Party (Terenure branch), 1983 to date. Director of election campaigns for her brother, Pat Upton. Chairperson, Radiological Protection Institute of Ireland. Chairperson, National Council for Educational Awards. Member, Microbiology Panel, Food Safety Authority.

ADDRESS: LABOUR PARTY CONSTITUENCY OFFICE, 61 KEEPER ROAD, DRIMNAGH, DUBLIN 12

MARY UPTON was elected to the Dáil in a by-election in Dublin South Central, in October 1999. She had previously been director of election campaigns for her brother, Pat Upton, whose death had caused the by-election.

The Seanad

1921-1937

Under the *Government of Ireland Act, 1920*, the Senate of the southern Ireland parliament, which was based on that proposed by the 1917 Irish convention, consisted of nominated members representing a range of interests in Ireland, particularly business, the professions and education. Fifteen senators, nominated by the Lord Lieutenant, met in June 1921, but the assembly was adjourned following the truce which ended the Anglo–Irish War, and was abolished in the *Irish Free State (Agreement) Act, 1922*.

The constitution of the Irish Free State provided for a Senate of sixty members who had to take the oath of allegiance. Southern Unionists were guaranteed special representations by Cosgrave, who, as president of the Executive Council, nominated half of the first Senate, including Jennie Wyse Power and the Countess of Desart. The election process was considerably amended. Senators were elected for a twelve-year term, later reduced to nine, with one-third retiring every three years. Popular elections were abolished in 1928, when Senators were elected by the Dáil and Senate. One member of the Senate could sit on the Executive Council.

Although the Senate could initiate legislation, it had no authority over money bills. If the Senate rejected a bill, the Dáil could, within a year, pass a resolution to send it back to the Senate, and within sixty days it would pass. The Senate could also suspend for ninety days any Bill passed by both Houses if a majority of the Senate requested the President of the Executive Council to do so.

First Triennial Period, 1922-5

Women Members

COSTELLO, EILEEN (9 YEARS) (ELECTED BY DÁIL, 7 DECEMBER 1922)
DESART, ELLEN, COUNTESS OF (12 YEARS) (NOMINATED BY PRESIDENT OF THE EXECUTIVE COUNCIL, 6 DECEMBER 1922)
GREEN, ALICE STOPFORD (9 YEARS) (ELECTED BY DÁIL, 7 DECEMBER 1922)
POWER, J. WYSE (12 YEARS) (NOMINATED BY PRESIDENT OF THE EXECUTIVE COUNCIL, 6 DECEMBER 1922)

Second Triennial Period, 1925-8 —————————————

Election: 17 September 1925. No women elected

Women Members
COSTELLO, EILEEN (6)
DESART, ELLEN, COUNTESS OF, (9)
GREEN, ALICE STOPFORD (6)
POWER, J. WYSE (9)

Eileen Costello, née Edith Drury

DATE/PLACE OF BIRTH: 1870, LONDON
PARTY: FINE GAEL
SEANAD: 1ST TO 5TH TRIENNIAL PERIODS INCLUSIVE
(7 DECEMBER 1922-20 MAY 1936)
AGE AT ENTRY TO SEANAD: 52
OCCUPATION: HEAD TEACHER, AUTHOR AND FOLKLORIST
FAMILY: MARRIED DR THOMAS BODKIN COSTELLO MD, MRIA, 1903;
ONE DAUGHTER
CAREER:
Member, Seanad Committee on Irish Manuscripts, 1923-4; Select Committee to Consider the *Dublin Reconstruction (Emergency Provisions) Bill, 1924*. Worker in Irish language movement in London and Ireland; Member, Gaelic League, 1896. First woman Tuam District Councillor and Town Commissioner, Chairman, 1921. Tuam Board of Guardians, 1921. Judge, Sinn Féin Arbitration Courts, 1921-2. Founder Member and Chair, Committee of Coláiste Connacht, Spiddal; Vice-president, Irish Folk Song Society; Member, governing body of University College, Galway.

PUBLICATIONS:
Amhráin Mhuighe Seóla, Folk Songs of Galway and Mayo, 1919.
DATE OF DEATH: 14 MARCH 1962, TUAM
ADDRESS: BISHOP STREET, TUAM, COUNTY GALWAY

EILEEN COSTELLO (Edith Drury) was born in London of a Welsh father and a Limerick mother and was a member of the Irish Society there. She came to Ireland in 1903 for her marriage to Dr Thomas B. Costello, the antiquarian, and took a very active part in the Irish Revival Movement. They were associated with Dr Douglas Hyde and other leaders, and their home was a centre of Irish culture.

She accompanied her husband on his house calls to patients; while he attended them, she spoke to the people about their folklore and songs, collecting them for her book of Connacht folk songs. She took a prominent part in the Independence Movement.

It is said that Eileen Costello never missed a meeting of the Town Commissioners, even during the Black and Tans terror. She organised Red Cross services during the Second World War. She championed the cause of unmarried mothers, attempting to delete legislation refusing public assistance to un-married mothers who refused to enter Magdalen Asylums and other homes:

> *The lines I wish to have omitted read 'Persons in Class (b) (unmarried mothers) who refuse to enter such institutions (Magdalen Asylums or some other Homes) as may be selected shall not be allowed under any circumstances to become chargeable to the public rates.' ...In the preamble to the Bill it is stated it is to enable poor persons requiring relief to be relieved, but it seems that an exception is to be made in the case of unmarried mothers who, it is stated, are on no account to be chargeable to the rates if they will not go into a Magdalen Asylum. I think that under no circumstances could a County Authority get rid of its responsibility to a person who is destitute and in need of help.*

Official Report Seanad Éireann, vol. 1, 21 March 1923,
Local Government (Temporary Provisions) Bill, 1923, col. 548

She also opposed the *Civil Service Regulation(Amendment) Bill, 1925*, denying women access to senior posts in the Civil Service.

> *I think the bringing in of this Bill by the Government is unjust, that it is morally wrong, and I think it is monstrously unfair. The women are still to be subject to the obligation of citizenship, but their privileges are to be curtailed and restricted.... I admit that it is to a certain extent the fault of the women themselves that such a thing as this should be allowed. They had very high privileges conferred on them, but they have not lived up to these privileges. This has been shown in the recent Seanad elections and at other elections as well. I do hope that if actions such as the present one in bringing in this Bill are continued, that the women will very soon wake up. The explanation is that they have not realised their power as yet.*

Official Report Seanad Éireann, vol. 6, 17 December 1925,
Civil Service Regulation (Amendment) Bill, 1925, cols. 245–6

Eileen Costello also supported the *Illegitimate Children (Affiliation Orders) Bill, 1929*, providing unmarried mothers with the right to seek maintenance from the father, and she supported raising the age of consent.

Ellen Desart, Countess Dowager
(Ellen Odette O'Connor, née Bischoffsheim)

DATE OF BIRTH: 1857

PARTY: MEMBER OF THE UNIONIST PARTY BUT ON THE ADVENT OF THE TREATY
ACCEPTED THE NEW CONDITIONS WITH LOYALTY

CONSTITUENCY: EXECUTIVE COUNCIL'S NOMINEE

SEANAD: 1ST, 2ND, 3RD, 4TH TRIENNIAL PERIODS
(6 DECEMBER 1922-29 JUNE 1933(DEATH))

AGE AT ENTRY TO SEANAD: 65

FAMILY: MARRIED WILLIAM O'CONNOR, 4TH EARL OF DESART, 27 APRIL 1881.
WIDOWED 15 SEPTEMBER 1898

EDUCATION: EDUCATED PRIVATELY

OCCUPATION: COMPANY DIRECTOR

CAREER:
Member, Seanad Select Committee to Consider the *Dairy Produce Bill, 1924*. Member, Conference of Members representing the Dáil and Seanad on Certain Amendments made by the Seanad to the *Intoxicating Liquor (General) Bill, 1924*, (Disagreed to by Dáil, 1924). President, Kilkenny branch of Gaelic League, 1913-15. Member, Irish Industrial Development Association, 1926. *Particular policy interests*: Pro-divorce in debate on divorce, 1925.

PUBLICATIONS:
Co-author with Constance Hoster, *Style and Title: A Complete Guide to Social Forms of Address*, London: Christopher, 1924. Review and magazine articles.

DATE OF DEATH: 29 JUNE 1933

ADDRESS: AUT EVEN, TALBOT'S INCH, KILKENNY. 2 UPPER BERKELEY STREET, LONDON

ELLEN ODETTE, eldest daughter of Henry Bischoffsheim, a banker, of Bute House, South Audley Street, London, was married in 1881. Her husband was Ulick O'Connor, the fourth Earl of Desart, with a seat in Kilkenny. After the death of her husband in 1898, she returned to her country seat at Ascot, Berkshire, England, and devoted time to social and charitable work in the London Jewish and general community.

The Countess Dowager of Desart held strong anti-suffrage views and played an energetic part in combating the agitation for women's suffrage. She contended that women should not compete against men at work or play, and regretted the passing of the age of chivalry, commenting, 'Women cannot have it both ways.' In 1911 she joined a committee to protest against the *National Health Insurance Bill* introduced by Lloyd George. Her case against compulsory insurance was that, in a large house, the servants are, naturally, looked after during illness. In the smaller house, the servant who falls ill must go to hospital to make room for the healthy worker, and in hospital she would be looked after whether she was insured or not.

In 1912 the Countess Dowager returned to live at Aut Even, Talbot's Inch, Kilkenny, near her former residence, Desart Court. She contributed articles to reviews and magazines, and wrote two books. Her brother-in-law, Captain the Hon. Otway Cuffe, enlisted her support for national, cultural and industrial movements. She took a deep interest in the revival of Irish, and this led her to the movement for the revival of Irish industries. In conjunction with prominent Kilkenny people and clergymen, she started a company for the establishment of Kilkenny Woollen Mills at Greenvale, and became Chairman of the Board of Directors. She also erected a theatre in the centre of the city of Kilkenny, and presented to the city the site on which the Carnegie Library was erected.

The lands at Talbot's Inch were transformed by her into a garden village occupied by the workers at the Woollen Mills and the other industries which she started. She built over thirty picturesque villas in beautifully laid-out grounds on the banks of the Nore, and a spacious recreation hall with a dancehall and club rooms in which indoor sports were played. She also erected and equipped Aut Even Hospital, which she intended as a permanent memorial to her brother-in-law, Captain Cuffe. She was president of the Kilkenny branch of the Gaelic League from 1913 to 1915.

Among the people of Kilkenny she was spoken of with admiration as the 'Jewish Lady'. When, in 1910, the freedom of the city of Kilkenny was conferred on her, she claimed to be the only woman in Ireland thus honoured and the only Jewess in the world — until then — to be made an honorary citizen. For her services to the cultural and economic welfare of Ireland she was, on the nomination of President Cosgrave, made a Senator of the Irish Free State in December 1922.

In a debate on divorce in 1925, the Countess Dowager said:

In the name of woman I protest against the idea that it is divorce that destroys the sanctity of the home. Surely, the law laid down 3,000 years ago by the greatest legislator, took the more sensible view of the matter. The Mosaic law, as can be read in the Bible, not only permitted divorce but enjoined it. The law recognised that it was the seducer in the home or out of it, not the judge in court or Parliament, who breaks up the home.

It realised that it is the sanctity of the home far more than that of the contract that really matters; that to anchor the guilty man irremovably to the hearth he violates, or to cast the guilty woman on to the street, cannot make for morality or for a high standard of virtue. It would be a hideous injustice to the women of this country, because, as Senator Mrs. Wyse Power has stated, the man can go across the water and shake the dust of this country off his feet to a country where he can reacquire the freedom of which we would deprive him. The woman cannot go. You condemn her to a life of misery or isolation, for a woman in so false a position must be ten times more circumspect than any other, if she would safeguard her good name. If guilty, she must spend the rest of her days as an example of the wicked, flourishing like a bay tree or as an eyesore in a land hitherto famed for its high ideals of purity. We protest against the taking away from the minority of a right which it has enjoyed for nearly two hundred years.

SEANAD ÉIREANN OFFICIAL REPORT, VOL. 5, DEBATE ON DIVORCE LEGISLATION, 11 JUNE 1925, COLS. 463–4

In a letter to the editor of the Jewish Guardian of 12 September 1930, she wrote:

emphatically resenting the unwarrantable assumption in your issue of 5th September that I have 'deserted the faith' of my fathers. Will you please contradict that unfounded statement in your next issue? I am, as I have been all my life, a staunch and practising Jewess....

When Ellen, Countess Dowager of Desart, died in 1933, she was buried beside her husband in Falmouth cemetery. The funeral service was, at her request, conducted according to Jewish rites.

Alice Stopford Green

DATE/PLACE OF BIRTH: 30 MAY 1847/KELLS, COUNTY MEATH

PARTY: NON-PARTY

SENATE: 1ST, 2ND, 3RD TRIENNIAL PERIODS.
(7 DECEMBER 1922-28 MAY 1929 (DEATH))

AGE AT ENTRY TO SEANAD: 75

FAMILY: DAUGHTER OF ARCHDEACON EDWARD ADDERLEY STOPFORD AND ANNE DUKE. MARRIED JOHN RICHARD GREEN (AUTHOR AND HISTORIAN), 1878

EDUCATION: PRIVATELY EDUCATED AT HOME. HONORARY LITT. DEGREE, UNIVERSITY OF LIVERPOOL, 1913

OCCUPATION: HISTORIAN

CAREER:
Founder Member, School of Irish Studies, 1903. Member, Seanad Committee on Irish Manuscripts, 1923-4. Member, Select Committee to consider the *Garda Síochána Bill, 1924*. *Particular policy interests*: Pro-Treaty.

PUBLICATIONS:
Short Geography of the British Isles, 1880; *Henry 11 (Twelve English Statesmen)*, 1888; *Town Life in the 15th Century*, 2, 1894; (ed.) *The Conquest of England*, revised ed. of the *Short History*, 1888; illustrated ed. of *Short History* (with Kate Norgate), 1892; *Oxford Studies* (with Kate Norgate), 1901; (ed.) *Historical Studies*, 1903; *The Making of Ireland and its Undoing*, 1908; *Irish Nationality*, 1911; *The Old Irish World*, 1912; *Women's Place in the World of Letters*, 1913; *The History of the Nineteenth Century*, 1916. New Edition of the *Short History*, with an

added epilogue. Pamphlets: *Ourselves Alone in Ulster, Loyalty and Disloyalty: What it Means in Ireland*, 1918. McDowell, R.B., *Alice Stopford Green: A Passionate Historian*, Dublin: A. Figgis, 1967.

DATE/PLACE OF DEATH: 28 MAY 1929/DUBLIN

ADDRESS: 90 ST STEPHEN'S GREEN, DUBLIN

ALICE STOPFORD was born into a landed unionist family in Kells, County Meath. Her father disagreed with the disestablishment of the Church of Ireland and visited Gladstone to influence the Bill leading to the *Irish Church Act, 1869*. She was educated by a succession of governesses. When the family moved to Dublin in 1873 she tried to get permission to attend lectures at the College of Science. The professor of physics told her that it was unheard of for a lady to do so, but agreed to admit her if she was accompanied by another lady. She persuaded Louisa La Touche to go with her, and they attended physics lectures, attracting considerable attention.

Her marriage in London, to Richard Green, a convinced nationalist, became a working partnership. She assisted him with his research, learning scholarly methods, until his death in 1883, and completed the books on which he was working. They were friends of Beatrice and Sidney Webb and of Tennyson, who 'read his poems grandly' to them. At the close of the nineteenth century a woman historian was unusual, and Alice Stopford Green's writings gave her considerable prestige. Her house was a centre where English politicians, Irish nationalists and men of letters exchanged ideas. In 1891 she invited five young liberals to dinner, to meet five Fabian essayists. All of the young liberals went on to become cabinet ministers.

Sir Roger Casement was a close friend and, at his suggestion, Alice Stopford Green organised the 'London Committee' to collect money for arms for the Irish Volunteers. The sum of £1,500 was used by Darrell Figgis to purchase the arms which were brought to Ireland in the Howth gun-running. When Roger Casement was arrested, she wrote to the Prime Minister about his treatment, received permission to visit him, lent him books, found a solicitor and raised funds for his defence. His trial, together with events following the Rising, had a profound effect on her, although she disapproved of the Rising itself. From 1916 she was completely absorbed in Irish affairs, and frequently visited Ireland; in 1918 she moved to Dublin. She became a strong liberal, which meant she supported Home Rule and later believed that Ireland must control its own resources.

The Gaelic revival and the language movement inspired some of her most striking work on Irish history, providing formidable propaganda for the nationalist cause. She responded to a request from Kuno Meyer in 1900 by helping him to found the School of Irish Studies. She was one of its first governors, contributed generously to its funds, financed a series of lectures and founded travelling scholarships.

In 1919 she produced pamphlets denouncing the union with Britain. She was visited by Michael Collins and persuaded Tom Casement, Roger's brother, to hand over his gun. Her house was raided on several occasions at night by the military.

Alice opposed violence, believed in the Commonwealth and was a strong supporter of the Treaty. She and her brother distributed pro-treaty leaflets in the streets. Her acceptance of the Senate seat exposed her to risk because Republicans began to burn down Senators' residences, and a military guard was installed in her house. She made a powerful speech for reconciliation, arguing that it was essential 'to create a new sense of law in this land, law coming from the will of the people and serving as their guardian'. (*Seanad Éireann Official Report*, vol. 1, cols. 1437–40). She voted in favour of divorce in 1925.

On 19 April 1923, Alice Stopford Green was appointed to the Committee on Irish Manuscripts, under the chairmanship of W.B. Yeats, to prepare a scheme for the publication of manuscripts in the Irish language, the study of dialects and the compilation of an Irish dictionary, with Eileen Costello and Edward MacLysaght. The Final Report, R22, published in May 1924, recommended that the publication of Irish manuscript material should be entrusted to an authoritative body, handling a substantial amount of money.

In 1924 Alice Stopford Green presented to the Senate a casket of bronze and silver, incorporating in its decoration ancient Gaelic motifs, containing a scroll to be inscribed with the names of all senators.

Jennie Wyse Power, née O'Toole

DATE/PLACE OF BIRTH: MAY 1858, BALTINGLASS, COUNTY WICKLOW
PARTY: SINN FÉIN, LATER CUMANN NA NGAEDHEAL
CONSTITUENCY: PRESIDENT OF EXECUTIVE COUNCIL'S NOMINEE
SEANAD: 1ST–5TH TRIENNIAL PERIODS (6 DECEMBER 1922–20 MAY 1936)
NOMINATED BY PRESIDENT OF THE EXECUTIVE COUNCIL
AGE AT ENTRY TO SEANAD: 64
FAMILY: DAUGHTER OF ÉAMONN Ó TUATHAIL, BALTINGLASS. MARRIED TO JOHN
WYSE POWER (HONORARY SECRETARY OF THE GAA, WHO IN 1881 LOST HIS
POSITION IN DUBLIN CASTLE FOR HIS LAND LEAGUE ACTIVITIES.);
TWO DAUGHTERS, ONE SON
EDUCATION: NOT RECORDED. FAMILY LIVED AT 6, JOHNSON PLACE, ON SOUTH SIDE OF DUBLIN.
PROBABLY WARRENMOUNT NATIONAL SCHOOL (CARMELITE NUNS)
AND/OR LORETO CONVENT, ST STEPHEN'S GREEN
OCCUPATION: SHOPKEEPER, RESTAURATEUR, 21 HENRY STREET, DUBLIN.
FOUNDER, IRISH FARM PRODUCE COMPANY, DUBLIN

CAREER:
Member, Seanad Committee on Irish Manuscripts, 1922; on Standing Orders, 1922. Member, Committee on Articles 21 and 23 of the Constitution and appointments and remuneration of Officers of the Seanad, 1922. Member, Special Committee on Standing Committees, 1923; Committee on the Appointment of the Clerks, 1924; Joint Committee on the Temporary Accommodation of the Oireachtas, 1924; Select Committee to Consider the *Dublin Reconstruction (Emergency Provisions) Bill, 1924*; Select Committee to Consider the *Garda Síochána Bill, 1924*. Executive member, Ladies' Land League, 1881; its Librarian to the prisoners in the Irish gaols during the Land War, 1881-2. Member, Gaelic League from its inception, 1893. Founder Member, Irish College, Ring, County Waterford. Executive Member, Sinn Féin organisation from its foundation, 1908, and for many years one of its Honorary Treasurers. Founder Member, Cumann na mBan, 1913, its first President and an active member until January 1922. Honorary Treasurer, Republican Prisoners' Dependants' Fund, 1917-22. Member, North Dublin Board of Guardians, 1903-12; Governor, Grangegorman Mental Hospital, 1914; Chair of the Board, 1920-21. Member, Dublin Corporation, 1920; Chair of its Finance and Public Health Committees, 1920-22. Member, Commission of Inquiry into the Resources and Industries of Ireland; Local Government Commission established by Dáil Éireann. District Justice, City of Dublin, from 1920 until the dissolution of the Dáil Courts. *Particular policy interests*: Pro-Treaty. Accepted the Treaty as 'a big step on the road to the Republic'.

PUBLICATIONS:
O'Neill, Marie, *From Parnell to De Valera: A Biography of Jennie Wyse Power, 1858-1941*, Dublin: Blackwater Press, 1991

DATE OF DEATH: 5 JANUARY 1941

ADDRESS: 15 EARLSFORT TERRACE, DUBLIN (1929); BUSINESS: 21 HENRY STREET, DUBLIN (1928)

JENNIE WYSE POWER played a part in three revolutions in Irish life — the abolition of landlordism, the establishment of self-government, and the achievement of a distinguished place in political life for women. Her public career started in 1881 with the Ladies' Land League in which she served as librarian to imprisoned members, and ended only with the abolition of the Senate in 1936. She was active in local government, in Cumann na mBan and in the Senate.

Jennie Wyse Power was a follower of Parnell, and helped William Rooney and Arthur Griffith to start the Celtic Library Society. She attended the foundation meeting of Sinn Féin in the Rotunda and was an honorary treasurer of the organisation for many years. Her café at 21 Henry Street became the rendezvous where Arthur Griffith, John Sweetman, Tom Kelly and other leaders met for informal discussions of their plans. General Michael Collins, Éamon de Valera, and other well-known figures from the fight for independence were frequent visitors, and, at the height of the struggle, it was raided daily by the British forces. The British authorities thought to trace there the Dáil funds and funds of the Prisoners' Dependants' organisation. This café was burned down in the conflagration which followed the destruction of the General Post Office in 1916, and later, after its reconstruction, the café became one of the principal meeting places for IRA chiefs during the Black-and-Tan period. The 1916 Proclamation was signed in Jennie Wyse Power's shop, which was mentioned in James Joyce's Ulysses 'Bloom emerged carrying a jug of cream from "that Irish Farm Dairy" John Wyse Nolan's wife has in Henry Street'.

Jennie Wyse Power strongly opposed the *Civil Service Regulation (Amendment) Bill, 1925* because it aimed to confine state examinations for senior civil-service positions to men. She and Eileen Costello convinced the Seanad to reject the Bill at Second Stage, and thereby held up the introduction of the Act for twelve months. Her experience as a judge in the Dáil courts convinced her to oppose the *Juries Act 1927*. She supported the *Illegitimate Children (Affiliation Orders) Bill, 1929*, which was intended to improve the lot of the unmarried mothers by providing the mother with the right to seek financial maintenance from the father for the upkeep of her child. She proposed raising the age of consent from fifteen to eighteen in the case of sexual assault, but without success. She strongly opposed the *Conditions of Employment Bill, 1935*, which gave power to the Minister for Industry to restrict the employment of women in industry.

Her daughter, Dr Nancy Wyse Power, a distinguished Celtic scholar, was one of the messengers sent by Patrick Pearse during the Easter Rising to provincial commanders to countermand Eoin MacNeill's orders; on her return, she made her way to the GPO, then under siege, to report back to Pearse. She was sent on behalf of the Dáil to Berlin in 1921 to establish a propaganda centre for Irish freedom. She was one of the first women to reach the rank of principal officer in the civil service; her criticisms of the discrimination women encountered in the Department of Local Government and Public Health resulted in the elimination of some inequalities. Jennie's second daughter, whose early death was a source of great distress, was a distinguished Celtic scholar; her son was a Circuit Court judge on the Western Circuit.

Third Triennial Period
6 December 1928–5 December 1931

Election: December 1928

Women Members
CLARKE, KATHLEEN (9) (*SEE P. 75*)
COSTELLO, EILEEN (3) (*SEE P. 158*)
DESART, COUNTESS OF, ELLEN (*SEE P. 160*)
GREEN, ALICE STOPFORD (3) DIED 28 MAY 1929 (*SEE P. 162*)
POWER, JENNIE WYSE (6) (*SEE P. 164*)
BROWNE, KATHLEEN (ELECTED 20 JUNE 1929 TO FILL VACANCY CAUSED
    BY ALICE STOPFORD GREEN'S DEATH)

Fourth Triennial Period
6 December 1931–5 December 1934

Women Members
BROWNE, KATHLEEN (3) (CUMANN NA NGAEDHEAL)
CLARKE, KATHLEEN (6) (*SEE P. 75*)
COSTELLO, EILEEN (3) (*SEE P. 158*)
DESART, COUNTESS OF, ELLEN (3) DIED 29 JUNE 1933 (*SEE P. 160*)
POWER, JENNIE WYSE (3) (*SEE P. 164*)

Fifth Triennial Period
6 December 1934–29 May 1936

Women Members
BROWNE, KATHLEEN (CUMANN NA NGAEDHEAL)
POWER, JENNIE WYSE (*SEE P. 164*)
CLARKE, KATHLEEN(*SEE P. 75*)
COSTELLO, EILEEN (*SEE P. 158*)

NOTE: Final Meeting of Irish Free State Senate: 19 May 1936; Senate abolished on 29 May 1936

Kathleen Anne Browne

DATE/PLACE OF BIRTH: OCTOBER 1878/BRIDGETOWN, COUNTY WATERFORD
PARTY: SINN FÉIN (1912-27), CUMANN NA NGAEDHEAL AND ARMY COMRADES
    ASSOCIATION (BLUESHIRTS) DURING SEANAD CAREER
SEANAD: 3RD TRIENNIAL – ELECTED 20 JUNE 1929 TO FILL VACANCY CAUSED BY
    ALICE STOPFORD GREEN'S DEATH, 4TH TRIENNIAL, 5TH TRIENNIAL TO
    19 MAY 1936
AGE AT ENTRY TO SEANAD: 50
FAMILY: DAUGHTER OF MICHAEL BROWNE (MEMBER OF THE FIRST WEXFORD COUNTY COUNCIL, 1898).
    AUNT OF DR IVOR BROWNE (NOTED PSYCHIATRIST)
EDUCATION: BRIDGETOWN NATIONAL SCHOOL; LORETO CONVENT, WEXFORD
OCCUPATION: FARMER, WRITER, HISTORIAN, ARCHAEOLOGIST
CAREER:
Close associate of Arthur Griffith. Fifteen years' active work in Gaelic League; Secretary, Wexford County Committee. Member, Irish Volunteers 1914-22; National Army during Civil War. Member, Irish Farmers Union; Wexford Agriculture Society; Managing Committee of Loch Garmáin Co-operative Society. Member, United Irishwomen. Lecturer in Dairying under Department of Agriculture. Member, Royal Society of Antiquaries of Ireland; Society for the

Protection of the Memorials of the Dead. Member, Council of Uí Céinnsealagh Historical Society. Branch Secretary, Cumann na nGaedheal. Member, Ladies' Land League, 1881. Member, Army Comrades Association/National Guard (popularly known as Blueshirts), 1933. Peace Commissioner for County Wexford. Particular policy interests: on Free State side in Civil War. Supporter of Hunting as a national sport and industry. Actively interested in promoting Afforestation to give employment and improve the country.

PUBLICATIONS:

History of County Wexford (adopted by the Department of Education for schools); *Castles and Antiquities of Wexford*. Articles in historical journals, including 'The Ancient Dialect of the Baronies of Forth and Bargy, County Wexford', *Journal of the Royal Society of Antiquaries of Ireland*, 1927. 'Was Wexford Betrayed to Cromwell – The Truth (1940). Articles in *An Cosantóir*.

ADDRESS: RATHRONAN CASTLE, BRIDGETOWN, COUNTY WEXFORD

KATHLEEN BROWNE belonged to a well-known Wexford family, which had included bishops to the Sees of Kilmore and Ferns. Her family had managed to regain control and ownership of some of their ancestral lands which had been confiscated during the Cromwellian settlement. Her father, a prominent nationalist, was the organiser of the 1798 centenary celebrations in County Wexford. He served on the Wexford Public Boards of his county, and took a particular interest in the welfare and rights of farm labourers who had no organisation to represent them.

During the 1916 Rising Kathleen Browne flew a tricolour from the roof of Rathronan Castle and attempted to reach the GPO in Dublin. With her friend Nell Ryan she was arrested near Bray and jailed in Kilmainham and Mountjoy. She was an acknowledged authority on Wexford history and in 1927 published a history which became a textbook for primary schools.

Kathleen Browne was conspicuous in the Seanad for her constant wearing of a blue shirt. In 1934 she asked for permission to bring into the Visitors' Gallery two visitors wearing blue shirts. This request was granted by the Cathaoirleach but on the visitors' arrival they were refused admittance on orders of the Minister for Defence, sanctioned by the Ceann Comhairle. The episode led to a clash between the Speakers of the Seanad and Dáil.

She played a crucial role in 1938 in the preservation of the Great Saltee Island as a bird sanctuary. An expert in the Yola dialect, she wrote what is believed to be the last letter written in it.

To Miss Kathleen Browne
Rathronan Castle, Wexford
The noblest of a noble family,
You chose the thorny way to make us free.
You worked and planned and dreamed that in our days,

Ireland might bask in Freedom's glorious rays.
Brave girl, your heart beat with the faithful few,
Who swore to God and Erin to be true —
True to the dead who for their country fell:
And now, your lot is in a prison cell.
All honour to this heroic girl then!
Who braved the frowns and sneers of coward men,
Her name shall shine with Ireland's gallant band,
Who suffered to redeem their native land. (1916)

EXTRACT FROM POEM BY MILES O'BYRNE, LEISURE LAYS, BUENOS AIRES, 1925

Seanad 1937

In 1936 Éamon de Valera abolished the Senate, which had earlier rejected the bill to abolish the oath of allegiance and other legislation. Contrary to expectations, the 1937 Constitution of Ireland revived the concept of the Upper House. There are sixty senators, forty-nine elected and eleven nominated by the Taoiseach. Two members of the Government can be Senators, and Ministers can attend both Houses. Of the forty-nine elected members, six members represent universities; the other forty-three members are elected from five panels, representing language and culture, agriculture, labour, industry and commerce, and public administration. The constitution also provides for direct election by vocational groups.

Under the 1947 *Seanad Electoral Act*, members of the Dáil and Seanad and county council members constitute the electorate for these panels; this has meant that panel members, despite their ostensibly vocational character, have tended to be party politicians. The Seanad can, like its predecessor, initiate legislation, but it cannot amend money bills. A Bill rejected by the Seanad can be passed after 180 days. The Seanad and the Dáil can address a joint petition to the President, requesting him or her not to sign a bill unless the 'will of the people' has been ascertained. With the Dáil, the Seanad can declare a national emergency in time of war or armed rebellion. The Seanad has always been subordinate to the Dáil and has not, until recently, actively used its revising and initiating powers. This changed with the introduction in the 1980s of more Oireachtas committees and with more crowded Dáil agendas.

1938 (a) Seanad Election: 28 March 1938 ————————————————

Women Members

CONCANNON, HELENA (*SEE P. 91*) (UNIVERSITY MEMBER, NATIONAL UNIVERSITY OF IRELAND)
KEARNS MACWHINNEY, LINDA (FF, PANEL MEMBER, INDUSTRIAL & COMMERCIAL PANEL. NOMINATING
    BODIES SUB-PANEL)
KENNEDY, MARGARET L. (NOMINATED MEMBER) (NOMINATED BY TAOISEACH — ÉAMON DE VALERA —
    1 APRIL 1938)
PEARSE, MARGARET MARY (*SEE P. 94*) (FF, PANEL MEMBER, ADMINISTRATIVE PANEL,
    DÁIL SUB-PANEL)

Linda Kearns-MacWhinney

DATE/PLACE OF BIRTH: JULY 1888/DROMARD, COUNTY SLIGO
PARTY: FIANNA FÁIL
CONSTITUENCY: SEANAD INDUSTRIAL AND COMMERCIAL PANEL
SEANAD: 1938 (A) ONLY (28 MARCH–16 AUGUST 1938)
AGE AT ENTRY TO SEANAD: 49
FAMILY: MARRIED MR MACWHINNEY
EDUCATION: DROMARD NATIONAL SCHOOL. SECONDARY SCHOOL IN BELGIUM
QUALIFIED AS A NURSE AT BAGGOT STREET HOSPITAL, DUBLIN
OCCUPATION: NURSE. MATRON/OWNER OF A NURSING HOME AT 29 GARDINER PLACE, DUBLIN

CAREER:
Founder member, Fianna Fáil; member of its National Executive. Founder member, Women's
Industrial Development Association. Honorary secretary, Irish Nurses' Association.

PUBLICATIONS:
Kearns, Linda. *In Times of Peril: Leaves from the Diary of Nurse Linda Kearns from Easter
Week, 1916 to Mountjoy*, 1921, Edited by Annie M.P. Smithson, Dublin: Talbot Press, 1922.

DATE/PLACE OF DEATH: 5 JUNE 1951/HOWTH, COUNTY DUBLIN

LINDA KEARNS joined Cumann na mBan and was associated in particular with
Countess Markievicz and Hanna Sheehy Skeffington. She set up a Red Cross
hospital on Wednesday of Easter Week 1916 in an empty house in North Great
George's Street. She refused to comply with the British military's demand to
attend British personnel only and closed it on Thursday morning on the instructions of the British Army. She acted as dispatch-carrier and nurse for the rebels.
during 1916–17. She smuggled arms, mostly in the Sligo area, and had many dar-
ing escapes from detection.

Linda Kearns nursed in Achill for a short time during the influenza epidemic of 1918, and afterwards opened a nursing home in Gardiner Place,
Dublin, which became a 'safe house' for Volunteers on the run. In November
1920, while driving three Volunteers and a consignment of explosives from

Sligo to Ballymote, she was arrested by a Black and Tan patrol and sent to Belfast with the others for trial. She claimed full responsibility in an unsuccessful attempt to save the men, and was sentenced to ten years' penal servitude.

> *In 1921 a sentence was passed by a Court Martial in Belfast on Nurse Linda Kearns. Miss Kearns had been captured in Sligo when driving some Republican men in a motor car which contained military supplies. The Auxiliaries who took her prisoner spent the night in trying to make her give information concerning the Sligo Volunteers. They used bribes and threats alternately, finally striking her in the face and breaking her teeth. At her trial, realising that the Republican men with her would, if convicted, receive very severe sentences, she declared herself responsible for the car and the contents. She was sentenced to ten years' penal servitude, the men each to thirteen years.*
>
> IRISH INDEPENDENT, 12 APRIL 1921

Linda Kearns was sent to Walton Prison, Liverpool, as a common criminal, but protests and lobbying succeeded in having her transferred to Mountjoy Prison in Dublin. From there she and two other republicans, with the help of a female warder, escaped by rope-ladder to an IRA camp at Duggett's Grove, County Carlow. Linda resumed active service with the Republicans when the Civil War began.

During the bombardment of the Republican garrison in the Hammam Hotel, O'Connell Street, Dublin, on 5 July 1922, she remained with the besieged and tended the dying commander, Cathal Brugha. She was imprisoned again and, on her release in 1923, immediately went to the US, at Éamon de Valera's request, to raise support for the republican cause. She toured Australia before returning home to become a founder member of Fianna Fáil, making a significant contribution to the creation of the party organisation throughout the country — a physically draining mission. She was one of five women elected to the Fianna Fáil Executive.

Although a staunch supporter of De Valera, Linda Kearns joined with the National Council of Women to fight for women's equality when Fianna Fáil introduced the discriminatory *Conditions of Employment Bill* in 1935 and the Constitution in 1937. She contested local elections in the Dublin North constituency.

In 1938, Linda Kearns MacWhinney (as she now was) was nominated to the Seanad by the Women's Industrial Development Association of which she had been a founder member. She had time to make only one speech on a motion on the extension of vocational organisation, which discussed discrimination against women's organisations.

I think [the motion] would be more acceptable if it suggested that the Act as it now exists might be examined with the object of including amongst the nominating bodies vocational bodies which have not the right to nominate [Seanad candidates] now. For example, there is the nursing council which was established in 1919. It is a statutory body, and I think it is the best organised vocational body in Ireland today. Yet, for some reason, it has not the right to nominate. It has a membership of 16,000.... Against that you have a veterinary vocational body with the right to nominate. It seems strange to me that the people who look after the animals of the country are regarded as being more important than the people who look after human beings.... You have the Amalgamated Society of Social Services. This society of women is representative of quite a big number of social service bodies. They have not the right to nominate. Against that you have the Mount Street Club which has the right to nominate.

OFFICIAL REPORT. SEANAD ÉIREANN, VOL. 21, 21 JULY 1938, COL. 456

In 1945 Linda Kearns MacWhinney set up a nursing home at Kilrock, Howth, Dublin. She died there on 5 June 1951, shortly after receiving the Florence Nightingale Medal from the International Committee of the Red Cross, for her work on behalf of the nursing profession.

Margaret L. Kennedy

DATE/PLACE OF BIRTH: 1892/DUBLIN

PARTY: FIANNA FÁIL

CONSTITUENCY: TAOISEACH'S NOMINEE (NOMINATED BY ÉAMON DE VALERA)

SEANAD: 1 APRIL 1938 (NOMINATION)–6 APRIL 1948.

DID NOT CONTEST 1948 SEANAD ELECTION

AGE AT ENTRY TO SEANAD: 46

FAMILY: SINGLE

EDUCATION: SISTERS OF CHARITY, BASIN STREET, DUBLIN

CAREER:

Member, Cumann na mBan, 1915-23. Captain 1917; Commandant of Dublin City, March 1919– October 1921; President of the Association of Old Cumann na mBan.

ADDRESS: 17, DONORE TERRACE, SOUTH CIRCULAR ROAD, DUBLIN

MARGARET KENNEDY was attached to Ceannt's battalion at Marrowbone Lane in 1916 which, on Easter Thursday, saw some of the fiercest fighting of the Rising when they experienced an attack by over 500 British troops. On the *Military Service Pensions (Amendment) Bill, 1945*, she declared:

> *Speaking for the women of Ireland, I should like to clear the air of the impression that has been given for some years back, that everybody who gave voluntary service from 1916 to 1921, or afterwards, immediately clamoured for a pension, as soon as a national government came into being. We did not. We never thought of it; we never looked for it. Even in 1934, under a Fianna Fáil government, as far as I am aware, the Cumann na mBan organisation never made any approach with regard to pensions.*

Official Report, Seanad Éireann, vol. 29, 13 March 1945, col. 1682

1938 (b) Seanad Election: 17 August 1938 ————————————

Women Members

Concannon, Helena (*see p. 91*) (University Member, National University of Ireland)

Kennedy, Margaret L. (*see p. 172*) (Nominated Member) (Nominated by Taoiseach – Éamon de Valera – 22 August 1938)

Pearse, Margaret Mary (*see p. 94*) (FF, Panel Member, Administrative Panel, Dáil Sub-Panel)

1943 Seanad Election: 25 August 1943 ————————————

Women Members

Concannon, Helena (*see p. 91*) (University Member, National University of Ireland)

Kennedy, Margaret L. (*see p. 172*) (Nominated Member) (Nominated by Taoiseach – Éamon de Valera – 31 August 1943)

Pearse, Margaret Mary (*see p. 94*) (Nominated by Taoiseach – Éamon de Valera – 31 August 1943)

1944 Seanad Election: 1 August 1944 ————————————

Women Members

Concannon, Helena (*see p. 91*) (University Member, National University of Ireland)

Kennedy, Margaret L. (*see p. 172*) (Nominated Member) (Nominated by Taoiseach – Éamon de Valera – 11 August 1944)

Pearse, Margaret Mary (*see p. 94*) (Nominated by Taoiseach – Éamon de Valera 11 August 1944)

1948 Seanad Election: 7 April 1948 ————————————

Women Members

Butler, Eleanor J. (Nominated Member) (Nominated by Taoiseach – John A. Costello – 14 April 1948)

Concannon, Helena (*see p. 91*) (University Member, National University of Ireland)

Pearse, Margaret Mary (*see p. 94*) (FF, Panel Member, Administrative Panel, Nominating Bodies Sub-Panel)

Seanad By-election: 16 June 1950 ———————————————————————

DAVIDSON, MARY F. (LAB, PANEL MEMBER, INDUSTRIAL & COMMERCIAL PANEL, OIREACHTAS SUB-PANEL)

Eleanor Butler, later Clonmore Countess of Wicklow

DATE/PLACE OF BIRTH: C.1915, DUBLIN

PARTY: LABOUR

CONSTITUENCY: TAOISEACH'S NOMINEE (NOMINATED BY JOHN A. COSTELLO)

SEANAD: SEANAD 14 APRIL 1948-31 JULY 1951

AGE AT ENTRY TO SEANAD: C. 33

FAMILY: DAUGHTER OF PROFESSOR RUDOLPH M. BUTLER (ARCHITECT WHO DESIGNED THE EARLSFORT TERRACE FAÇADE OF UCD). MARRIED WILLIAM HOWARD, 8TH EARL OF WICKLOW, 1959

EDUCATION: COEDUCATIONAL BOARDING SCHOOL IN ENGLAND FROM AGE 10 ALEXANDRA COLLEGE, DUBLIN. UNIVERSITY COLLEGE, DUBLIN. B.ARCH. (FIRST CLASS), MA, ARIBA, MRIAI

OCCUPATION: ARCHITECT (IN PRIVATE PRACTICE WITH PROFESSOR BUTLER)

CAREER:
Member, Dublin Corporation, 1943. 1947/48: Member, Corporation Scholarships Committee, Town Planning and Streets Committee; Representative of School Attendance Area No.1. Member, Coombe Hospital Board; Dublin Housing Consultative Council (appointed by the Minister for Local Government, 1949). Governor, Cork Street Fever Hospital, National Children's Hospital. Member, Architectural Record Society. First Chair, Library Council (An Chomhairle Leabharlanna), 1948-52. Founder, Centre for Peace and Reconciliation at Glencree. Founder Member, Co-operation North. *Particular policy interests*: Active in campaigns on poverty, travellers, adult education, the elderly, social housing, Cheshire Homes and many others.

PUBLICATIONS:
Betjeman, John and Eleanor Butler, *Life of Francis Johnson*.

DATE OF DEATH: FEBRUARY/MARCH 1997

ELEANOR BUTLER contracted polio at the age of six, after which she did not walk for a number of years and was partially disabled all her life. Interviewed in 1978 about her childhood, she said:

> *When I grew up on Ailesbury Road, the difference between rich and poor was extreme. I can remember as a child the General Strike in London and later in the Thirties I saw the Jarrow Marchers. In the early Twenties, a sizeable Catholic middle class had not yet emerged in Ireland; as a family, we were per-haps somewhat unusual in that my father, Professor Butler — a Loyalist*

Protestant — had married a Catholic, and therefore we knew both sides and points of view. The sad thing is that, when many Catholics did achieve affluence, they proved to be singularly lacking in social conscience. In the period after the Civil War, both political parties seemed locked in an impasse of recrimination and bitterness. Their response to the problems of the socially deprived around them then seemed negative and at best of secondary importance so I joined the Labour Party and was soon elected a member of the Dublin Corporation. My area stretched from Ringsend to Ranelagh, encompassing great poverty alongside wealth. Bad housing encouraged disease, TB was widespread; in a time when unemployment assistance was minimal, sickness was a financial disaster to many families.

THE IRISH TIMES, 28 OCTOBER 1978

Eleanor Butler contested the General Election of 1948 for Labour, in the Dublin South East constituency; she was defeated by 400 votes by Noel Browne. She was nominated to the Seanad by John A. Costello. She was one of three Senators chosen to represent Ireland at the Congress of Europe in The Hague in May 1948. The removal of Ireland from Commonwealth deliberations strengthened the pull towards Europe. Since no place was available in the United Nations and a decision had been made not to seek membership of NATO, an invitation to take part in the Council of Europe in 1949 was considered to be important for Ireland. There was only one representative of Ireland at the first meeting to draft the Statute for the Council of Europe and draw up the agenda for the Consultative Assembly in Strasbourg: Senator Eleanor Butler. She recalled:

When I got to Paris the night before and found I was the only one, I was panic-stricken. I remember the Irish Ambassador telling me to stick to the Danish Foreign Minister and together we got our points on the agenda.

THE IRISH TIMES, 28 OCTOBER 1978

Eleanor Butler told *The Irish Times* that, when Nehru visited Dáil Éireann about this time, he looked around the Chamber and asked why there were so few women representatives. Someone was sent to the Senate to produce Senator Butler to meet him, and he invited her to visit India two years later.

Eleanor Butler was a member of the Architectural Record Society, founded by her father, which collected and catalogued the original drawings of buildings of architectural merit and placed them in the National Library.

Mary Frances Davidson

DATE OF BIRTH: C. 1902

PARTY: LABOUR

CONSTITUENCY: INDUSTRIAL & COMMERCIAL PANEL, OIREACHTAS SUB-PANEL

SEANAD: 16 JUNE 1950-31 JULY 1951. 14 JULY 1954-11 AUGUST 1969

AGE AT ENTRY TO SEANAD: C. 48

FAMILY: DAUGHTER OF WILLIAM DAVIDSON (PRINCIPAL, SCHOOL OF BUILDING
AND ARCHITECTURE, DUBLIN)

OCCUPATION: SECRETARY, IRISH LABOUR PARTY

CAREER:
Member, Central Council, Irish Red Cross Society. *Particular policy interests*: wrote on social
subjects, particularly women's and children's issues, such as legal adoption,
and equal pay for equal work

DATE OF DEATH: 29 MAY 1986

ADDRESS: 105 WEIR VIEW DRIVE, STILLORGAN, DUBLIN

MARY DAVIDSON worked with William O'Brien in the ITGWU and entered the service of the Labour Party as a clerk during the Civil War (1922–3). She served under four leaders — Tom Johnson, Thomas J. O'Connell, William Norton and Brendan Corish. She retired as Secretary of the Party on 31 December 1967.

In her Seanad speeches, Senator Davidson drew on her knowledge of the trade union and labour movements. She opposed the extension of licensing hours, the fluoridation of water, corporal punishment and the abolition of PR. She moved a Motion urging the government to institute legislation to control nursing homes in which neglect had been discovered, describing in graphic detail cruelty and the helplessness of patients. (Control of Nursing Homes: Motion. *Seanad Éireann Official Report*, vol. 56, 3 April 1963, col. 760). She mentioned her shock at the 'horrible attack' the Minister made on her in response. Her efforts, nevertheless, led to the *Health (Homes for Incapacitated Persons) Act, 1964.*

1951 Seanad Election: 1 August 1951 ————————————————————

Women Members

CONCANNON, HELENA (*SEE P. 91*) (UNIVERSITY MEMBER, NATIONAL UNIVERSITY OF IRELAND)
(DIED FEBRUARY 1951)

DOWDALL, JANE (FF, PANEL MEMBER, INDUSTRIAL & COMMERCIAL PANEL; NOMINATING BODIES
SUB-PANEL)

PEARSE, MARGARET MARY (*SEE P. 94*) (NOMINATED MEMBER) (NOMINATED BY TAOISEACH —
ÉAMON DE VALERA — 9 AUGUST 1951)

1954 Seanad Election: 14 July 1954 ——————————————

Women Members

DAVIDSON, MARY F. *(SEE P. 176)* (LAB, PANEL MEMBER, INDUSTRIAL & COMMERCIAL PANEL, OIREACHTAS SUB-PANEL)

DOWDALL, JANE (FF, PANEL MEMBER, INDUSTRIAL & COMMERCIAL PANEL; NOMINATING BODIES SUB-PANEL)

PEARSE, MARGARET MARY *(SEE P. 94)* (PANEL MEMBER, ADMINISTRATIVE PANEL; OIREACHTAS SUB-PANEL)

1957 Seanad Election: 9 May 1957 ——————————————

Women Members

CONNOLLY-O'BRIEN, NORA (NOMINATED MEMBER) (NOMINATED BY TAOISEACH — SEÁN LEMASS — 15 MAY 1957)

DAVIDSON, MARY F. *(SEE P. 176)* (LAB, PANEL MEMBER, INDUSTRIAL & COMMERCIAL PANEL, OIREACHTAS SUB-PANEL)

DOWDALL, JANE (FF, PANEL MEMBER, INDUSTRIAL & COMMERCIAL PANEL; NOMINATING BODIES SUB-PANEL)

PEARSE, MARGARET MARY *(SEE P. 94)* (NOMINATED MEMBER) (NOMINATED BY TAOISEACH — SEÁN LEMASS — 15 MAY 1957)

1961 Seanad Election: 5 December 1961 ——————————————

Women Members

CONNOLLY-O'BRIEN, NORA (NOMINATED MEMBER) (NOMINATED BY TAOISEACH — SEÁN LEMASS — 9 DECEMBER 1961

DAVIDSON, MARY F. *(SEE P. 176)* (LAB, PANEL MEMBER, INDUSTRIAL & COMMERCIAL PANEL)

PEARSE, MARGARET MARY *(SEE P. 94)* (NOMINATED MEMBER) (NOMINATED BY TAOISEACH — SEÁN LEMASS — 9 DECEMBER 1961

1965 Seanad Election: 8 June 1965 ——————————————

Women Members

AHERN, KIT *(SEE P. 111')* (NOMINATED MEMBER) (NOMINATED BY TAOISEACH — SEÁN LEMASS — 11 JUNE 1965)

CONNOLLY-O'BRIEN, NORA (NOMINATED MEMBER) (NOMINATED BY TAOISEACH — SEÁN LEMASS — 11 JUNE 1965)

DAVIDSON, MARY F. *(SEE P. 176)* (LAB, PANEL MEMBER, INDUSTRIAL & COMMERCIAL PANEL, OIREACHTAS SUB-PANEL)

PEARSE, MARGARET MARY *(SEE P. 94)* (NOMINATED MEMBER) (NOMINATED BY TAOISEACH — SEÁN LEMASS — 11 JUNE 1965)

Jane Dowdall, née Doggett

DATE/PLACE OF BIRTH: 29 SEPTEMBER 1899/SMITHFIELD, DUBLIN
PARTY: FIANNA FÁIL
CONSTITUENCY: INDUSTRIAL AND COMMERCIAL PANEL
SEANAD: 1 AUGUST 1951–4 DECEMBER 1961. DEFEATED IN 1961 ELECTION
AGE AT ENTRY TO SEANAD: 51
FAMILY: WIDOW OF SENATOR J.C. DOWDALL; ONE SON.
SISTER-IN-LAW OF T.P. DOWDALL (TD)
EDUCATION: CENTRAL DUBLIN CONVENT
OCCUPATION: NURSE. LATER COMPANY DIRECTOR
CAREER:
First woman Member, Council of State, 1964; first woman Lord Mayor of Cork (1959-1960); first woman member of Cork Corporation, 1950-67. Member, Irish Countrywoman's Association and Red Cross. Member, committee of the South Infirmary, 1945. Founder member, Women's Industrial Development Association. Executive member, Irish Tourist Board. Patron, Cork Ballet Company. President, Cork Orchestral Society. Member, Cork Tóstal Council. Member, Cork City Vocational Education Committee.

DATE OF DEATH: 10 DECEMBER 1974
ADDRESS: CARRIGDUBH, BLACKROCK, COUNTY CORK

JENNIE DOGGETT was a nurse on duty in 1920 when the victims of Bloody Sunday were brought in. She had a life-long friendship with Éamon De Valera. Her commercial interest centred on the firm of Dowdall & O'Mahony and Company, margarine manufacturers. On her suggestion, a committee was formed which led to the establishment of the Cork Museum. As a member of the Cork City Vocational Education Committee, her activities led to improvements in the School of Music and the School of Art.

Nora Connolly-O'Brien

DATE/PLACE OF BIRTH: 1893/EDINBURGH
PARTY: FIANNA FÁIL
CONSTITUENCY: TAOISEACH'S NOMINEE (NOMINATED BY SEÁN LEMASS)
SEANAD: 15 MAY 1957–11 AUGUST 1969
AGE AT ENTRY TO SEANAD: 64
FAMILY: DAUGHTER OF JAMES CONNOLLY (EXECUTED AFTER THE 1916 RISING)
MARRIED TO SÉAMUS O'BRIEN
CAREER:
Founder Member, Young Republican Party; Member Sinn Féin; Cumann na mBan
PUBLICATION
Portrait of a Rebel Father, Dublin: Talbot Press, 1935
DATE OF DEATH: 17 JUNE 1981

NORA CONNOLLY was the daughter of the executed 1916 leader and socialist revolutionary, James Connolly. Her family moved from Edinburgh to Dublin when she was three. In her book, *Portrait of a Rebel Father*, she describes the poverty in which she was brought up. As a child, she attended meetings in Dublin of her father's Irish Socialist Republican Party, and her father introduced her to Irish language classes. She also accompanied him on a lecture tour to England and Scotland. When the family moved to the US in the early 1900s James Connolly founded a small journal called *The Harp*, of which Nora later became manager. The Connollys returned to Ireland in 1910 and lived in Belfast, where she became active in revolutionary politics. She joined Fianna Éireann, founded the Young Republican Party with a group of friends, organised the Belfast branch of Cumann na mBan, and was involved in the anti-recruitment campaign during the First World War.

During the week of the Easter Rising, Nora set out for Dublin to join the fighting but, having had to walk from Dundalk, arrived too late. She visited her father in prison the night before his execution, and later wrote of how he advised her mother to return to the US with the children in case there would be resentment against them among employers. Later that year, Nora went to the US herself, speaking to Clann na Gael and Friends of Irish Freedom at mass meetings.

After eighteen months, Nora Connolly tried to return via Britain, but was refused permission to enter Ireland. She was smuggled back to Dublin on board a cargo vessel, and addressed Republican meetings throughout the country. She was active in the 1918 Sinn Féin general election campaign. In 1922 she married Séamus O'Brien a former courier for Michael Collins. Both were arrested during the Civil War and imprisoned in separate jails. She joined the new Labour Party, but left when the party gave up the objective of a workers' republic. She served in the Seanad for fifteen years, as Taoiseach's nominee of Seán Lemass. During her time in the Seanad, she always remained dedicated to her father's ideals of national freedom and social justice. She opposed the Fianna Fáil proposal to abolish proportional representation and fought legislative measures that were aimed against striking electricity workers.

During the Northern Ireland Troubles, she attended many meetings there, and in 1977 visited the US again where she was fêted by NorAid. Up to her death she remained opposed to partition and maintained that those who fought the British presence in Northern Ireland were 'still following the unbroken tradition of every generation rising in arms against the British occupation of any part of Ireland'.

Nora Connolly-O'Brien is buried in Glasnevin Cemetery.

1969 Seanad Election: 12 August 1969 ————————————————————————

Women Members

AHERN, KIT (*SEE P. 111*) (FF, PANEL MEMBER CULTURAL & EDUCATIONAL PANEL; OIREACHTAS
 SUB-PANEL)
BOURKE, MARY J.W. (UNIVERSITY MEMBER, UNIVERSITY OF DUBLIN)
DESMOND, EILEEN (*SEE P. 107*) (LAB, PANEL MEMBER, INDUSTRIAL & COMMERCIAL PANEL;
 OIREACHTAS SUB-PANEL)
FARRELL, PEGGY (NOMINATED MEMBER) (NOMINATED BY TAOISEACH — JACK LYNCH —
 19 AUGUST 1969)
OWENS, EVELYN P. (LAB, PANEL MEMBER, LABOUR PANEL, NOMINATING BODIES SUB-PANEL)

Evelyn P. Owens
DATE/PLACE OF BIRTH: 22 JANUARY 1931/DUBLIN
PARTY: LABOUR
CONSTITUENCY: LABOUR PANEL. NOMINATING BODIES SUB-PANEL
(IRISH CONGRESS OF TRADE UNIONS/ICPSA NOMINATION).
SEANAD: 12 AUGUST 1969–16 AUGUST 1977
AGE AT ENTRY TO SEANAD: 38
FAMILY: SINGLE
EDUCATION: HOLY FAITH CONVENT, CLONTARF, DUBLIN. TRINITY COLLEGE DUBLIN
(DIPLOMA IN PUBLIC ADMINISTRATION)
OCCUPATION: LOCAL GOVERNMENT OFFICIAL, DUBLIN CORPORATION (TO 1984). LABOUR COURT,
DEPUTY CHAIR (1984–94), CHAIR, (1994–8)
CAREER:
First woman Leas-Cathaoirleach (Deputy Chairman), and office-holder, Seanad Éireann 1973–7.
Member, Committee of Selection, 1973–7; Committee on Procedure and Privileges, 1973–7 (ex-
officio); Select Committee on Statutory Instruments, 1969–79. Member and first woman
president, Irish Local Government Officials' Union, later Local Government and Public Services
Union, 1948, Vice-president 1964–7, first woman President 1967–9; representative on Dublin
Trades Council, 1971–2. Member, Women's Advisory Committee, Irish Congress of Trade
Unions, 1965 (chairman, 1968–71). Member, Council for the Status of Women, 1971. Member,
Administrative Council, Labour Party. Chair, Labour Women's National Council (two terms).
Member, Special Advisory Committee on setting up Office of Ombudsman; Chair, Commission
on Minimum Wage; Chair, National Partnership Centre, 1999. *Particular policy interests*: indus-
trial relations, local government, women's affairs.
ADDRESS: STILES ROAD, CLONTARF, DUBLIN 3

EVELYN OWENS was the first woman to be appointed deputy chairwoman of the
Labour Court. The Minister for Labour, Ruairí Quinn, described the appointment as an 'historic one' when he announced it on 11 May 1984, and said that it
was in recognition of the important role the Labour Court had to play in the
establishment of women's rights in areas such as equal pay, access to work and

access to fair promotional opportunities. She became the first woman Chair in 1994.

In her job at Dublin Corporation, Evelyn Owens had been responsible for the investigation of labour disputes, deciding appeals against recommendations of rights commissioners and overseeing the work of joint labour committees and joint industrial councils. In her Seanad speeches, she advocated the case of women workers. She supported co-education, a return of power to community control, and the recognition of motherhood as social work. She was critical of the effect of mass media advertising. She was nominated by *The Irish Times* to an all-woman fantasy cabinet (*The Irish Times*, 14 February 1973).

Mary Bourke, later Robinson

DATE/PLACE OF BIRTH: 21 MAY 1944/BALLINA, COUNTY MAYO

PARTY: LABOUR

CONSTITUENCY: UNIVERSITY OF DUBLIN (TRINITY COLLEGE)

SEANAD: 12 AUGUST 1969-15 AUGUST 1989). PRESIDENT, 7 NOVEMBER
1990-12 SEPTEMBER 1997

AGE AT ENTRY TO SEANAD: 25

FAMILY: MARRIED NICHOLAS ROBINSON, 1970; ONE DAUGHTER, TWO SONS

EDUCATION: HOLLYMOUNT, MAYO. CONVENT OF SACRED HEART, MOUNT ANVILLE, DUNDRUM 1954-61;
MADEMOISELLE ANITA'S, PARIS, 1961-2; ENTRANCE SCHOLARSHIP (FRENCH AND ENGLISH) TO
TRINITY COLLEGE, DUBLIN, 1963; SCHOLARSHIP IN LEGAL SCIENCE, 1965; HENRY HAMILTON
HUNTER MEMORIAL PRIZE, 1965; MODERATORSHIP IN LEGAL SCIENCE (FIRST CLASS), 1967; LLB
DEGREE (FIRST CLASS), 1967; DEGREE OF BARRISTER-AT-LAW (FIRST CLASS), 1967; FELLOWSHIP TO
HARVARD UNIVERSITY, 1967; MA, LLB, LLM HARVARD LAW SCHOOL (FIRST CLASS), 1968

OCCUPATION: BARRISTER, 1967; SENIOR COUNSEL, 1980; MEMBER OF THE ENGLISH BAR (MIDDLE
TEMPLE), 1973. REID PROFESSOR OF CONSTITUTIONAL AND CRIMINAL LAW, TRINITY COLLEGE,
DUBLIN, 1969-75

CAREER:

Senator, 1969-89. President of Ireland, 1990-97. United Nations High Commissioner for Human Rights, 1997 to date. Member, Select Committee on Statutory Instruments 1969. Member, Joint Committee on Secondary Legislation of the European Communities, 1973-89; Chair of its Social Affairs Sub-Committee 1977-87, Chair of its Legal Affairs Committee 1987-1989. Member, Joint Committee on Marital Breakdown, 1983-5; Member, New Ireland Forum, 1983-4. Member, Dublin Corporation, 1979-83. Vice-Chair, Irish Council of European Movement, 1972. Irish member of Vedel Group on powers of the European Parliament set up by the EEC Commission, 1971-2; President of Cherish (Irish Association of Single Parents), 1973-90. Director of Centre International de Formation Européenne, 1973. Member, Trilateral Commission, 1973-80. Member, Saint-Geours Committee on Energy Efficiency, EC, 1978-9; Member, Executive Committee of Amnesty. Member, International Commission of Jurists (1987-90). Member, Advisory Commission of Inter-Rights (1984-90). Founder and director, Irish Centre for European Law, 1988-90. Reid Professor of Constitutional and Criminal Law, Trinity College, Dublin, 1969-75; Lecturer in European Community Law, TCD, 1975-90.

Member, Editorial Board of Irish Current Law Statutes, Annotated 1984-90. Chair of its Social Affairs Sub-Committee, 1977-87. Chair of its Legal Affairs Committee, 1987-9. Member, Advisory Board of *Common Market Law Review*, 1976-90. Member, Advisory Committee of Interights, London, 1984-90. Member, International Commission of Jurists, Geneva 1987-90. Member, Committee of Management, European Air Law Association 1989-90. Member, Scientific Council of European Review of Public Law, 1989-90. Member of Chambers, 2 Hare Court, London, 1989-90. Member of Royal Irish Academy, 1991. General Rapporteur, 'Human Rights at the Dawn of the 21st Century', Council of Europe, Strasbourg, 1993. *Particular policy interests*: introduced in 1973 the first Bill to make contraceptives available in the Republic, the *Family Planning Bill, 1973*, defeated at Second Stage on 27 March 1974. Introduced Private Members Bills: *Adoption Bill, 1971*, given Second Reading 29 June 1972, withdrawn in favour of promised government measure; *Criminal Law Amendment Bill, 1971*, refused First Reading on 7 July 1971; *Criminal Procedure (Amendment) Bill, 1973*, withdrawn in favour of Government Bill, 25 July, 1973; *Family Planning Bill, 1978*, lapsed 8 November 1978, defeated at First Stage; *Illegitimate Children (Maintenance & Succession) Bill, 1974*, reached Second Stage and withdrawn on 13 February 1975.

PUBLICATIONS:

Robinson, Mary, *The Special Criminal Court*, Dublin University Press, 1974. Numerous papers published by the Irish Centre for European Law. O'Sullivan, Michael, Mary Robinson: *The Life and Times of an Irish Liberal*, Dublin: Blackwater, 1993. O'Leary, Olivia and Helen Burke. Mary Robinson: *The Authorised Biography*, London: Hodder and Stoughton, 1998. Horgan, John, Mary Robinson: *An Independent Voice*, Dublin: O'Brien, 1997.

ADDRESS: 17 WELLINGTON PLACE, DUBLIN 4. LATER 43 SANDYFORD ROAD, RANELAGH, DUBLIN 6

MARY ROBINSON, in her role as a lawyer, was successful in landmark constitutional cases in Ireland and the European courts, in areas such as women's right to serve on juries, access to legal aid, decriminalisation of homosexual activity and equalisation of social welfare payments. She was counsel for Josie Airey who won a case against Ireland in the European Court of Human Rights when the State was found to be in breach of the European Convention for the Protection of Human Rights because of its failure to provide free legal aid in a family law matter. The government then put in place a limited scheme for civil legal aid. She acted for Mary McGee whose contraceptives delivery from England was intercepted by customs officers under the *Criminal Law Amendment Act, 1935*. The 1973 Supreme Court judgement in Mrs McGee's favour established the right of married couples to import contraceptives for their own use and enabled family planning clinics to act as suppliers within Ireland.

Elected to the Seanad as an Independent (DU) in 1969, she held her seat until 1989. In 1970 she led a protest against the Senate's long holidays during a period of national crisis. She said that she was disappointed with the Seanad and that parliament was becoming irrelevant.

In 1971 she asked why the recommendation on divorce of the 1967 Report of the Committee on the Constitution had not been implemented. In 1972 she pressed the government to amend the adoption law by putting forward her own

Bill. *The Adoption Act, 1974* was the result. When she introduced the first bill to make contraceptives available in the Republic in 1973, it gained minimal support and she received hate mail during this time.

She was a constructive critic of Ireland's negotiations with the EEC and opposed the *Prisons Bill, the Prohibition of Forcible Entry Bill, 1970* and the *Offences Against the State Amendment Bill, 1972*. In 1976 she joined the Labour Party and in 1977 and 1981 unsuccessfully contested Dáil elections in Dublin. She resigned from the party after the 1985 Anglo–Irish Agreement in protest at the exclusion of Unionists from the prior negotiations.

When she decided not to run for the Seanad in 1989 it appeared that Mary Robinson's political career was at an end. But in 1990 Dick Spring asked her to accept a Labour party nomination for the presidential election later that year. She agreed, on the condition that she would not have to rejoin the party or run strictly as a Labour candidate. Few expected her to win. She threw herself into the nationwide campaign and struck a chord with community groups all over the country. Attempts were made to accuse her of anti-family radicalism but she brushed aside an attempt to label her as pro-abortion and polled exceptionally well among women, even in rural areas thought to be conservative. Her surprise defeat of the Fianna Fáil candidate, Brian Lenihan, by a large margin on the second count was helped by the sacking of the latter from the Haughey government during the campaign over allegations that Lenihan had sought to bring pressure on President Hillery in 1982 to refuse dissolution of the Dáil. But it was also viewed as a desire by women to end male dominance at the top of the establishment and to recognise Mary Robinson's devotion to women's causes and support for a more liberal spirit in Irish affairs. Her election as Ireland's first woman president was widely welcomed, even by many of those who had opposed her. She promised Irish women that 'the hand that rocks the cradle can rock the system'.

Unionists in Northern Ireland had noted her resignation from the Labour party in protest at the Anglo–Irish Agreement and cautiously welcomed her victory. But as guardian of the Constitution she could not court controversy or voice doubts about the nature of the constitutional claim to Northern Ireland. She spoke eloquently about extending friendship across the border and entertained many groups and individuals from Northern Ireland. When, in February 1992, she visited Northern Ireland, she was, however, denied a reception at Belfast City Hall and Unionist Councillors stayed away from the functions linked with her first official visit to Derry in May 1992. She appointed Quintin Oliver, chairman of the Northern Ireland Council for Voluntary Action, to her Council of State.

In April 1993, President Robinson attended a memorial service in Warrington, Cheshire, for two young boys killed in the town by Provisional IRA bombs. In May 1993 she met President Clinton in Washington and paid a courtesy call on the Queen at Buckingham Palace — the first such meeting between the British and Irish Heads of State. In June 1993, she provoked controversy when she shook hands with Gerry Adams at a West Belfast reception. The British Government and Unionists were particularly hostile, but she argued that the encounter had no significance. In October she launched a new peace project in Warrington. She visited Manchester to show solidarity with the victims of paramilitary violence. In 1996 she became the first Irish head of state to pay an official visit to Britain, where she was received by Queen Elizabeth at Buckingham Palace.

Mary Robinson was the most active president in the history of the State, one of her priorities being visits to deprived and disaster-stricken areas of the world. Among the numerous international activities relating to human rights in which she participated, she served as Special Rapporteur to the Interregional Meeting of the Council of Europe as part of its preparation for the 1993 Vienna World Conference on Human Rights. She delivered the keynote address at the Council of Europe preparatory meeting for the Beijing Fourth World Conference on Women.

President Robinson was the first Head of State to visit Rwanda in the aftermath of the genocide there. After her second visit to Rwanda, in October 1995, she went on to focus on Rwanda her address to the United Nations 50th anniversary session. She made another visit, on which she addressed the Pan-African Conference on 'Peace, Gender and Development'. She was also the first Head of State to visit the International Criminal Tribunal for the Former Yugoslavia, and the first Head of State to visit Somalia following the crisis there in 1992. The President received the Special CARE Humanitarian Award in 1993 in recognition of her efforts for Somalia.

Mary Robinson developed a new sense of Ireland's economic, political and cultural links with other countries and cultures. She emphasised the needs of developing countries, linking the history of the Great Famine of 1845 to today's nutrition, poverty and policy issues, creating a bridge between developed and developing countries.

Hers was a watershed presidency which redefined the primarily ceremonial role of Head of State. She embodied some of the contradictions and concerns of modern Ireland — a Catholic married to a Protestant, she visited the Queen and shook hands with Gerry Adams, leader of Sinn Féin. Her approach gained her a 93 per cent approval rating with the Irish electorate. She was voted 'Woman of the Century' on the eve of the millennium by *Sunday Independent* readers (*Sunday Independent*, 2 January 2000). President Robinson has received honours and awards from Ireland, England, Australia, America, Portugal, Spain, Tanzania, Italy, the Netherlands, New Zealand and Switzerland.

In 1997 Mary Robinson was appointed United Nations High Commissioner for Human Rights.

'Óid Insealbhaite'
Éire, Banba, Fódhla
Cuirimid ainm eile leosan
Máire ó Mhaigh Eo sin.
Ní h-aisling í ach beobhean
A mhisneoidh croíte scólta.
Flaitheas Éireann faoi do láimhse
Thoirbhir an ínion is an mháthair
An mac, an t-athair, is fiú an garlach.
Deir siad uile leat go grámhar:
'Fáilte romhat san Áras.
Cosain beachtaigh agus deársnaigh
Ár gcatrt, ár gceart, ár náisiun,
Díbir uainn béalchráifeacht,
Gura fíor flatha iad do ráite'
—sliocht,

PÁDRAIG Ó FIANNACHTA,
AN SAGART, EARREACH, 1991

'Inauguration Ode'
Éire, Banba, Fódhla,
We place with them another name;
Mary from Mayo.
No dream but living woman
Who will encourage scalded hearts.
In your hands the sovereignty of Ireland
the mother, the daughter, the father
and son and even the child repose.
With love they say as one:
'Welcome to the Áras.
Defend, define, distinguish
Our laws, our rights, our nation,
Rid us of hypocrisy,
Be the truth of kingship in your speech'.
— extract,

PÁDRAIG Ó FIANNACHTA
AN SAGART, SPRING 1991
(WITH THANKS TO BRIAN Ó CLÉIRIGH FOR THE TRANSLATION)

Peggy Farrell

DATE/PLACE OF BIRTH: 15 NOVEMBER 1920/BANTRY, COUNTY CORK
PARTY: FIANNA FÁIL
CONSTITUENCY: TAOISEACH'S NOMINEE (NOMINATED BY JACK LYNCH)
SEANAD: 19 AUGUST 1969-31 APRIL 1973
AGE AT ENTRY TO SEANAD: 48
FAMILY: MARRIED TO THOMAS P. FARRELL; TWO DAUGHTERS, TWO SONS.
NIECE OF TED O'SULLIVAN (FF TD FOR CORK WEST,
1937-54, LATER SENATOR)
EDUCATION: CONVENT OF MERCY, BANTRY; RURAL SCHOOL, CLIFDEN;
MUNSTER INSTITUTE, CORK
OCCUPATION: POULTRY INSTRUCTOR; LATER MANAGING DIRECTOR
CAREER:
Only woman Founder Member, Small Firms Association of Confederation of Irish Industry. First woman Chairperson, Small Firms Association. First woman Member, Council of Confederation of Irish Industry. Director, Irish Small and Medium Enterprises Association, 1997-8. Winner, Veuve Cliquot Business Woman of the Year Award, 1981. Member, Irish Countrywomen's Association (ICA), 1962; President for County Cavan, 1965; National President, 1968. Founder Member, Slieve Bawn Handcraft Co-operative Market. *Particular policy interests*: development of the West and small industry. Promotion, development and education of women, particularly rural women.

PUBLICATIONS:
Cookery book, published by the Irish Countrywoman's Association for the conference of Associated Countrywomen of the World in Dublin, 1965.
ADDRESS: ARDSALLAGH, ROSCOMMON

PEGGY FARRELL had to resign her post as poultry instructor in the Munster Institute because of the ban on married women enforced in the Department of Agriculture. She accepted this and believed that in many cases married women shouldn't work outside the home:

> *I feel that in a country like ours when we haven't full employment that we have gone too fast with women working after marriage. Economic necessity apart I think it is unjust and nearly unchristian that in some families you have two salaries coming in and in others none at all.*
>
> THE IRISH TIMES, 18 DECEMBER 1981

She campaigned for the women in rural Ireland to have the same standard of living as urban women, including intellectual and cultural outlets, protested against policies which depopulated the West, and demanded educational programmes relevant to rural life. In 1969 she was nominated for the Senate in recognition of the work she had done for the ICA.

Peggy Farrell said about the ICA:

I emerged under the ICA which I love. It is a tremendous organisation but I don't know how many members it has now, because you see they fired me. I was six years in it when I became National President. No one ever went to the top of it faster than I did, and no one was turfed out faster either.

THE IRISH TIMES, 18 DECEMBER 1981

The trouble started when she accepted a Senate nomination as a Fianna Fáil nominee.

The Association is non-political and non-sectarian, at least it used to be, though looking at some of their actions I don't think it is. In my case, without consulting the members, the Executive Committee took a decision to ask me to resign. I expected to be allowed to stay on as vice-president, but I was told since I resigned, I couldn't be one. Even twelve years later this still stings, because I feel I made my National Presidency a 24-hour day seven-days-a-week job, and I straightened out its finances.

THE IRISH TIMES, 18 DECEMBER 1981

She ran a hatchery business with her husband before going into the clothing business to provide an alternative to emigration for young Roscommon women. In the early 1970s she was granted an IDA factory where her Chixwear firm was started. In 1974 she took over another factory in Athlone. In all, she employed 96 women.

Peggy Farrell was nominated by *The Irish Times* to an all-woman fantasy cabinet (*The Irish Times*, 14 February 1973).

1973 Seanad Election: 23 February 1973 ——————————————

Women Members
AHERN, KIT (*SEE P. 111*) (FF, PANEL MEMBER, CULTURAL & EDUCATIONAL PANEL; OIREACHTAS SUB-PANEL)
BOURKE, MARY J.W. (*SEE P. 181*) (UNIVERSITY MEMBER, UNIVERSITY OF DUBLIN)
OWENS, EVELYN P. (*SEE P. 180*) (LAB, PANEL MEMBER, LABOUR PANEL, NOMINATING BODIES SUB-PANEL)
WALSH, MARY (FG, CULTURAL & EDUCATIONAL PANEL, OIREACHTAS SUB-PANEL)

Mary Walsh

DATE/PLACE OF BIRTH: OCTOBER 1929/TINAHELY, COUNTY WICKLOW
PARTY: FINE GAEL
CONSTITUENCY: CULTURAL & EDUCATION PANEL; OIREACHTAS SUB-PANEL
SEANAD: 1 MAY 1973-AUGUST 1976 (DEATH)
AGE AT ENTRY TO SEANAD: 43
FAMILY: SINGLE
EDUCATION: LORETO ABBEY, GOREY; UNIVERSITY COLLEGE, DUBLIN (BCOMM, H.DIP.ED.)
OCCUPATION: PUBLICAN

CAREER:
Member, Dáil and Seanad Joint Restaurant Committee, 1973. Member, Wicklow County Council, 1960. First woman Chair, Wicklow County Council, 1969-70. First woman Chair, General Council of County Councils, 1973-74; Vice-chair 1972-3, Member, 1969. Member, Wicklow County Committee of Agriculture, 1960; Wicklow Vocational Education Committee, 1960-76; Eastern Regional Tourism Organisation; Arklow Harbour Authority, 1967-76. Chair, Wicklow Library Committee, 1971-6. Member, Standing Committee, Irish Vocational Education Committee, 1972-6, An Foras Forbartha (The National Institute for Physical Planning and Construction Research), 1973-6. Member, Tinahely Development Association; Arklow Branch, Wicklow County Association of Parents and Friends of Mentally Handicapped Children, 1970-76, Shillelagh Old Age Pensions Committee.

DATE OF DEATH: AUGUST 1976

ADDRESS: BRIDGE HOUSE, TINAHELY, COUNTY WICKLOW

MARY WALSH was a candidate for Fine Gael in the Wicklow constituency in the 1973 Dáil general election and in the Seanad by-election of 1970. She was elected to the Seanad in 1973.

1977 Seanad Election: 17 August 1977 ————————————————

Women Members

CASSIDY, EILEEN (FF, NOMINATED MEMBER) (NOMINATED BY TAOISEACH — JACK LYNCH — 25 AUGUST 1977)

GOULDING, LADY VALERIE (FF) (NOMINATED MEMBER) (NOMINATED BY TAOISEACH — JACK LYNCH — 25 AUGUST 1977)

HARNEY, MARY (*SEE P. 120*) (FF, NOMINATED MEMBER) (NOMINATED BY TAOISEACH — JACK LYNCH — 25 AUGUST 1977)

HONAN, TRAS (FF, PANEL MEMBER, ADMINISTRATIVE PANEL, NOMINATING BODIES SUB-PANEL)

HUSSEY, GEMMA (*SEE P. 124*) (IND, UNIVERSITY MEMBER, NATIONAL UNIVERSITY OF IRELAND)

ROBINSON, MARY T.W. (*SEE P. 181*) (LAB, UNIVERSITY MEMBER, UNIVERSITY OF DUBLIN)

Seanad By-election: 11 December 1979

McGUINNESS, CATHERINE (IND, UNIVERSITY MEMBER; UNIVERSITY OF DUBLIN)

Eileen Cassidy, née Foreman

DATE/PLACE OF BIRTH: AUGUST 1932/DUBLIN

PARTY: FIANNA FÁIL

CONSTITUENCY: TAOISEACH'S NOMINEE (NOMINATED BY JACK LYNCH)

SEANAD: 25 AUGUST 1977-11 AUGUST 1981

AGE AT ENTRY TO SEANAD: 45

FAMILY: MARRIED TO JOHN B. CASSIDY SC; FOUR DAUGHTERS, THREE SONS

EDUCATION: HOLY FAITH CONVENT, DOMINICK STREET, DUBLIN; UNIVERSITY COLLEGE, DUBLIN (BA)

OCCUPATION: LIBRARIAN, MARSH'S LIBRARY; PEARSE STREET LIBRARY

CAREER:
Member, Committee on Selection, 1977-81; Select Committee on Statutory Instruments, 1978-81; Joint Committee on the *Royal College of Physicians of Ireland (Charters and Letters Patent Amendment) Bill, 1979.* .Member, Gorta, Saint Vincent de Paul, KARE.

DATE OF DEATH: 6 OCTOBER 1995

ADDRESS: BROADLEAS, BALLYMORE EUSTACE, COUNTY KILDARE (ADDRESS WHILE IN SEANAD)

EILEEN CASSIDY was politicised through her family's attempts to persuade the local authority to provide a water supply to their rural neighbourhood. She became a Fianna Fáil activist, in the tradition of her father and husband, and campaigned on numerous issues. While campaigning for candidates in Kildare/Wicklow for the 1977 general election she impressed the Taoiseach, Jack Lynch, with her vigorous defence of the election manifesto. He phoned her out of the blue to ask if she would accept his nomination to the Seanad.

She contributed to the *Housing Bill, Consumer Information Bill, 1976, Industrial Development Bill, 1977, Health Contributions (Amendment) Bill, 1978, Medical Practitioners Bill, 1977, Social Welfare Bills, 1979* and *1980* and *Employment Guarantee Fund Bill, 1980,* among others.

In her speech on the *Health (Family Planning) Bill, 1978,* which made contraceptives available to married couples through pharmacies and medical practitioners, she expressed her opposition to artificial contraception and abstained on the vote (*Official Report Seanad Éireann, vol. 92, cols. 741–5, 811–4*). As a Taoiseach's nominee, she was expected to support the government, and this stand weighed against her receiving another nomination.

Eileen Cassidy returned to local political activism at the end of her Seanad term.

Lady Valerie Goulding, née Monckton

DATE/PLACE OF BIRTH: SEPTEMBER, 1918/KENT, ENGLAND

PARTY: FIANNA FÁIL

CONSTITUENCY: TAOISEACH'S NOMINEE (NOMINATED BY JACK LYNCH)

SEANAD: 25 AUGUST 1977-11 AUGUST 1981

AGE AT ENTRY TO SEANAD: 58

FAMILY: DAUGHTER OF VISCOUNT MONCKTON OF BRENCHLEY, ENGLAND
(A CONSERVATIVE MINISTER). MARRIED SIR BASIL GOULDING, 1939;
THREE SONS

EDUCATION: DOWNE HOUSE, READING, BERKSHIRE. DUBLIN SCHOOL OF PHYSIOTHERAPY

OCCUPATION: CHAIR, MANAGING DIRECTOR, CENTRAL REMEDIAL CLINIC

CAREER:
Member, Committee on Procedure and Privileges, 1977. Founder member, National Rehabilitation Board. Governor, St Patrick's Hospital. Founder member, Union of Voluntary

Organisations for the Handicapped. Member, Eastern Area Committee of the National Association for Cerebral Palsy. Founder, Central Remedial Clinic, Dublin, 1951. Founder member, Peace Point. Advisory member, Ireland Funds Committee.

ADDRESS: DARGLE LODGE, ENNISKERRY, COUNTY WICKLOW

LADY VALERIE GOULDING was a candidate on the Administrative Panel in the Senate elections of 1977. She was unsuccessful in her candidacy, but was then nominated to the Seanad by the Taoiseach, Jack Lynch. She has been conferred with the honorary degree of Doctor of Laws by the National University of Ireland.

Tras Honan, née Barlow

DATE/PLACE OF BIRTH: 4 JANUARY 1930/TIPPERARY
PARTY: FIANNA FÁIL
CONSTITUENCY: ADMINISTRATIVE PANEL; NOMINATING BODIES SUB-PANEL
SEANAD: 17 AUGUST 1977-31 JANUARY 1993
AGE AT ENTRY TO SEANAD: 47
FAMILY: DAUGHTER OF COMDT. MATT BARLOW (THIRD TIPPERARY BRIGADE,
OLD IRA). MARRIED TO DERRY HONAN, MCC, LIDC
(SENATOR 1965-73, INDUSTRIAL AND COMMERCIAL PANEL); ONE DAUGHTER, ONE SON.
DAUGHTER-IN-LAW OF THOMAS V. HONAN (SENATOR, 1934-6, 38-54);
SISTER OF CARRIE ACHESON (TD FOR TIPPERARY SOUTH (*SEE P. 116*))
EDUCATION: ST. LEO'S CONVENT, CARLOW; MERCY CONVENT, CLONMEL, COUNTY TIPPERARY
OCCUPATION: BUSINESSWOMAN
CAREER:
Member, Joint Committees on Health, Justice, Local Government. First woman Cathaoirleach of Seanad, 13 May 1982-23 February 1983, 25 April 1987-1 November 1989. Leas Chathaoirleach 9 March 1983-3 April 1987. Chair (25 years), Clare Federation of Friends of the Mentally Handicapped. Member, Mid-Western Committee for the Mentally Handicapped since 1965. Member, Clare Health Board 1974. First woman member, then first woman Chair, Ennis Urban District Council. Director, Deputy Chair, CIE board, 1994. *Particular policy interests*: Local government, health, transport, justice.

ADDRESS: HEATHERLEA, CUSACK ROAD, ENNIS, COUNTY CLARE (ADDRESS WHILE IN SEANAD)

TRAS HONAN joined the Fianna Fáil party in January 1948. She was the only woman amongst the forty-three Senators elected from the five vocational panels in 1977.

Catherine McGuinness, née Ellis

DATE/PLACE OF BIRTH: 14 NOVEMBER 1934/DUNMURRY, BELFAST
PARTY: INDEPENDENT, 1968 TO DATE. LABOUR PARTY, 1961-7
CONSTITUENCY: UNIVERSITY OF DUBLIN
SEANAD: 11 DECEMBER, 1979 (BY-ELECTION)-20 APRIL 1982;
    31 JANUARY 1983-13 APRIL 1987
AGE AT ENTRY TO SEANAD: 45
FAMILY: MARRIED TO PROINSÍAS MACAONGHUSA; ONE DAUGHTER, TWO SONS
EDUCATION: DUNMURRY PUBLIC ELEMENTARY SCHOOL; ALEXANDRA COLLEGE, DUBLIN (CLERGY
    DAUGHTERS' SCHOOL), TRINITY COLLEGE DUBLIN (BA MOD (FRENCH, IRISH); MA) KING'S INNS,
    DUBLIN, BL, 1974-7. D.LITT. (HONORIS CAUSA) UNIVERSITY OF ULSTER, 1998
OCCUPATION: BARRISTER-AT-LAW. SENIOR COUNSEL. JUDGE OF THE HIGH COURT. JUDGE OF THE
    SUPREME COURT
CAREER:
Irish Bar, 1977; Inner Bar, 1989. First woman Judge of the Circuit Court –Dublin Circuit –
1994-6, Judge of the High Court, 1996-2000. Judge of the Supreme Court, 2000 to date.
Member, Council of State, 1988-90. Chairperson, Forum for Peace and Reconciliation, 1994-6.
Member, Second Commission for the Status of Women, 1990-93; Chair, Kilkenny Incest
Investigation, 1993. Chairperson, National College of Art and Design, 1987-93. Chairperson,
Employment Equality Agency, 1987-92. Member, An Bord Uchtala (Adoption Board), 1971-8.
First woman Member, Voluntary Health Insurance Board, 1977-9. Member, National Economic
and Social Council, 1982-4. Chair, National Social Service Board, 1975-82. Member, General
Synod, Church of Ireland; Chancellor of the Dioceses of Dublin and Glendalough; Trustee
and member of the Academic Council of the Irish School of Ecumenics; Judicial Fellow
of International Academy of Matrimonial Lawyers; Past President, Family Lawyers'
Association. *Particular policy interests*: foreign affairs, education, Northern Ireland, family law.
Other interests: choral singing (President, Culwick Choral Society, 1998 to date), gardening,
travel.
PUBLICATIONS: ARTICLES AND BOOK REVIEWS ON FAMILY LAW SUBJECTS, FORUM FOR PEACE AND
    RECONCILIATION
ADDRESS: 4 NEW PARK ROAD, BLACKROCK, COUNTY DUBLIN

CATHERINE MCGUINNESS is the daughter of a Catholic mother from Tullamore
and Canon Robert Ellis, a Church of Ireland rector from County Clare, who was
based in Belfast during her childhood. She is a fluent Irish speaker.

She worked as a teacher, freelance writer and parliamentary officer with the
Labour Party in the 1960s, when she was scriptwriter for Brendan Corish and
most Labour deputies. She wrote the Labour Party pamphlet on education in 1966.
She advocated comprehensive schools, co-education, non-sectarian control,
parental participation, equal opportunities for girls and boys and an emphasis on
cultural subjects such as music, art and drama. When her husband, Proinsías
MacAonghusa, was expelled from the Labour Party in 1967, she resigned her post.
She served on a number of State boards in the 1970s in areas of social policy.

Catherine McGuinness studied in the King's Inns as a mature student and qualified as a barrister in 1977, aged 42. At the Bar she highlighted family law issues and was involved in a number of landmark cases, becoming an authority on family law. Family law cases are not reported and she was seen as an unknown quantity when she was appointed first woman judge of the Circuit Court in 1994. Her involvement in family law strengthened her interest in social policy. She has been a liberal voice in social controversies. She told the Social Studies Conference in the early 1990s that the Protestant churches took too negative an approach to mixed marriages. When she became a Senior Counsel in 1989 her focus on family law continued and she made a challenge to the legislation governing the property rights of women. Throughout her judicial career she stood for the rights of the individual against the State.

Her 1993 report, *Kilkenny Incest Investigation*, revealed a horrendous history of abuse, exposed many of the shortcomings in the social and legal systems, and led to the government's introduction of unprecedented amendments to the law to strengthen the rights of children.

Her Protestant background played a role in her appointment as Chair of the Forum for Peace and Reconciliation in 1994, as it was felt that this would help her to be accepted by the unionist parties who were refusing to come to the table for all-party talks held by the Forum on the future of Northern Ireland.

She was the first judge to be raised through the ranks through the Circuit Court to the High Court to the Supreme Court.

Catherine McGuinness was nominated by *The Irish Times* to an all-woman fantasy cabinet (*The Irish Times*, 14 February 1973).

1981 Seanad Election: 17 August 1981 ——————————————————————

Women Members

BOLGER, DEIRDRE (FG, PANEL MEMBER, INDUSTRIAL & COMMERCIAL PANEL, NOMINATING BODIES SUB-PANEL)

BULBULIA, KATHARINE (FG, PANEL MEMBER, ADMINISTRATIVE PANEL, OIREACHTAS SUB-PANEL)

HONAN, TRAS (*SEE P. 190*) (FF, PANEL MEMBER, ADMINISTRATIVE PANEL, NOMINATING BODIES SUB-PANEL)

HUSSEY, GEMMA (*SEE P. 124*) (FG, UNIVERSITY MEMBER, NATIONAL UNIVERSITY OF IRELAND)

MIRIAM KEARNEY (FG, NOMINATED MEMBER) (NOMINATED BY TAOISEACH — GARRET FITZGERALD — 19 AUGUST 1981)

PATSY LAWLOR (FG, PANEL MEMBER, CULTURAL & EDUCATIONAL PANEL, NOMINATING BODIES SUB-PANEL)

MCGUINNESS, CATHERINE (*SEE P. 191*) (IND, UNIVERSITY MEMBER; UNIVERSITY OF DUBLIN)

MARY O'ROURKE (*SEE P. 130*) (FF, CULTURAL & EDUCATIONAL PANEL, OIREACHTAS SUB-PANEL

ROBINSON, MARY T.W. (*SEE P. 181*) (LAB, UNIVERSITY MEMBER, UNIVERSITY OF DUBLIN)

Deirdre Bolger, née Boland

DATE/PLACE OF BIRTH: 27 JULY 1938/DUBLIN

PARTY: FINE GAEL

CONSTITUENCY: INDUSTRIAL & COMMERCIAL PANEL; NOMINATING BODIES
SUB-PANEL (AUGUST 1981-APRIL 1982), OIREACHTAS SUB-PANEL
(APRIL 1982-JANUARY 1983)

SEANAD: 12 AUGUST 1981-30 JANUARY 1983

AGE AT ENTRY TO SEANAD: 43

FAMILY: MARRIED TO DAVID F. BOLGER; FIVE SONS

EDUCATION: CONVENT OF THE HOLY CHILD, KILLINEY, COUNTY DUBLIN; GUY'S HOSPITAL, LONDON
(STATE REGISTERED NURSE)

OCCUPATION: COMPANY DIRECTOR. DIRECTOR OF JOHN BOLGER AND CO., LTD., FERNS,
COUNTY WEXFORD

CAREER:
Member, Wexford County Council 1978 to date. Gorey Town Commissioner, 1978 (Chairperson 1979-80). Chair, South Eastern Health Board, 1979; Chair, General Council of County Councils. Member, South East Regional Authority; European Committee of the Regions, 1994-8. Member, Gorey Community Development; House Committee of Cheshire Homes, Shillelagh, County Wicklow. *Particular policy interests*: health, environment, social issues. *Other interests*: Bridge, golf, music. Member, past captain and past president of Courtown Golf Club.

ADDRESS: MILLMOUNT, GOREY, COUNTY WEXFORD

Katharine Bulbulia, née O'Carroll

DATE/PLACE OF BIRTH: JULY 1943/DUBLIN

PARTY: FINE GAEL; LATER PROGRESSIVE DEMOCRATS

CONSTITUENCY: ADMINISTRATIVE PANEL; OIREACHTAS SUB-PANEL (AUGUST
1981-APRIL 1982), NOMINATING SUB-PANEL APRIL 1982-AUGUST 1989)

SEANAD: 12 AUGUST 1981-15 AUGUST 1989

AGE AT ENTRY TO SEANAD: 38

FAMILY: MARRIED TO DR ABDUL BULBULIA; ONE DAUGHTER, TWO SONS

EDUCATION: SACRED HEART OF MARY CONVENT, ROSLYN PARK, FERRYBANK, WATERFORD; ST MARY'S
COLLEGE, CATHAL BRUGHA STREET (DIPLOMA IN HOUSEHOLD MANAGEMENT); UNIVERSITY
COLLEGE, DUBLIN (BA, H.DIP.ED.)

OCCUPATION: TEACHER

CAREER:
First woman Member, Waterford County Council, 1979. First woman Chairperson, Local Health Committee; first woman Chairperson, National Monuments Advisory Committee. Member, South Eastern Health Board, 1979; General Council of County Councils, 1979. Director, Tramore Fáilte. Member, Board of Governors of Newtown School, Waterford. Member, Women's Political Association; founder member of Waterford branch. Member, Concordia-Waterford; Soroptimists; An Taisce.

ADDRESS: UPPER WOODSTOWN, WATERFORD

KATHARINE BULBULIA joined Fine Gael and in the 1979 local elections topped the poll in the Tramore Electoral Area, becoming the first woman elected to Waterford County Council. She was a Fine Gael candidate in the Waterford constituency in the 1981 general election. She was appointed as a programme manager for the Progressive Democrats in 1997.

Miriam Kearney

DATE/PLACE OF BIRTH: JULY 1959/CORK
PARTY: FINE GAEL
CONSTITUENCY: TAOISEACH'S NOMINEE (NOMINATED BY GARRET FITZGERALD)
SEANAD: 19 AUGUST 1981-20 APRIL 1982
AGE AT ENTRY TO SEANAD: 22
FAMILY: SINGLE
EDUCATION: ST ANGELA'S COLLEGE, CORK; UNIVERSITY COLLEGE, CORK;
INCORPORATED LAW SOCIETY OF IRELAND (BCL)
OCCUPATION: FINE GAEL ASSISTANT DIRECTOR OF ORGANISATION
WITH SPECIAL RESPONSIBILITY FOR YOUNG FINE GAEL
CAREER:
Chairperson, Young Fine Gael International Affairs Committee. Assistant General Secretary, European Union of Young Christian Democrats. Member, Women's Political Association.
ADDRESS: MOUNT ALTO, GLANMIRE, COUNTY CORK (ADDRESS WHILE IN SEANAD)

MIRIAM KEARNEY was the youngest member of the Upper House during her tenure.

Patsy Lawlor

DATE/PLACE OF BIRTH: MARCH 1933/KILL, COUNTY KILDARE
PARTY: FINE GAEL
CONSTITUENCY: CULTURAL & EDUCATIONAL PANEL,
NOMINATING BODIES SUB-PANEL
SEANAD: 12 AUGUST 1981-20 APRIL 1982
AGE AT ENTRY TO SEANAD: 48
FAMILY: MARRIED TO TONY LAWLOR; ONE DAUGHTER, THREE SONS
EDUCATION: KILL NATIONAL SCHOOL. ST MARY'S SECONDARY SCHOOL, NAAS, COUNTY KILDARE
OCCUPATION: NURSE. BUSINESSWOMAN
CAREER:
Member, Kildare County Council, 1974. First woman Chair, Kildare County Council and Kildare VEC. Member, General Council of County Councils, 1979; Vice-chairperson, 1980-81; chairperson, 1981-2. Chairperson, Kildare Vocational Education Committee, 1979. Chairperson, County Kildare Library Committee, 1974-80. Member, Kildare County Committee of

Agriculture. Founder Kill Guild, ICA, 1961; national President ICA, 1976-9. Member, Arts Council, 1975-8; Irish Council for the European Movement 1977-9.

DATE OF DEATH: FEBRUARY 1998

ADDRESS: JOHNSTOWN HOUSE, NAAS, COUNTY KILDARE

PATSY LAWLOR contested the 1981 general election as a Fine Gael candidate in the Kildare constituency; she was defeated by less than fifty votes. In 1985 she stood for election to the board of the Bank of Ireland, an exclusive male preserve for more than two centuries, and was defeated by 120 votes to 50.

1982 Seanad Election: 21 April 1982 ——————————————————

Women Members

BARNES, MONICA (*SEE P. 127*) (FG, PANEL MEMBER, LABOUR PANEL, OIREACHTAS SUB PANEL)

BOLGER, DEIRDRE (*SEE P. 193*) (FG, PANEL MEMBER, INDUSTRIAL & COMMERCIAL PANEL, OIREACHTAS SUB PANEL)

BULBULIA, KATHARINE (*SEE P. 193*) (FG, PANEL MEMBER, ADMINISTRATIVE PANEL, NOMINATING BODIES SUB PANEL)

HANNON CAMILLA (FF, NOMINATED MEMBER) (NOMINATED BY TAOISEACH – CHARLES HAUGHEY – 10 MAY 1982)

HONAN, TRAS (*SEE P. 190*) (FF, PANEL MEMBER, ADMINISTRATIVE PANEL, NOMINATING BODIES SUB-PANEL)

O'ROURKE, MARY (*SEE P. 130*) (FF, PANEL MEMBER, CULTURAL & EDUCATIONAL PANEL, OIREACHTAS SUB PANEL)

ROBINSON, MARY T.W. (*SEE P. 181*) (LAB, UNIVERSITY MEMBER, UNIVERSITY OF DUBLIN)

TAYLOR-QUINN, MADELEINE (*SEE P. 123*) (FG, PANEL MEMBER, CULTURAL & EDUCATIONAL PANEL, NOMINATING BODIES SUB-PANEL)

Camilla Hannon, née Begley

DATE OF BIRTH: 21 JULY 1936/BALLYMOTE, COUNTY SLIGO

PARTY: FIANNA FÁIL

CONSTITUENCY: TAOISEACH'S NOMINEE (NOMINATED BY CHARLES J HAUGHEY)

SEANAD: 10 MAY 1982-30 JANUARY 1983

AGE AT ENTRY TO SEANAD: 45

FAMILY: MARRIED TO JOSEPH HANNON, A DAIRY FARMER; TWO DAUGHTERS, THREE SONS

EDUCATION: MERCY CONVENT, BALLYMOTE, COUNTY SLIGO. LORETO ABBEY, RATHFARNHAM

OCCUPATION: HOMEMAKER

CAREER:

President, ICA, 1979-82; Member since 1971. Member, EEC Committee on Social and Family matters. Member, World Association of Countrywomen. In January 1982 appointed to ACOT, the Agriculture Council, Boyle, County Roscommon. Particular policy interests: women's affairs, agriculture, Third World. Other interests: winner of five Leinster League titles, four Leinster

Cups and three All-Ireland titles with Loreto Past Hockey Club. Member of Leinster Senior Hockey team for four years and substitute on the Irish team.

ADDRESS: DERRYPATRICK, DRUMREE, COUNTY MEATH

1983 Seanad Election: 31 January 1983 ————————————————

Women Members

BULBULIA, KATHARINE (*SEE P. 193*) (FG, PANEL MEMBER, ADMINISTRATIVE PANEL, NOMINATING BODIES SUB PANEL)

FENNELL, NUALA (*SEE P. 116*) (FG, NOMINATED MEMBER (CASUAL VACANCY)). NOMINATED 20 FEBRUARY 1987)

HONAN, TRAS (*SEE P. 190*) (FF, PANEL MEMBER, ADMINISTRATIVE PANEL, NOMINATING BODIES SUB-PANEL)

MCAULIFFE-ENNIS, HELEN (LAB, PANEL MEMBER, CULTURAL & EDUCATIONAL PANEL, OIREACHTAS SUB PANEL)

MCGUINNESS, CATHERINE (*SEE P. 191*) (IND, UNIVERSITY MEMBER; UNIVERSITY OF DUBLIN)

ROGERS, BRÍD (IND, NOMINATED MEMBER) (NOMINATED BY TAOISEACH – GARRET FITZGERALD – 7 FEBRUARY 1983)

ROBINSON, MARY T.W. (*SEE P. 181*) (LAB, UNIVERSITY MEMBER, UNIVERSITY OF DUBLIN)

Helena McAuliffe-Ennis

DATE/PLACE OF BIRTH: 1 APRIL 1951/MILLTOWNPASS, COUNTY WESTMEATH

PARTY: LABOUR, 1970S-1985; PROGRESSIVE DEMOCRATS, 1985-7; LABOUR, 1988 TO DATE

CONSTITUENCIES: CULTURAL & EDUCATION PANEL

SEANAD: 31 JANUARY 1983-13 APRIL 1987

AGE AT ENTRY TO SEANAD: 31

FAMILY: DAUGHTER OF TIMOTHY MCAULIFFE (LAB, SENATOR, CULTURAL & EDUCATION PANEL 1961-9, 1973-83)

EDUCATION: MILLTOWNPASS NATIONAL SCHOOL TO 1963; ROCHFORDBRIDGE NATIONAL SCHOOL 1963-4; SCOIL CAITRÍONA, ECCLES STREET, DUBLIN, 1964-8; CRAIGLOCKHART COLLEGE OF EDUCATION, TEACHER TRAINING COLLEGE, EDINBURGH 1969-72; NUI MAYNOOTH 1989-90 (POST GRAD DIP. IN ADULT AND COMMUNITY EDUCATION)

OCCUPATION: ADULT LITERACY ORGANISER

CAREER:

Member, Joint Committee on Small Businesses, 1985-9; Westmeath County Council, 1985-90/91; Westmeath VEC until local elections, 1991. Fundraiser, IWA, Parents and Friends of Mentally Handicapped, Order of St Camillus – Hospice/Terminal Care. Local community activist. *Particular policy interests*: education and children's rights.

ADDRESS: 22 CHESTNUT GROVE, MULLINGAR

Bríd Rodgers, née Stratford

DATE/PLACE OF BIRTH: 20 FEBRUARY 1935/GWEEDORE, COUNTY DONEGAL

PARTY: INDEPENDENT (NO WHIP)

CONSTITUENCY: TAOISEACH'S NOMINEE (NOMINATED BY GARRET FITZGERALD)

SEANAD: 7 FEBRUARY 1983-13 APRIL 1987

AGE AT ENTRY TO SEANAD: 47

FAMILY: MARRIED TO ANTOIN RODGERS; THREE DAUGHTERS, THREE SONS

EDUCATION: ST LOUIS CONVENT SECONDARY SCHOOL, MONAGHAN;
    UNIVERSITY COLLEGE, DUBLIN

OCCUPATION: SECONDARY SCHOOLTEACHER (LANGUAGES), 1957-60, 1988-92

CAREER:
Minister for Agriculture and Rural Development in power-sharing Northern Ireland Executive, 29 November 1999-11 February 2000 [date Executive was suspended], 30 May 2000 to date. Founder Member, Social Democratic and Labour Party (SDLP), Northern Ireland. Member, SDLP Executive, 1974-80, Chair 1978-80. General Secretary, SDLP, 1981-3. Member, Advisory Commission on Human Rights, 1977-80. Member, Craigavon Borough Council, 1985-93. Delegate, Brooke/Mayhew talks on political future of Northern Ireland, 1992-93. In 1991, appointed to a new Government water and sewage company. Member, Southern Education and Library Board. Delegate, Multi-Party Talks, 1996-8, and Chair, SDLP Negotiating Team at Multi-Party Talks which culminated in Belfast/Good Friday Agreement, 10 April 1998. Northern Ireland Assembly: Member for Upper Bann, 1998 to date. Member, Forum for Peace and Reconciliation, 1997. *Particular policy interests*: Education, human rights. *Other interests*: reading, music, golf.

ADDRESS: 20 CHURCH PLACE, LURGAN, COUNTY ARMAGH

BRÍD RODGERS is a native Irish speaker from Gweedore, County Donegal. She is related through her grandmother to Patrick MacGill of Glenties, author of *Children of the Dead End*. She has lived since 1960 in sectarian mid-Ulster. Her involvement in the civil rights movement and politics began in 1965 when she and her husband, also from Gweedore, were asked to become involved in the Campaign for Social Justice, the predecessor to the Northern Ireland Civil Rights Association. In 1969 she led the first civil rights march through Lurgan. She contested general elections in the Upper Bann constituency in 1987 and 1992.

She was the SDLP's political representative from 1995 during the various Drumcree disputes, providing an alternative nationalist viewpoint to that of local activists and republicans. She supported the Garvaghy Road Residents' Coalition in their attempts to prevent the Orange Order from marching in the predominantly nationalist area of Portadown.

1987 Seanad Election: 14 April 1987 _____

Women Members

KATHARINE BULBULIA (*SEE P. 193*) (FG, PANEL MEMBER, ADMINISTRATIVE PANEL, NOMINATING BODIES SUB PANEL)

FENNELL, NUALA (*SEE P. 116*) (FG, PANEL MEMBER, LABOUR PANEL, OIREACHTAS SUB PANEL)

HONAN, TRAS (*SEE P. 190*) (FF, PANEL MEMBER, ADMINISTRATIVE PANEL, NOMINATING BODIES SUB-PANEL)

ROBINSON, MARY T.W. (*SEE P. 181*) (LAB, UNIVERSITY MEMBER, UNIVERSITY OF DUBLIN)

WALLACE, MARY (*SEE P. 137*) (FF, PANEL MEMBER, ADMINISTRATIVE PANEL, OIREACHTAS SUB PANEL)

1989 Seanad Election: 16 August 1989 _____

Women Members

BENNETT, OLGA (FF, NOMINATED MEMBER) (NOMINATED BY TAOISEACH – CHARLES J. HAUGHEY – 27 OCTOBER 1989)

DOYLE, AVRIL (*SEE P. 129*) (FG, PANEL MEMBER, AGRICULTURAL PANEL, NOMINATING BODIES SUB PANEL)

HEDERMAN, CARMENCITA (IND, UNIVERSITY MEMBER; UNIVERSITY OF DUBLIN)

HONAN, TRAS (*SEE P. 190*) (FF, PANEL MEMBER, ADMINISTRATIVE PANEL, NOMINATING BODIES SUB-PANEL)

KEOGH, HELEN (*SEE P. 142*) (PD, NOMINATED MEMBER) (NOMINATED BY TAOISEACH – CHARLES J. HAUGHEY –27 OCTOBER 1989)

JACKMAN, MARY (FG, PANEL MEMBER, LABOUR PANEL, NOMINATING BODIES SUB-PANEL)

Olga Bennett

DATE/PLACE OF BIRTH: OCTOBER 1947/DUBLIN

PARTY: FIANNA FÁIL

CONSTITUENCY: TAOISEACH'S NOMINEE (NOMINATED BY CHARLES J. HAUGHEY)

SEANAD: 27 OCTOBER 1989-31 JANUARY 1993

AGE AT ENTRY TO SEANAD: 42

FAMILY: MARRIED TO EAMON BENNETT

EDUCATION: CONVENT OF MERCY DUBLIN. COLLEGE OF COMMERCE, RATHMINES, DUBLIN

OCCUPATION: FASHION BUYER

CAREER: Member, third Joint Committee on Women's Rights, 1989-92. Member, Dublin City Council, 1985.

ADDRESS: 104 INCHICORE ROAD, DUBLIN 18

OLGA BENNETT was a candidate in the 1989 General Election in the Dublin West constituency.

Carmencita Hederman, née Cruess-Callaghan

DATE/PLACE OF BIRTH: 23 OCTOBER 1939/DUBLIN
PARTY: INDEPENDENT
CONSTITUENCY: UNIVERSITY OF DUBLIN
SEANAD: 16 AUGUST 1989-31 JANUARY 1993
AGE AT ENTRY TO SEANAD: 49
FAMILY: MARRIED TO WILLIAM HEDERMAN (SURGEON, MATER HOSPITAL);
THREE DAUGHTERS, TWO SONS
EDUCATION: SACRED HEART CONVENTS, LEESON STREET, DUBLIN, AND WOLDINGHAM, SURREY;
    TRINITY COLLEGE DUBLIN (MA, 1964); SORBONNE, PARIS (FINE ARTS AND MODERN
    LANGUAGES); SCHOLARSHIP, INSTITUTO PALLADIO, VICENZA, FLORENCE. HONORARY DEGREE OF
    LAWS, TRINITY COLLEGE, DUBLIN (1988) AND NATIONAL UNIVERSITY OF IRELAND (1988)
OCCUPATION: BOARD MEMBER, FIRST ACTIVE PLC
CAREER:
Alderman, Dublin City Corporation (Community Group, i.e., non-party), 1974-99;
Commissioner for Irish Lights; Lord Mayor of Dublin, 1987-8. Director, First National Building
Society (head of its sponsorship of Tidy Towns Competition, 1989-91); Vice-chair, 1993;
Director, People in Need Trust; Board Member, Dublin City Food Bank; Life Governor, Royal
Hospital, Donnybrook; Governor, National Maternity Hospital, Holles Street; Founder, Upper
Leeson Street Area Residents' Association. Chair, Civics Institute, St Brigid's Nursery Centre.
Member, An Taisce – the National Trust; Women's Political Association; Irish Countrywoman's
Association; Cycle Action Trust; Inland Waterways Association; Irish Association for Cultural,
Economic and Social Relations; Editorial Board of *Studies*; Council Member, Friends of the
National Collections of Ireland. Honorary Member, An Óige, TCD Women's Graduates
Association. Patron, War on Want; AIDS Fund, Ballymun Job Centre Co-op; Alzheimer Society
of Ireland; Clongowes Youth Fundraising; Methodist Widows Home; Irish National Council for
Soviet Jewry; Kiltalown House, Tallaght; Friends of St Anne's Cancer Therapy; Carlingford
Lough Heritage Trust. *Other interests*: gardening, riding, patchwork.
ADDRESS: 92 UPPER LEESON STREET, DUBLIN 4

CARMENCITA HEDERMAN toured the United States as a guest of the Federal
Government, addressing local authorities and other bodies in the US
Bicentennial Year (1976). She travelled to Lisbon to meet mayors of EEC cities
during her year as Lord Mayor, and toured the US and Europe promoting
Ireland during the Dublin Millennium. She received the People of the Year
Award, 1988; the Spirit of Dublin Award, 1988; and was nominated for the
European of the Year Award, 1989.

Mary Jackman, née Furlong

DATE/PLACE OF BIRTH: APRIL, 1943/CAPPAWHITE, COUNTY TIPPERARY

PARTY: FINE GAEL

CONSTITUENCY: LABOUR PANEL, NOMINATING BODIES SUB-PANEL

SEANAD: 16 AUGUST 1989-31 JANUARY 1993. 7 AUGUST 1997 TO DATE

AGE AT ENTRY TO SEANAD: 46

FAMILY: DAUGHTER OF GEORGE FURLONG (INDEPENDENT CANDIDATE, TIPPERARY
NORTH, 1951 GENERAL ELECTION). GRANDDAUGHTER OF PATRICK DUGGAN
(MEMBER OF FIRST LIMERICK COUNTY COUNCIL, 1899)
MARRIED TO NICHOLAS JACKMAN; ONE DAUGHTER

EDUCATION: CONVENT OF MERCY, DOON, COUNTY LIMERICK; UNIVERSITY COLLEGE CORK

OCCUPATION: SECONDARY SCHOOLTEACHER

CAREER:
Member, Third Joint Committee on Women's Rights, 1989-92. Member, Joint Committee on
Health and Children, 1997. Member, Limerick County Council, 1985; Cathaoirleach, 1998.
Member, County Limerick VEC, 1985. Chairperson, Network, 1987. Member, Association of
Secondary Teachers of Ireland. Member, National Council, Fine Gael.

ADDRESS: 5 NEWTOWN, CASTLETROY, LIMERICK

MARY JACKMAN contested the June 1989 general election in Limerick East for
Fine Gael. She was unsuccessful but was elected to the Seanad in August of the
same year — the first woman Senator from Limerick. On 24 July 1998 she
became the first woman Cathaoirleach of Limerick County Council in its 100-
year history. She was also the first woman to receive an ASTI nomination.

1993 Seanad Election: 1 February 1993 ————————————————————————

Women Members

GALLAGHER, ANN (LAB, PANEL MEMBER, INDUSTRIAL & COMMERCIAL PANEL, OIREACHTAS SUB-PANEL)

HENRY MARY, E.F. (IND, UNIVERSITY MEMBER, UNIVERSITY OF DUBLIN)

HONAN, CATHY (PD, PANEL MEMBER, INDUSTRIAL & COMMERCIAL PANEL, OIREACHTAS SUB-PANEL)

KELLY, MARY (LAB, CULTURAL & EDUCATIONAL PANEL, OIREACHTAS SUB-PANEL)

McGENNIS, MARIAN (*SEE P. 152*) (FF, (NOMINATED MEMBER, NOMINATED BY TAOISEACH –
ALBERT REYNOLDS –10 FEBRUARY 1993)

ORMONDE, ANN (FF, PANEL MEMBER, CULTURAL & EDUCATIONAL PANEL, NOMINATING BODIES
SUB PANEL)

O'SULLIVAN, JAN (*SEE P. 154*) (LAB, PANEL MEMBER, ADMINISTRATIVE PANEL, OIREACHTAS SUB-PANEL)

TAYLOR-QUINN, MADELEINE (*SEE P. 123*) (FG, CULTURAL & EDUCATIONAL PANEL, NOMINATING
BODIES SUB-PANEL)

Casual Vacancies ——————————————————————————————

BHREATHNACH, NIAMH (*SEE P. 139*) (LAB, NOMINATED MEMBER, NOMINATED BY TAOISEACH –
JOHN BRUTON – 13 JUNE 1997)

COSGRAVE, NIAMH (NOMINATED MEMBER, NOMINATED BY TAOISEACH – JOHN BRUTON –
13 JUNE 1997)

Ann Gallagher

DATE/PLACE OF BIRTH: MARCH 1967/DONEGAL

PARTY: LABOUR

CONSTITUENCY: INDUSTRIAL & COMMERCIAL PANEL, OIREACHTAS SUB-PANEL

SEANAD: 1 FEBRUARY 1993-6 AUGUST 1997

AGE AT ENTRY TO SEANAD: 25

FAMILY: GREAT-GRANDNIECE OF JOHN HANNIGAN (CUMANN NA NGAEDHEAL
    DEPUTY SLIGO/LEITRIM, 1922-33)

EDUCATION: KINLOUGH, COUNTY LEITRIM; ST LOUIS SECONDARY SCHOOL, COUNTY DONEGAL;
    TRINITY COLLEGE, DUBLIN

OCCUPATION: PUBLIC REPRESENTATIVE

CAREER:
Member, Joint Committee on Women's Rights, 1993-7. Member, Forum for Peace and
Reconciliation, 1997.

ADDRESS: YORK STREET, CASTLEBLAYNEY, COUNTY MONAGHAN (WHILE IN SEANAD)

ANN GALLAGHER was an unsuccessful Dáil candidate in Cavan–Monaghan in the
1992 general election. She was the youngest member of the Seanad on taking up
office in 1993.

Mary E.F. Henry

DATE/PLACE OF BIRTH: 11 MAY 1940/BLACKROCK, CORK

PARTY: INDEPENDENT

CONSTITUENCY: UNIVERSITY OF DUBLIN, TRINITY COLLEGE

SEANAD: 1 FEBRUARY 1993 TO DATE

AGE AT ENTRY TO SEANAD: 52

FAMILY: MARRIED TO JOHN MCENTAGART; ONE DAUGHTER, TWO SONS

EDUCATION: ST MICHAEL'S NATIONAL SCHOOL, BLACKROCK, CORK;
    ROCHELLE SCHOOL, CORK; ALEXANDRA COLLEGE, DUBLIN; UNIVERSITY OF DUBLIN (TRINITY
    COLLEGE) (FIRST NON-FOUNDATION SCHOLAR IN MEDICINE, 1962; BA IN ENGLISH AND HISTORY OF
    MEDICINE, 1963; MB (HONOURS) (1965), MA (1966), MD (1968). OVER A DOZEN ACADEMIC
    PRIZES)

OCCUPATION: MEDICAL PRACTITIONER

CAREER:
Member, Joint Committee on Women's Rights, 1995; Joint Committee on Enterprise and Small
Business, 1997. Member, British-Irish Interparliamentary Body. Consultant, Varicose Veins and
Thromboembolic Clinics, Rotunda Hospital and Adelaide Hospital, Dublin. Editor, *Trinity
Alumni Medical News*. Member, Ethics Committee of the Irish Hospitals Consultant Association.
President, The Irish Association (which promotes cross-border co-operation). Trustee, Trinity
College Dublin Association and Trust. Member, Royal Irish Academy of Medicine. Member,
Council of Alexandra College, Dublin. Member, European Parliamentary Network on

HIV/AIDS. Member, National Economic and Social Forum. Governor, Adelaide Hospital, Dublin. Patron, Irish Raynaud's and Scleroderma Society. Member, Comhairle na n-Ospidéal, 1992. President, Cherish. Patron, Irish Penal Reform Trust. Member, European Committee of the International Medical Parliamentarians' Organisation. Alternate Delegate, Forum for Peace and Reconciliation. Chairperson, Fund-raising Committee of the Rape Crisis Centre. Member, Board of the Well Woman Centre. Member, Irish Congress of Trade Unions Advisory Committee on Women's Health. Member, Executive of the Irish Red Cross, Chairperson of Overseas Committee. Member, National Health Council of Ireland. President, Dublin Biological Society, Trinity College Dublin 1986-7. Founder Member, Women's Political Association. Member, Postgraduate Medical and Dental Board. Member, Rotunda Hospital Research Committee. Member, Eastern Health Board. Council Member, Irish Medical Organisation. Member, Government Committee to establish Sexual Assault Unit.

ADDRESS: 12 BURLINGTON ROAD, DUBLIN 4

MARY HENRY initiated adjournment debates on topics from the need to promote Irish-made goods to the problem of Ecstasy consumption in nightclubs. During Private Members' Time she initiated debates on the prison and probation services. Her Private Member's Bill, *Child Sex Tours Bill, 1995*, to stop child-sex tourism was incorporated into a government *Sexual Offences (Jurisdiction) Act, 1996*. Amendments put forward or supported by her — such as to the *Powers of Attorney Bill, 1995* and the *Refugee Bill, 1995* — were frequently accepted.

She opposed the *Universities Bill, 1996* because of anxieties about the autonomy of Trinity. After her extensive amendments, the *Universities Act, 1997*, providing for the appointment of government nominees to university boards, and promoting the aim of the Dublin Institute of Technology to become a university, became acceptable to the board of Trinity and was passed, although a private Bill was required in 2000 to facilitate Trinity's compliance. She introduced a Private Member's Bill, *Regulation of Assisted Human Reproduction Bill, 1999*, to regulate in-vitro fertilisation, which was defeated at Second Stage. The government responded by saying that it would ask the Law Reform Commission to study the subject. Privately, Mary Henry is a supporter of the Labour Party.

Cathy Honan, née O'Brien

DATE/PLACE OF BIRTH: 16 SEPTEMBER 1951/CLONMEL, COUNTY TIPPERARY
PARTY: PROGRESSIVE DEMOCRATS
CONSTITUENCY: INDUSTRIAL & COMMERCIAL PANEL, OIREACHTAS SUB-PANEL
SEANAD: 1 FEBRUARY 1993-6 AUGUST 1997
AGE AT ENTRY TO SEANAD: 41
FAMILY: MARRIED TO ADRIAN HONAN; THREE SONS
EDUCATION: PRESENTATION CONVENT, CLONMEL; UNIVERSITY COLLEGE CORK (BCOMM)
OCCUPATION: ACCOUNTANT

CAREER:
Member, Laois County Council 1991-9; its Finance and Arts Committees. Member, Second Commission on the Status of Women. Member, National Economic and Social Forum. Member, An Taisce, Amnesty International, Women's Political Association. *Particular policy interests:* equal participation of women in all aspects of life. Equal opportunity for all to benefit from economic growth. Other interests: theatre, art galleries, hill-walking, tennis, travel.

ADDRESS: AUSTEN HOUSE, PORTARLINGTON, COUNTY LAOIS (WHILE IN SEANAD)

Mary Kelly

DATE/PLACE OF BIRTH: MAY 1952/CROOM, COUNTY LIMERICK

PARTY: LABOUR

CONSTITUENCY: CULTURAL AND EDUCATIONAL PANEL, OIREACHTAS SUB PANEL

SEANAD: 1 FEBRUARY 1993-6 AUGUST 1997

AGE AT ENTRY TO SEANAD: 40

FAMILY: MARRIED TO SEÁN KELLY; SIX DAUGHTERS

EDUCATION: SCOIL CARMEL, LIMERICK; UNIVERSITY COLLEGE CORK (BA, H.DIP.ED.)

OCCUPATION: TEACHER AND BOOKSHOP PROPRIETOR

CAREER:
Member, Joint Committee on the Irish Language, 1993-7. Chairperson, Task Force on the Travelling Community; Member, Limerick County Council 1991-9. Member, VEC. Member, Macra Na Feirme, 1973-6. Member, Newcastle West Chamber of Commerce, 1990.

PUBLICATIONS:
Report of the Task Force on the Travelling Community (Pn. 1726, Dublin: Stationery Office, July 1995).

ADDRESS: MAIDEN STREET, NEWCASTLE WEST, COUNTY LIMERICK

Ann Ormonde

PLACE OF BIRTH: KILMACTHOMAS, COUNTY WATERFORD

PARTY: FIANNA FÁIL

CONSTITUENCY: CULTURAL & EDUCATIONAL PANEL, NOMINATING BODIES SUB-PANEL

SEANAD: 1 FEBRUARY 1993-6 AUGUST 1997. 7 AUGUST 1997 TO DATE

FAMILY: DAUGHTER OF JOHN ORMONDE (FIANNA FÁIL MINISTER, WATERFORD, 1947-65). SISTER OF DONAL ORMONDE (TD FOR WATERFORD, NOVEMBER 1982-3)

EDUCATION: UNIVERSITY COLLEGE DUBLIN (MA (PSYCH.), BCOMM, H.DIP.ED., DIPLOMA IN CAREER GUIDANCE

OCCUPATION: CAREER GUIDANCE COUNSELLOR

CAREER:
Member, Joint Committee on Education and Science, 1997. Alternate Member, Forum for Peace and Reconciliation, 1997. Member, Dublin County Council, 1985, now South Dublin County

Council; Planning, Environment, Community and Parks Committees; County Dublin VEC. Member, Boards of Management, Firhouse, Deansrath and Stillorgan Community Colleges.

ADDRESS: 2 AUBURN ROAD, DUBLIN 4

ANN ORMONDE contested the general elections of 1987, 1989, 1992 and 1997.

Niamh Cosgrave

DATE/PLACE OF BIRTH: 9 OCTOBER 1964/DUBLIN

PARTY: FINE GAEL

CONSTITUENCY: TAOISEACH'S NOMINEE (CASUAL VACANCY)

(NOMINATED BY JOHN BRUTON)

SEANAD: 13 JUNE-6 AUGUST 1997

AGE AT ENTRY TO SEANAD: 32

FAMILY: DAUGHTER OF MICHAEL JOE COSGRAVE (TD FOR DUBLIN-CLONTARF AND DUBLIN NORTH EAST, 1977-92, 1997 TO DATE). MARRIED TO MYLES DUNNE; THREE SONS

EDUCATION: ST MARY'S PRIMARY AND SECONDARY SCHOOL, BALDOYLE, DUBLIN; CERTIFICATE IN SUPERVISORY MANAGEMENT, IRISH MANAGEMENT INSTITUTE

OCCUPATION: TECHNICAL WRITER AT COMPUTER FIRM

CAREER: Member, Dublin Borough Council, Donaghmede ward, 1999. *Particular policy interests*: healthcare, childcare, senior citizens, housing.

ADDRESS: 6 FOXFIELD ROAD, RAHENY, DUBLIN 5

NIAMH COSGRAVE joined the Fine Gael party at the age of 14. She missed a seat for the Donaghmede ward by one vote in the 1991 local elections. In 1994, she discovered that she had Hepatitis C as a result of receiving a contaminated blood product. She stood in the 1997 general election for Fine Gael in Dublin North-Central. She campaigned for restitution for people affected by Hepatitis C induced by contaminated blood. Her filling of the Seanad vacancy had a political importance as members of the Oireachtas are entitled to vote in the election for the new Seanad.

My aim was always to get into politics, but I had put my life on hold because I didn't know what was wrong with me.

THE IRISH TIMES, 29 MAY 1997

1997 Seanad Election: 7 August 1997 ——————————————————

Women Members

Cox, Margaret (FF, Panel Member, Industrial & Commercial Panel, Oireachtas Sub Panel)

Doyle, Avril (*see p. 129*) (FG, Panel Member, Agricultural Panel, Nominating Bodies Sub Panel)

Henry, Mary (*see p. 201*) (Ind, University Member; University of Dublin)

Jackman, Mary (*see p. 200*) (FG, Panel Member, Labour Panel, Nominating Bodies Sub Panel)

Keogh, Helen (*see p. 142*) (PD, Nominated Member) (Nominated by Taoiseach – Bertie Ahern – 12 September 1997)

Leonard, Ann (FF, Nominated Member) (Nominated by Taoiseach – Bertie Ahern – 12 September 1997)

O'Meara, Kathleen (Lab, Panel Member, Agriculture Panel, Oireachtas Sub-Panel)

Ormonde, Ann (*see p. 203*) (FF, Panel Member, Cultural & Educational Panel, Nominating Bodies Sub-Panel)

Quill, Máirín (*see p. 135*) (PD, Nominated Member) (Nominated by Taoiseach – Bertie Ahern – 12 September 1997)

Ridge, Therese (FG, Panel Member, Labour Panel, Nominating Bodies Sub Panel)

Taylor-Quinn, Madeleine (*see p. 123*) (FG, Panel Member, Cultural & Educational Panel)

Margaret Cox

Date/Place of Birth: September 1963/Birmingham, England

Party: Fianna Fáil

Constituency: Industrial & Commercial Panel, Oireachtas Sub-Panel

Seanad: 7 August 1997 to date

Age at Entry to Seanad: 34

Family: Married to Felim McDonnell; two daughters, two sons

Education: Meánscoil Mhuire, Galway; University of Limerick (Dip. Personnel Management; Dip. Accounting and Finance); University College Galway (Dip. System Analysis)

Occupation: Managing director, ICE Group, Galway

Career:
Member, Joint Committee on Enterprise and Small Business, 1997. Member, Joint House Services Committee, 1997. Fianna Fáil Spokesperson for Enterprise, Trade and Employment. Member, Western Health Board; Western Regional Authority; Galway County and City Enterprise Board; General Council of County Councils. Member of Galway County Council, 1995; Galway Corporation, 1999.

Address: 7 Father Griffin Road, Galway

Margaret Cox stood in the Dáil general election in 1997.

Ann Leonard

DATE/PLACE OF BIRTH: JANUARY 1969/SMITHSBORO, COUNTY MONAGHAN
PARTY: FIANNA FÁIL
CONSTITUENCY: TAOISEACH'S NOMINEE (NOMINATED BY BERTIE AHERN)
SEANAD: 12 SEPTEMBER 1997 TO DATE
AGE AT ENTRY TO SEANAD: 28
FAMILY: DAUGHTER OF JIMMY LEONARD (TD, CAVAN/MONAGHAN, 1973-97)
EDUCATION: ST LOUIS SECONDARY SCHOOL, MONAGHAN; ST PATRICK'S COLLEGE,
MAYNOOTH; OUR LADY'S HOSPITAL FOR SICK CHILDREN, CRUMLIN; IRISH INSTITUTE OF
REFLEXOLOGISTS; ROTUNDA HOSPITAL; THE MISSIONARY TRAINING HOSPITAL, DROGHEDA
OCCUPATION: PAEDIATRIC NURSE. MIDWIFE.
CAREER:
Member, Joint Committee on Family, Community and Social Affairs, 1997; Monaghan County
Council, 1999. Secretary, Monaghan Fianna Fáil Women's Forum since it was established in 1993.
ADDRESS: STRANAGARVAGH, SMITHBORO, COUNTY MONAGHAN

ANN LEONARD contested the Dáil seat held by her father, Jimmy, in
Cavan–Monaghan in the general election of 1997.

Kathleen O'Meara

DATE/PLACE OF BIRTH: JANUARY 1960/ROSCREA, COUNTY TIPPERARY
PARTY: LABOUR
CONSTITUENCY: AGRICULTURE PANEL, OIREACHTAS SUB-PANEL
SEANAD: 7 AUGUST 1997 TO DATE
AGE AT ENTRY TO SEANAD: 37
FAMILY: MARRIED TO KEVIN DOLAN; ONE DAUGHTER, ONE SON
EDUCATION: SACRED HEART COLLEGE, ROSCREA; UNIVERSITY COLLEGE, GALWAY
(BA (HONS)), ENGLISH, HISTORY). NATIONAL INSTITUTE FOR
HIGHER EDUCATION, DUBLIN (DIPLOMA IN JOURNALISM)
OCCUPATION: JOURNALIST
CAREER:
Member, Joint Committee on Health and Children, 1997. Member, Joint Committee on Justice,
Equality and Women's Rights, 1998; its Sub-Committee on Women's Rights, 1998. Member, All-
Party Oireachtas Committee on the Constitution and allied Joint Committee on the Constitution,
May 2000 (which conducted public hearings on abortion). Special Adviser to Minister of State,
Eithne Fitzgerald (*see p. 141*) 1994-7, working on press and media relations and legislation,
including the Freedom of Information Act. Press Officer for Labour Party 1985-8. Journalist in
RTÉ newsroom, 1988-94, working on *Morning Ireland, News at One, Oireachtas Report* and
the foreign desk. Freelance journalist, 1983-4.
ADDRESS: LISHEEN, PORTROE, NENAGH, COUNTY TIPPERARY

KATHLEEN O'MEARA was a candidate in the general election of 1997 in the
Tipperary North constituency.

Therese Ridge

DATE/PLACE OF BIRTH: MARCH 1941/DUBLIN

PARTY: FINE GAEL

CONSTITUENCY: LABOUR PANEL, NOMINATING BODIES SUB-PANEL

SEANAD: 7 AUGUST 1997 TO DATE

FAMILY: MARRIED TO JAMES RIDGE; TWO DAUGHTERS, ONE SON

EDUCATION: GOLDENBRIDGE COLLEGE, DUBLIN; ST PATRICK'S COLLEGE,
MAYNOOTH

OCCUPATION: TEACHER; EXTERNAL TUTOR, MAYNOOTH ADULT EDUCATION DEPARTMENT

AGE AT ENTRY TO SEANAD 56

CAREER:

Member, Joint Committee on Family, Community and Social Affairs, 1997. Member, Dublin County Council, 1985-93; Chairperson 1992-3; Member South Dublin County Council since 1993; chairman 1996-7. Chairperson, Irish Pre-School Playgroups Association. *Particular policy interests*: Fine Gael Seanad Spokeswoman for Family, Community and Social Affairs.

ADDRESS: 4 ST PATRICK'S AVENUE, CLONDALKIN, DUBLIN 22

The inauguration ceremony of Mary Robinson as President of Ireland, 3 December 1990. (Courtesy *The Irish Times*)

The Presidency

Under Articles 12–14 of the 1937 Constitution, the President is the head of State, elected by popular vote for a seven-year term. The President is also commander-in-chief of the armed forces, though this command is 'regulated by law'. Éamon de Valera stated in 1937 that the President's function was 'to guard the people's rights and mainly to guard the constitution'. Most of the President's powers and functions are exercised on the advice of the Government and on the advice of the Council of State, whose function is 'to aid and counsel the President' on the matters defined by the constitution. The President cannot leave the State without the Government's permission; an address to the Oireachtas must be approved by the Government; and the President can be impeached, although this process requires a two-thirds majority of the Oireachtas.

The most important discretionary powers exercised on the President's own initiative are: to refuse 'in his absolute discretion' a dissolution to a Taoiseach who has no Dáil majority; to convene a meeting of the Oireachtas after consulting the Council of State; and to refer a bill to the Supreme Court for a decision on its constitutionality.

Prior to 1990 there were no women candidates for the presidency.

1990: Presidential Election: 7 November 1990

Elected: Mary Robinson (*see p. 181*)

The Presidential election of 1990 was contested by three candidates: Austin Currie, member of Dáil Éireann; Brian Lenihan, Tánaiste and Minister for Defence; Mary Robinson, Senior Counsel. The result of the voting was as follows:

Electorate:	2,471,308	**Total Valid Poll**:	1,574,65163	72 per cent
Percentage Poll:	64.10	**Spoiled Votes**:	9,4440	60 per cent
Total Poll:	1,584.095	**Quota**:	787,326	

	First Count			**Second Count**			
Candidate	Party	1st Pref	%	Transfer of Currie' vote	%	Result	%
Currie	FG	267,902	17.01	-267,902			
Lenihan	FF	694,484	44.10	+36,789	13.73	731,273	47.21
Robinson	NP	612,265	38.89	+205,565	76.73	817,830	52.79
Non-trans papers		—		25,548	9.54		
Total		1,574,651	100.00		100.00	1,549,103	100.00

1997: Presidential Election: 30 October 1997 _____

Elected: Mary McAleese

The presidential election of 1997 was contested initially by four women: Mary Banotti, Member of the European Parliament, nominated by Fine Gael; Mary McAleese, university professor, nominated by Fianna Fáil; Adi Roche, charity worker, nominated by Labour, Democratic Left and the Greens; and Dana Rosemary Scallon, entertainer, nominated by the county councillors of Donegal, Kerry, Wicklow, Longford and Tipperary North. By nominating only women candidates, it seemed that the parties in their selection processes were hoping to emulate the Mary Robinson phenomenon. This scenario was attracting international headlines. Then Derek Nally, a company director from County Wexford, gained a nomination from a sufficient number of local authorities to enter the race, declaring that the voters should have the choice of a male candidate. The result of the voting was as follows:

Electorate:	2,688.316	Total Valid Poll	1,269,836	47.24 per cent
Percentage Poll:	64.10	Spoiled Votes	9,852	0.77 per cent
Total Poll:	1,279.688	Quota	634,919	

Candidate	Party	First Count 1st Pref	%	Second Count Transfer of Nally, Roche & Scallon's Vote	%	Result	%
Banotti	FG	372,002	29.30	+125,514	38.81	497,516	41.35
McAleese	FF	574,424	45.24	+131,835	40.76	706,259	58.67
Nally	NP	59,529	4.69	-59,529			
Roche	NP	88,423	6.96	-88,423			
Scallon	NP	175,458	13.82	-175,458			
Non-trans. papers				66,061	20.43		
Total		1,269,836	100.00		100.00	1,203,775	100.00

Elected: Mary McAleese

Mary McAleese, née Leneghan

DATE/PLACE OF BIRTH: 27 JUNE 1951/BELFAST

PARTY: FIANNA FÁIL

CONSTITUENCY: REPUBLIC OF IRELAND

PRESIDENCY: 30 OCTOBER 1997 TO DATE

AGE AT ENTRY TO PRESIDENCY: 46

FAMILY: MARRIED MARTIN MCALEESE, 1976; TWO DAUGHTERS, ONE SON

EDUCATION: ST DOMINIC'S HIGH SCHOOL, FALLS ROAD, BELFAST; QUEEN'S UNIVERSITY BELFAST; INNS OF COURT OF NORTHERN IRELAND, KING'S INNS, DUBLIN, UNIVERSITY OF DUBLIN. LLB, MA, MILL, FRSA. HON. LLD (QUEEN'S, BELFAST), (NOTTINGHAM), 1998

OCCUPATION: BARRISTER. LAW LECTURER. UNIVERSITY ADMINISTRATOR.

CAREER:
Pro-Vice-Chancellor, Queen's University Belfast, 1994-7; Director of the Institute of Professional Legal Studies, 1987-97. Director, Channel 4 Television, 1993-7; of Northern Ireland Electricity Plc, 1992-7, and Chairwoman of its remuneration committee; of Royal Group of Hospitals Trust. Delegate to 1995 White House Conference on Trade and Investment in Ireland and follow-up Pittsburgh Conference in 1996. Member, Campaign for Homosexual Law Reform, 1977. Co-founder of Belfast Women's Aid refuge; Chairperson, Royal Victoria Hospital's complaints board. Member, Strategy for Sport steering group; Northern Ireland Rapporteur for International Bar Association. Honorary President, Newry and Mourne Royal College of Midwives Association; Northern Ireland Housing Rights Association. Member, National Institute of Trial Advocacy in Britain and Northern Ireland; British and Irish Legal Technology Association; Society of Public Teachers of Law; European Bar Association; Institute of Advanced Legal Studies.

PUBLICATIONS:
The Irish Martyrs, 1995; *Reconciled Being*; *Love in Chaos: Spiritual Growth and the Search for Peace in Northern Ireland*, 1997. Academic articles on crime, punishment, prisons and childcare in custody, e.g., 'Just what is recklessness?' *Dublin University Law Journal*, 1981. McCarthy, Justine, *Mary McAleese: The Outsider*, Dublin: Blackwater, 1999

ADDRESS: ÁRAS AN UACHTARÁIN, PHOENIX PARK, DUBLIN 8

MARY MCALEESE's early experiences included privilege and suffering. She witnessed and experienced in her Belfast neighbourhood the effects of violence and sectarian hatred. Her brother was beaten, her home was attacked and a bomb exploded outside her father's business in Belfast.

On graduation from Queen's University, Belfast, in 1973, she became a barrister and was called to the Northern Ireland Bar in 1974, where she specialised mainly in criminal and family law. From 1975 to 1979, she was Reid Professor of Criminal Law, Criminology and Penology in Trinity College, Dublin, engaging in research on the Constitution, prisons, computerisation of prison records, child custody and attitudes to crime. In 1979, she joined RTÉ as a current affairs journalist and presenter on *Frontline* and *Today Tonight*. She returned to the Reid Professorship at Trinity in 1981, continuing with RTÉ, presenting the first dedicated EU current affairs programme, *Europa*, and a current affairs programme, *Studio 10*. She was involved in the campaigns to have a ban on abortion added to the Constitution and the ban on divorce retained.

In 1987, she was appointed Director of the Institute on Legal Studies, which trains barristers and solicitors for the legal profession in Northern Ireland, and set about reinventing the Institute as a pioneering department in Queen's University. She is familiar with sign language and introduced the first module in sign language in a European legal training module.

In 1994 Mary McAleese was appointed Pro-Vice-Chancellor, the first woman in the history of the university to hold one of the three Pro-Vice-Chancellor positions. She established outreach campuses of Queen's at Armagh and Omagh, and developed links between these and Dublin City University and other universities in the Republic of Ireland. She has spoken as a guest lecturer at Minneapolis, the International School, Paris, Bristol University, and Newcastle University. She was a course consultant at Nottingham Law School, and an external examiner for the King's Inns, Dublin.

She is fluent in Spanish and is a Member of the Institute of Linguists. She has a long-standing interest in the rights of the disabled, and in the implementation and management of change, particularly equal opportunities and fair employment.

In May 1983 Mary McAleese was a delegate to the Ecumenical Conference in Ballymascanlan and became involved in Corrymeela, an interdenominational peace group. In 1983 also she was co-opted onto a working group of the Council for Social Welfare, which reported to the Catholic Bishops' Conference. She promoted the Church's moral teaching on contraception, abortion and divorce, and forged a reputation as an able and influential lay Catholic. She stood out as the only woman member of the Catholic Church Episcopal Delegation to the New Ireland Forum in 1984, arguing in opposition to Senator Mary Robinson (*see p. 181*) of the Labour Party against integrated education in Northern Ireland.

In February 1987 she stood unsuccessfully as a Fianna Fáil candidate in Dublin South East, added to the ticket by the National Executive with the backing of Charles Haughey.

In the 1990s she publicly criticised the Catholic Church for its exclusion of women from the priesthood, its anachronism, its position on the IRA, its handling of the Father Brendan Smyth case and some papal views. Her support for liberal causes such as homosexual law reform and woman priests, and also for conservative ones, such as opposition to contraception, abortion and divorce, made her difficult to pigeonhole.

In October 1995 she attended a celebration in St James's Palace for the 150th anniversary of Queen's, UCC and UCG. She was afterwards invited to a private lunch with Queen Elizabeth.

She was a founder member of the Irish Commission for Prisoners Overseas, and a campaigner on behalf of the Maguire family and the Birmingham Six. She was a member of the Catholic Church's five-person delegation, led by Cardinal Daly and Archbishop Sean Brady in December 1996, to the North Commission on Contentious Parades. In 1996 she became a member of Fr Alex Reid's Redemptorist Peace Ministry which worked to re-establish the second IRA ceasefire.

Mary McAleese has been the subject of Ulster Television and Radio documentaries. She has presented a series of radio programmes for BBC Radio 4 and was a regular contributor to newspapers, journals and radio and TV, and has been invited to be a guest lecturer in Sydney, Australia. She received the Gilmartin Medal for a lecture she gave at the Royal College of Surgeons in Dublin in 1996.

During her presidential campaign, and again at her inauguration, Mary McAleese announced that bridge-building across the sectarian and political divides would be the theme of her presidency. In December 1997 she gave tan-gible expression to this promise by taking communion at a Church of Ireland service in Christ Church Cathedral. It was an unexpected move which Church of Ireland clergy believed may have been the first for an Irish President from the Roman Catholic tradition. The Catholic hierarchy, including the Archbishopof Dublin, announced their disapproval on the grounds that this action wascontrary to Canon Law. An opinion poll, however, showed an over-whelming approval of her stance.

In general, she retreated from the fray to exercise the constitutional role of the presidency, and distanced herself from political causes with which she had been associated. She declined an invitation in 1998 to address the 5000 Too Many conference on abortion. She hosted a reception for southern members of the Orange Order on the eve of the Twelfth of July 1998. She opened Áras an Uachtaráin to the public and met Tony Blair, the UK prime minister, there. She has focused on being a figurehead at ceremonies such as the opening of the park at Messines in Belgium to commemorate the British and Irish war dead, and the millennial address to the Oireachtas in December 1999

In an outspoken speech, 'Hopes for the new Millennium', on 11 June 2000, Mary McAleese entered the debate over sleaze in political life, saying, 'The sordid side of the country's secret life is now under the spotlight and we are deeply challenged by the evidence of many different forms of corruption'. One of her hopes was that this would be 'a chastening period, of purging and purification radically calling us to higher values instead of providing self-justification for low standards whether in business, the church, politics, the street or the home.' Voices were needed to insist on humanity's ability to be decent, and to live authentic lives that could withstand the searching scrutiny of the spotlight.

Irish Women in the European Parliament

An Assembly was established in 1957 when the member states signed the Treaty of Rome establishing the European Economic Community (EEC). The Assembly brought together delegations from the national parliaments of member states to oversee the work of the community institutions. The first three Irish delegations established in January 1973, March 1973 and December 1977 included no women.

The 410 seats, of which the Republic of Ireland had fifteen, and Northern Ireland three, were divided between the political groups: Socialists, 113; European People's Party (Christian Democrat), 107; European Democrats, 64; Communists, 44; Liberals and Democrats, 40; European Progressive Democrats, 22; Independent Group, 11; and non-attached (as at January 1980). The parliament now has 626 members of whom 15 are Irish.

The first elections 'by direct universal suffrage' took place in 1979. The elections in Ireland, which were governed by the *European Assembly Elections Act, 1978*, were conducted under the normal electoral system of the single transferable vote, in four multi-member constituencies: Connacht–Ulster, Dublin, Leinster and Munster. The breakdown of of the 15 members is as follows:

Constituencies:

Dublin	4 Members
Leinster	3 Members
Munster	5 Members
Connaught–Ulster	3 Members

The Northern Ireland (United Kingdom) constituency has 3 Members. To date no women have been elected to represent the constituency of Northern Ireland.

Election 7 June 1979

Women Elected
DE VALERA, SÍLE (*SEE P. 112*) (FF, DUBLIN)
DESMOND, EILEEN (*SEE P. 107*) (LAB, MUNSTER)

Election 14 June 1984

Women Elected
BANOTTI, MARY (FG, DUBLIN)
LEMASS, EILEEN (*SEE P. 114*) (FF, DUBLIN)

Mary Banotti, née O'Mahony

DATE/PLACE OF BIRTH: 29 MAY 1939/DUBLIN

PARTY: FINE GAEL

CONSTITUENCY: DUBLIN

EUROPEAN PARLIAMENT: 1984 TO 2004 (SHE HAS ANNOUNCED HER INTENTION

TO RETIRE)

AGE AT ENTRY TO EUROPEAN PARLIAMENT: 45

FAMILY: SISTER OF NORA OWEN (*SEE P. 122*), GRANDNIECE OF MARGARET

COLLINS-O'DRISCOLL (*SEE P. 85*), AND OF MICHAEL COLLINS. SEPARATED, ONE DAUGHTER

EDUCATION: DOMINICAN CONVENT, WICKLOW; LONDON HOSPITAL; HUNTER COLLEGE, NEW YORK

OCCUPATION: STATE REGISTERED NURSE. INDUSTRIAL SOCIAL WORKER

CAREER:
Member, Environment, Public Health and Consumer Protection Committee, 1984-9; substitute 1989. Member, Women's Rights Committee, 1984-6, 1995; substitute 1989-95. Member, Culture, Youth, Education and Media Committee, 1989, vice-chair, 1989-97. Member, Petitions Committee, 1994; Mashreq Countries Delegation, 1984-6, Sweden Delegation, 1986-9; Finland Delegation, 1986-9; Iceland Delegation, 1986-9; and USA Delegation, 1989. President's Mediator for Transnationally Abducted Children. One of five quaestors in the European Parliament; Member, Committee on Citizens' Freedom and Rights, Justice and Home Affairs. Group of European People's Party (Christian Democrats) and European Democrats, Member, Quaestor Bureau, College of Quaestors. Member, Committee on Petitions; Substitute, Committee on Women's Rights and Equal Opportunities. Co.-founder, Rutland Centre for alcoholic treatment; Chairperson, Rutland Centre Board 1975-87. Founder member, ADAPT and Women's Aid. Member, AIM Group. *Particular policy interests*: environment, youth, culture.

ADDRESS: RINGSEND, DUBLIN/EUROPEAN PARLIAMENT OFFICE, 43 MOLESWORTH STREET, DUBLIN 2

MARY BANOTTI worked as a nurse and travelled extensively in Europe, Africa and America. She met her husband, Giovanni Banotti, in Kenya. She was a social worker with Irish Distillers from 1972 to 1984. Mary Banotti was a regular presenter of an RTÉ programme on social welfare.

This was Mary Banotti's first elective office. She was a Senate candidate in 1982–3 and a candidate in a by-election in the Dublin Central constituency in November 1983. She was also the Fine Gael candidate in the 1997 Irish Presidential election.

In 1989, Mary Banotti was named by the European Environmental Bureau, Brussels, as one of the best legislators in the European Parliament on environmental issues. She won Ireland's 1997 European of the Year Award. She was appointed United Nations Population Fund Goodwill Ambassador for Ireland in October 1999, to campaign for reproductive health care and education.

Election: 15 June 1989 ————————————————————————

Women Elected
BANOTTI, MARY (*SEE P. 216*) (FG, DUBLIN)

Election: 9 June 1994 ————————————————————————

Women Elected
AHERN, NUALA (GREEN PARTY, LEINSTER)
BANOTTI, MARY (*SEE P. 216*) (FG, DUBLIN)
MCKENNA, PATRICIA (GREEN PARTY, DUBLIN)
MALONE, BERNIE (LAB, DUBLIN)

Nuala Ahern, née McDowell

DATE/PLACE OF BIRTH: 5 FEBRUARY 1949/BELFAST

PARTY: GREEN PARTY

CONSTITUENCY: LEINSTER

EUROPEAN PARLIAMENT: JUNE 1994 TO DATE

AGE AT ENTRY TO EUROPEAN PARLIAMENT: 45

FAMILY: DAUGHTER OF VINCENT MCDOWELL (FOUNDER MEMBER AND VICE-
CHAIRMAN, CIVIL RIGHTS MOVEMENT IN NORTHERN IRELAND). MARRIED TO
BARRY AHERN

EDUCATION: OMEATH; DOMINICAN CONVENT, DÚN LAOGHAIRE; BRUNEL UNIVERSITY, UK
(BSc (PSYCHOLOGY))

OCCUPATION: COUNSELLING PSYCHOLOGIST

CAREER:
Member, Wicklow County Council, 1991-4. Chairperson, Committee on Industry, External
Trade, Research and Energy. Member, Earthwatch. Founder Member, Irish Women's
Environment Network. Member, Research, Technological Development and Energy/Research;
Technological Development and Energy Committee, 1994; Vice-chair Petitions Committee,
1994-7, substitute, 1997. Substitute, Culture, Youth Education and Media Committee, 1996-7;
Regional Policy Committee 1997. Member USA Delegation 1997. Group of the Greens/European
Free Alliance; Member on Industry, External Trade, Research and Energy/Committee on Legal
Affairs and the Internal Market; substitute, Delegation to the EU-Romanian Joint Parliamentary
Committee. *Particular policy interests*: energy, civil rights, citizen's rights, anti-nuclear, environ-
ment, genetic engineering. *Other interests*: badminton, walking, swimming

ADDRESS: 5 OATLANDS, GREYSTONES, COUNTY WICKLOW

NUALA AHERN grew up in County Louth and became involved in politics in the
Dundalk area where she campaigned for the closure of the Sellafield nuclear
reprocessing plant, which remains her objective. She has developed a high profile because of her opposition to the use of genetically modified organisms in
the food chain.

Patricia McKenna

DATE/PLACE OF BIRTH: 13 MARCH 1957/CASTLESHANE, COUNTY MONAGHAN

PARTY: GREEN PARTY

CONSTITUENCY: DUBLIN

EUROPEAN PARLIAMENT: JUNE 1994 TO DATE

AGE AT ENTRY TO EUROPEAN PARLIAMENT: 37

FAMILY: MARRIED TO MARTIN GILLEN; ONE SON

EDUCATION: ST LOUIS CONVENT, MONAGHAN; DEGREE IN FINE ART FROM
LIMERICK COLLEGE OF ART AND DESIGN, STUDIED FOR TEACHER DIPLOMA IN ART AND DESIGN WITH
THE NATIONAL COLLEGE OF ART AND DESIGN, DUBLIN (1981-4)

OCCUPATION: ART TEACHER

CAREER:
Member, Committee on the Environment, Public Health and Consumer Policy; Committee on
Fisheries. Founder Member, Women's Environment Network. Co-secretary, European Greens.
MEP 1994. Vice-chair, Green group, 1994. Member, Environment, Public Health and Consumer
Protection Committee, 1994; Fisheries Committee, 1994; Women's Rights Committee, 1995-7;
substitute, 1997. Substitute, Budgetary Control Committee, 1994-7; Employment and Social
Affairs Committee, 1997. Member South-east Asia and SAARC Delegation, 1994-7 and ASEAN,
South-east Asia and Republic of Korea Delegation, 1997.

PUBLICATION:
Amsterdam Treaty: The Road to an Undemocratic and Military Superstate, Green Party, 1998.

ADDRESS: EUROPEAN PARLIAMENT OFFICE, 43 MOLESWORTH STREET, DUBLIN 2

PATRICIA MCKENNA worked with the Mid-West Arts Council and taught art in
Dublin. In 1987 she was an organiser of the Irish Campaign against the Single
European Act and became co-ordinator of the Green Party until 1989. In 1989 she
became an advisor to the first Green deputy, Roger Garland, and subsequently to
Trevor Sargent until she defied expectations by topping the poll in the Dublin
constituency, and being elected to the European Parliament in 1994, to become
Ireland's first Green Member of the European Parliament. In 1990 she was
elected co-secretary of the European Co-ordination of Green Parties and organised the first alternative EC summit during Ireland's presidency of the EC in
June 1990 in Dublin. In 1991 she stood in the local government elections in Dublin
and helped to organise the first public meeting against the Gulf War.

In 1992 she contested the general election in Dublin Central. She was a leader
of the anti-Maastricht campaign, and brought an unsuccessful High Court case
against the Government over the use of public money to fund its campaign. Two
weeks before the divorce referendum in 1995, she secured a Supreme Court ruling
that Government use of taxpayers' money on one-sided referendum campaigns
was unconstitutional (*McKenna v. An Taoiseach, Irish Reports 1995*, vol. 2). In 1995
also, she appeared before a Cumbrian public enquiry regarding an underground
nuclear waste dump near Sellafield. The case for this dump was rejected.

As an MEP, Patricia McKenna urged EU pressure on the Irish authorities to provide a light-rail link for both sides of Dublin city, highlighted the lack of cycle lanes in the city, and sought EU intervention in the dispute over the Dublin Port Tunnel plan. In 1998 she campaigned for a No vote in the referendum on the Amsterdam Treaty, to protect Irish neutrality.

Bernie Malone, née O'Brien

DATE/PLACE OF BIRTH: 26 MARCH 1948/CLONTARF, DUBLIN

PARTY: LABOUR

CONSTITUENCY: DUBLIN

EUROPEAN PARLIAMENT: JUNE 1994–JUNE 1999

AGE AT ENTRY TO EUROPEAN PARLIAMENT: 46

FAMILY: MARRIED FRANK MALONE, 1972

EDUCATION: DOMINICAN COLLEGE, ECCLES STREET, DUBLIN;
UNIVERSITY COLLEGE DUBLIN (BCL 1968); LAW SOCIETY (SOLICITOR 1970)

OCCUPATION: SOLICITOR; CORPORATE LAWYER, 1970–90; PARTNER 1990–94

CAREER:
Member, Dublin County Council 1979–94; Chair, 1984–5. MEP, 1994: Vice-chair, PES Group 1994. Vice-Chair, Foreign Affairs, Security and Defence Policy Committee, 1994–7; substitute, 1997. Substitute, Development and Co-operation Committee, 1994–7; vice-chair, Employment and Social Affairs Committee, 1997. Member, USA Delegation, 1994–7. Particular policy interests: foreign affairs, employment. Other interests: reading, television, walking, languages.

BERNIE MALONE's involvement in the Labour Party began in the late 1960s. In her first election in 1979, she won a seat on Dublin County Council, representing the Malahide area. She protested at the planning policies pursued by Dublin County Council and the majority of her colleagues. She retained her seat in 1985 when most outgoing Labour councillors lost theirs in the mid-term stage of the Fine Gael–Labour coalition. Despite her conscientious work on the Council, Bernie Malone was not warmly regarded by Dick Spring, the Labour leader; she was seen as someone who didn't quite fit the image he had in mind for 1990s Labour.

At the Labour Party selection convention in 1994, Bernie Malone overcame a challenge from Orla Guerin who had the active support of Dick Spring. Orla Guerin was added to the Labour ticket at Dick Spring's request. Bernie Malone won, polling 22,419 first-preference votes against Orla Guerin's 16,674. Orla Guerin's votes helped Bernie Malone to take the last seat. The publicity from Orla Guerin's imposition had benefited Bernie Malone.

Bernie Malone contributed to over ninety parliamentary debates on issues including employment action plans, nuclear energy, English football hooligans, child abduction and tobacco advertising. She asked over fifty oral questions of the Commission and the Council. In 1999 she lost her seat to former Democratic Left (DL) Leader, Proinnsías de Rossa, who had been imposed by the Labour leadership as her running mate as an outcome of the DL/Labour merger.

Election: 11 June 1999

Women Elected
AHERN, NUALA (*SEE P. 217*) (GREEN PARTY, LEINSTER)
BANOTTI, MARY (*SEE P. 216*) (FG, DUBLIN)
DOYLE, AVRIL (*SEE P. 129*) (FG, LEINSTER)
McKENNA, PATRICIA (*SEE P. 218*) (GREEN PARTY, DUBLIN)
SCALLON, DANA (ROSEMARY) (NON-PARTY, CONNAUGHT–ULSTER)

Dana (Rosemary) Scallon, née Brown

DATE/PLACE OF BIRTH: 30 AUGUST 1950/LONDON
PARTY: NON-PARTY
CONSTITUENCY: CONNAUGHT–ULSTER
EUROPEAN PARLIAMENT: JUNE 1999 TO DATE
AGE AT ENTRY TO EUROPEAN PARLIAMENT: 48
FAMILY: MARRIED DAMIEN SCALLON, 1979; TWO DAUGHTERS, TWO SONS
EDUCATION: THORNHILL CONVENT, DERRY
OCCUPATION: ENTERTAINER, TV PRESENTER
CAREER:
Candidate, Irish Presidency, 1997, the first-ever nominee of County Councils. Member on Regional Policy, Transport and Tourism. Group of the European People's Party (Christian Democrats) and European Democrats. MEP, Member, Committee on Regional Policy, Transport and Tourism; on Culture, Youth, Education, the Media and Sport, Substitute.
ADDRESS: EUROPEAN PARLIAMENT OFFICE, 43 MOLESWORTH STREET, DUBLIN 2

DANA (ROSEMARY) SCALLON was the first Irish winner of the Eurovision Song Contest. In 1970, as an 18-year-old, she sang 'All Kinds of Everything' in the Eurovision, and began a career as a singer. When her husband's hotel in Newry, County Down, was blown up for the seventh time, the couple left for Dublin. They later moved to London. In 1990, they began a television career in Alabama. Dana presented and sang on a bi-weekly chat show, Say Yes, at Eternal Word Television Network (EWTN), a Catholic cable channel. While working with the station, Dana sang at rallies and concerts. She sang for the Pope three times, and recorded an album of the Rosary. She composed a hymn, 'The Golden Rose'.

Damien Scallon resigned from EWTN in 1996 to manage his wife's career; he founded the Heartbeat Records label, for the Catholic market, which released a number of albums and videos by Dana.

Dana is on record for her anti-abortion stand and support for family values.

Northern Ireland Parliaments

The Parliament of Northern Ireland was established by the *Government of Ireland Act, 1920*; it was suspended on 30 March 1972, and abolished by the *Northern Ireland Constitution Act* on 18 July 1973. The three parliamentary assemblies that succeeded it were established by legislation enacted by the United Kingdom parliament; three were dissolved by statutory instrument and the current Assembly commenced in 1998.

General Election, 1921 (52 seats)

Polling Day: 24 May 1921

Women Elected

CHICHESTER, DEHRA (UNIONIST, LONDONDERRY CITY AND COUNTY)
McMORDIE, JULIA (UNIONIST, BELFAST SOUTH)

Dehra Chichester, née Kerr Fisher,
later Dame Dehra Parker, OBE (1949), JP

DATE/PLACE OF BIRTH: 1882/KILREA, COUNTY DERRY

PARTY: UNIONIST

CONSTITUENCY: LONDONDERRY CITY AND COUNTY (1921-9); SOUTH LONDONDERRY (1933-60)

FAMILY: ONLY CHILD OF JAMES KERR-FISHER. MARRIED 1901, LT. COL. ROBERT SPENCER CHICHESTER D.L. MP (DIED 1921). MARRIED 1928, ADMIRAL W.H. PARKER (DIED 1940). GRANDMOTHER OF CAPTAIN TERENCE O'NEILL AND MAJOR JAMES DAWSON CHICHESTER-CLARK (BOTH PRIME MINISTERS OF NORTHERN IRELAND)

EDUCATION: EDUCATED PRIVATELY

OCCUPATION: JUSTICE OF THE PEACE

CAREER:
Minister of Health and Local Government, 1949-57. Parliamentary Secretary to Ministry of Education, 1937-44. Chairman of Northern Ireland General Health Services Board 1948-9. Rural District Council, Magherafelt. Chair, Magherafelt Board of Guardians. Vice-chair, Ulster Women's Unionist Council. Member, Lynn Committee on Education. Chair, Magherafelt Regional Education Committee.

PUBLICATIONS:
See Urquhart, Diane, *Women in Ulster Politics, 1890-1940*, Dublin: Irish Academic Press, 2000, pp. 182-98.

ADDRESS: MOYOLA PARK, CASTLEDAWSON, COUNTY DERRY

DATE OF DEATH: 28 NOVEMBER 1963

DEHRA CHICHESTER entered politics after the death of her first husband, Robert Spencer Chichester, and was an important force in the Unionist Party. She was the first woman to sit in the Northern Ireland Cabinet. Following her election in 1921, she served until 1929. She was again elected in 1933, for South Londonderry, on the death of the sitting member, her son-in-law, Captain Chichester-Clark, RN.

In 1924 she was selected as the first woman in Britain to present the annual address on behalf of the House of Commons, following the King's speech at the opening of the parliamentary session.

Dehra Parker introduced several education bills to the House of Commons, including the *Physical Education Act, 1938*, the *Teachers' Salaries and Superannuation (War Service) Act, 1939*, the *Education (Evacuated Children Bill)* and the *Education (Emergency Provisions) Act, 1940*. Most importantly, she also introduced the *Education Act, 1938*, which reformed Northern Ireland's educa-tion system, making school attendance compulsory up to the age of fifteen, establishing nursery schools and technical classes, and recognising the right to education of every child — regardless of class or religion. The Act did not receive universal support as the costs were to be met by local authorities. Dehra Parker, however, persisted, stating that it was 'a crime to stop a child's education at 14' (Northern Ireland House of Commons, vol. xxi, col. 568, 30 March 1938).

She contributed to debates on women's issues and initiated important amendments to several legislative reforms, including the Illegitimate Children Act and Summary Jurisdiction Act.

According to Urquhart (p. 196 op. cit.)

Parker was as competent and self-assured in the position of parliamentary sec-retary as she had been throughout her earlier parliamentary career. J.A. Oliver, a civil servant who worked for Parker during the 1950s, described her as 'capricious, an adroit politician and a most formidable operator'.

Dehra Parker sat in the House of Commons for thirty-five years. The aver-age term of service for the other women who sat in the house from 1921 to 1972, was eight and a half years.

She resigned as Minister for Health and Local Government in 1957, at the age of seventy-five, having served for eight years. She resigned from Parliament on 15 June 1960. When she resigned her seat it was won by her grandson, Major James Dawson Chichester-Clark. It was believed that she directed that another grandson, Captain Terence O'Neill, should succeed Lord Brookeborough as Prime Minister, and that he, in turn, should be succeeded by Chichester-Clark; this was what happened.

Dehra Parker did not respond to the political grievances of nationalists under the Stormont government. Neither did she contribute to any feminist agenda in the house.

Julia McMordie, JP, OBE (1919), née Gray

DATE/PLACE OF BIRTH: 30 MARCH 1860/HARTLEPOOL, UK

PARTY: UNIONIST

CONSTITUENCY: BELFAST SOUTH

FAMILY: DAUGHTER OF SIR WILLIAM & DOROTHY GRAY. MARRIED, 8 APRIL 1885, R.J. MCMORDIE
(MP FOR EAST BELFAST AND LORD MAYOR OF BELFAST, 1910-14; DIED 1914); ONE DAUGHTER,
ONE SON

EDUCATION: COLD-BEL, CHISLEHURST

OCCUPATION: JUSTICE OF THE PEACE FOR BELFAST

CAREER:
Hon. Burgess of City of Belfast, 1914. First woman Member, Belfast City Council, 1917;
Alderman, 1920. First woman High Sheriff of Belfast, 1929. Vice-president, Ulster Women's
Unionist Council, 1919-40. Chairman, Tuberculosis Committee. Lady of Grace, Order of St
John of Jerusalem. President, St John's Women's VAD for Belfast, 1914-18. *Particular policy
interests*: social work, women police officers, education, unemployment

ADDRESS: CALRIE HILL, KNOCK, BELFAST

JULIA MCMORDIE's support for women's issues was apparent from her maiden
speech to the House of Commons on 5 April 1922. In it she defended the appointment of female police officers. At the time only two of the 3,000 police officers in
Belfast were women. She called for at least a doubling of their representation.
Although she did not support equal pay, she highlighted the necessity of providing equal allowances and pensions to female officers. She opposed the
Constabulary Bill in May 1922, as it contained no clause dealing with women
officers. Her stand was ultimately successful, as a clause was inserted which
defined the term 'constable' as inclusive of both sexes. Although a staunch
unionist, she did not feel that this demanded that she support any bill just
because it was backed by her party.

General Election, 1925 (52 seats) ————————————

Polling Day: 3 April 1925

Women Elected
CHICHESTER, DEHRA (*SEE P. 221*) (UNIONIST, LONDONDERRY)

General Election, 1929 (52 seats) ————————————

Polling Day: 22 May 1929

Women Elected
WARING, MARGARET ALICIA (UNIONIST, IVEAGH)

Margaret Alicia Waring JP, CBE (1933)

DATE/PLACE OF BIRTH: 19 NOVEMBER 1887/WARRINGTON, HEREFORDSHIRE

PARTY: UNIONIST.

CONSTITUENCY: IVEAGH, COUNTY DOWN

FAMILY: DAUGHTER OF JOSEPH CHARLTON PARR, WARRINGTON. MARRIED IN 1914 TO MAJOR HOLT WARING WHO WAS KILLED IN ACTION, 1918

EDUCATION: EDUCATED PRIVATELY

OCCUPATION: JUSTICE OF THE PEACE FOR COUNTY DOWN

CAREER:

Member, Unemployment Assistance Board, Northern Ireland, 1929-33.
Member, Ulster Women's Unionist Council.

DATE OF DEATH: 9 MAY 1968

ADDRESS: WARINGSTOWN HOUSE, WARINGSTOWN, COUNTY DOWN

MARGARET WARING served from 1929 to 1933, and did not stand for re-election. She was a liberal benefactor of Waringstown. She made her maiden speech during the Ministry for Education's estimates, highlighting the plight of mentally handicapped children in Northern Ireland, for whom there was a lack of institutional care available. She was selected to second the motion during the debate on the King's address at the opening of the 1931 parliamentary session. During her lengthy speech (reported in Hansard) she outlined her views on forthcoming legislative developments and on the economic situation in Northern Ireland:

> *Unfortunately there is still grave depression in our industries and in agriculture, with a corresponding lack of employment for our people. It is, therefore, more than ever necessary to economise our resources whenever and wherever possible.*

She also spoke about the Town Planning and Housing Bill which proposed to clear slums and improve houses. She said that this must be achieved in a non-partisan manner. The quality of her speech led one MP to say: 'We would like to hear more of the hon. Member for Iveagh than we have in the past.'

By-election, 1933 _____

Women Elected

PARKER, DEHRA (FORMERLY CHICHESTER) (*SEE P. 221*) (UNIONIST, LONDONDERRY SOUTH)

General Election, 1933 (52 seats) _____

Polling Day: 30 November 1933

Women Elected

PARKER, DEHRA (FORMERLY CHICHESTER) (*SEE P. 221*) (UNIONIST, LONDONDERRY SOUTH)

General Election, 1938 (52 seats) ——————

Polling Day: 9 February 1938

Women Elected

PARKER, DEHRA (FORMERLY CHICHESTER) (*SEE P. 221*) (UNIONIST, LONDONDERRY SOUTH)

General Election, 1945 (52 seats) ——————

Polling Day: 14 June 1945

Women Elected

CALVERT, LILIAN IRENE MERCER (INDEPENDENT, QUEEN'S UNIVERSITY, BELFAST)
PARKER, DEHRA (FORMERLY CHICHESTER) (*SEE P. 221*) (UNIONIST, LONDONDERRY SOUTH)
MCNABB, DINAH (UNIONIST, ARMAGH NORTH)

Lilian Irene Mercer Calvert, née Earls

DATE/PLACE OF BIRTH : 10 FEBRUARY 1909/BELFAST

PARTY: INDEPENDENT

CONSTITUENCY: QUEEN'S UNIVERSITY, BELFAST

FAMILY: DAUGHTER OF JOHN EARLS (PROFESSOR OF MATHEMATICS AT QUEEN'S; PRINCIPAL, BELFAST
    MUNICIPAL COLLEGE OF TECHNOLOGY) AND MARY ARNOLD. MARRIED RAYMOND CALVERT;
    ONE SON

EDUCATION: METHODIST COLLEGE, BELFAST (1919-25); QUEEN'S UNIVERSITY BELFAST
    (BA ECONOMICS, PHILOSOPHY, 1936)

OCCUPATION: CHIEF WELFARE OFFICER FOR NORTHERN IRELAND, MINISTRY OF HOME AFFAIRS, 1940.
    MANAGING DIRECTOR, THE ULSTER WEAVING CO., LTD. A BELFAST LINEN FIRM, 1952

CAREER:
Chair, Standing Conference of Women's Organisations for Northern Ireland, 1945-7. Member,
Board of Curators for university appointments, 1946. Member, Belfast Chamber of Commerce,
1946; Member of its Senate, 1958-71. First woman President, Belfast City Chamber of
Commerce, 1965-6. Group Chair, Duke of Edinburgh's Study Conference on Industry, 1956.
Member, Secretary, Irish Association for Cultural, Social and Economic Relations [an independ-
ent group set up to promote better relations between North and South], 1965. *Other interests*:
music, poetry, modern Irish art.

DATE OF DEATH: 19 MAY 2000

ADDRESS: DERAVOHER, BALLYGALLY, COUNTY ANTRIM (ADDRESS AT TIME OF SERVICE)

Irene Calvert was a candidate in a by-election in 1944 for a Queen's University
seat. While working as a wartime Chief Welfare Officer, she handled the re-
settlement in Northern Ireland of evacuated Gibraltarians in 1940 and the care of
people affected by the bombing of Belfast in April 1941. These experiences gave

her an insight into social deprivation and made her responsive to the suggestion of friends that she should go into politics as an economist and to 'put the women's point of view'.

During her years in Stormont, despite the limitations of being an Independent, Irene Calvert stood for progressive social legislation and introduced reforms to the education and child welfare laws. In 1953 she declared that the Northern Ireland statelet was not a viable economic unit and she hoped partition would be temporary. She resigned on the strength of that conviction in a storm of controversy. In her resignation speech she said:

> ... *as an economist I am now convinced that it is quite impossible for us to improve our tragic unemployment circumstances ... so long as we are deprived of control of our entire finances and trade.*

(QUOTED IN THE IRISH TIMES, 14 FEBRUARY 1973)

While working as an economist for the Ulster Weaving Company, she developed new markets, supplying linen to hospitals and other large public institutions, and was made a managing director in 1953.

In retirement in Dublin, she worked for the Irish Labour Party in the Dún Laoghaire constituency until she was over 80.

She was nominated to the fantasy all-woman cabinet by the Women First staff of *The Irish Times* (14 February 1973).

Dinah McNabb

PLACE OF BIRTH: LURGAN
PARTY: UNIONIST
CONSTITUENCY: ARMAGH NORTH (1945-69)
FAMILY: MARRIED TO THOMAS G. McNABB, DPH, BSc MRCVS
EDUCATION: QUEEN'S UNIVERSITY OF BELFAST (BA H.DIP.ED.)
OCCUPATION: TEACHER
CAREER:
Member, Public Accounts Committee, 1960. Chair of Committee, 1966-8. Member, Armagh County Council. Member, Orange Order. First Northern Ireland woman to be President of Federation of Soroptimists of Great Britain and Ireland. Address: Aughnacloy House, Lurgan, County Armagh.

DINAH McNABB did not seek re-election in 1969 because of ill health.

General Election, 1949 (52 seats) —————————

Polling Day: 10 February 1949

Women Elected

CALVERT, LILIAN IRENE MERCER (*SEE P. 225*) (INDEPENDENT, QUEEN'S UNIVERSITY, BELFAST)
HICKEY, DR EILEEN MARY (INDEPENDENT, QUEEN'S UNIVERSITY BELFAST)
PARKER, DEHRA (FORMERLY CHICHESTER) (*SEE P. 221*) (UNIONIST, LONDONDERRY SOUTH)
MCNABB, DINAH (*SEE P. 226*) (UNIONIST, ARMAGH NORTH)

Eileen Mary Hickey, MB, BCh, BAO (1921), BSc, DPh (1922) MD (Gold Medal) (1923), MRCP (1934), FRCPI (1937)

DATE OF BIRTH: C.1897

PARTY: INDEPENDENT

CONSTITUENCY: QUEEN'S UNIVERSITY, BELFAST (1949-58)

EDUCATION: QUEEN'S UNIVERSITY, BELFAST

OCCUPATION: SENIOR PHYSICIAN, MATER INFIRMORUM HOSPITAL, BELFAST

CAREER:
Examiner and Clinical Lecturer, Queen's University, Belfast. Member, Senate of Queen's University Belfast; Northern Ireland Medical Women's Federation

ADDRESS: 76 EGLANTINE AVENUE, BELFAST; 20 DONEGALL PARK AVENUE, BELFAST

General Election, 1953 (52 seats) —————————

Polling Day: 22 October 1953

Women Elected

HICKEY, DR EILEEN MARY (*SEE P. 227*) (INDEPENDENT, QUEEN'S UNIVERSITY BELFAST)
PARKER, DAME DEHRA (FORMERLY CHICHESTER) (*SEE P. 221*)
    (UNIONIST, LONDONDERRY SOUTH)
MCNABB, DINAH (*SEE P. 226*) (UNIONIST, ARMAGH NORTH)
MACONACHIE, ELIZABETH (BESSIE) HAMILL (UNIONIST, QUEEN'S UNIVERSITY BELFAST)

Elizabeth (Bessie) Hamill Maconachie

PARTY: UNIONIST

EDUCATION: QUEEN'S UNIVERSITY, BELFAST (BA)

CONSTITUENCY: QUEEN'S UNIVERSITY, BELFAST (1953-69)

OCCUPATION: SCHOOLTEACHER

CAREER: ELECTED IN 1953. RETIRED WITH ABOLITION OF UNIVERSITY SEATS IN 1969

ADDRESS: 24 DERRYVOLGIE AVENUE, BELFAST

General Election, 1958 (52 seats) ——————————————————

Polling Day: 20 March 1958

Women Elected

PARKER, DAME DEHRA (FORMERLY CHICHESTER) (*SEE P. 221*) (UNIONIST, LONDONDERRY SOUTH)

MCNABB, DINAH (*SEE P. 226*) (UNIONIST, ARMAGH NORTH)

MACONACHIE, ELIZABETH (BESSIE) HAMILL (*SEE P. 227*) (UNIONIST, QUEEN'S UNIVERSITY BELFAST)

By-elections, 1958-62 ————————————————————————

Women Elected

MURNAGHAN, SHEELAGH MARY (LIBERAL, QUEEN'S UNIVERSITY BELFAST)

Sheelagh Mary Murnaghan

DATE/PLACE OF BIRTH: 26 MAY 1924/DUBLIN

PARTY: LIBERAL

CONSTITUENCY: QUEEN'S UNIVERSITY, BELFAST (1961 (BE-ELECTION)-69)

FAMILY: GRANDDAUGHTER OF GEORGE MURNAGHAN (NATIONALIST MP AT WESTMINSTER FOR MID-TYRONE, 1895). GRANDNIECE OF JOHN MORROGH (MP FOR CORK AT WESTMINSTER, 1895)

EDUCATION: LORETO COLLEGE, RATHFARNHAM, DUBLIN; QUEEN'S UNIVERSITY, BELFAST

OCCUPATION: BARRISTER

CAREER:

MP for Queen's University Belfast, 1961-9. Member, Northern Ireland Advisory Commission and Community Relations Commission, 1972-3. Chairwoman, Industrial and National Insurance Tribunals. Member, United Nations Association, Protestant and Catholic Encounter, and a committee devoted to finding sites for the settlement of Travellers. *Particular policy interests*: Travellers, criminal law reform, human rights. *Other interests*: Irish Hockey International, 1948-58.

PUBLICATIONS:

See Gordon Gillespie, *The Ulster Liberal Party, 1956-73*. Dissertation, Master of Social Science, Queen's University of Belfast, 1984, pp. 24-32.

DATE OF DEATH: 14 SEPTEMBER 1993

SHEELAGH MURNAGHAN grew up in a Catholic nationalist family in Omagh and Dublin. At Queen's University, in 1947, she became President of the University Literary and Scientific Debating Society. On graduation, she became Northern Ireland's first woman barrister. For the next decade she devoted herself to her legal and sporting career. In 1959 she joined the Ulster Liberal Association (later the Ulster Liberal Party) and a few months later contested her home constituency of South Belfast. This attempt was unsuccessful but in 1961 she achieved an excellent victory for the Liberals in a Queen's University by-election. She became the only Liberal ever to serve in the Stormont parliament.

An outspoken and fearless critic of extremism (despite a bomb attack on her home in February 1970), she drew on her links with the Liberals in Britain in her strenuous attempt to bring about reform.

She spoke often and at length on reform of local government and its electoral system, aid to farmers, the need for a comprehensive planning system, an efficient transport system and the reform of the rating system.

Her first Private Members Bill in 1963 made provisions for certain types of homicide and aimed to abolish capital punishment. The Bill was narrowly defeated. The government's *Criminal Justice Bill* in 1969 was in many respects the same as hers, although the death penalty was retained for the murder of policemen or prison officers and for 'murder done in the cause of furtherance of any seditious conspiracy', a clause aimed at the IRA.

She devoted much time to producing a Human Rights Bill, first discussed on 16 June 1964, to make discrimination (on the basis of race, creed, colour or political belief) illegal and to provide a Commission to investigate complaints. The Bill was defeated; she introduced a modified Human Rights Bills in 1965, February 1967 and December 1967.

In 1969 she lost her parliamentary seat — ironically through the process of electoral reform, which abolished the university franchise and forced her into an unsuccessful fight with a unionist in North Down. This put an end to her plan to introduce a Human Rights Bill for the fifth time. By this time, events had begun to deteriorate beyond the point where such a Bill alone could have improved the situation in Northern Ireland.

In 1972, when direct rule from London had been introduced, the Secretary of State, William Whitelaw, appointed her to his special advisory committee.

General Election, 1962 (52 seats) ——————————————

Polling Day: 31 May 1962

Women Elected

McNABB, DINAH (*SEE P. 226*) (UNIONIST, ARMAGH NORTH)
MACONACHIE, ELIZABETH (BESSIE) HAMILL (*SEE P. 227*) (UNIONIST, QUEEN'S UNIVERSITY BELFAST)
MURNAGHAN, SHEELAGH MARY (*SEE P. 228*) (LIBERAL, QUEEN'S UNIVERSITY BELFAST)

General Election, 1965 (52 seats) ——————————————

Polling Day: 25 November 1965

Women Elected

McNABB, DINAH (*SEE P. 226*) (UNIONIST, ARMAGH NORTH)
MACONACHIE, ELIZABETH (BESSIE) HAMILL (*SEE P. 227*) (UNIONIST, QUEEN'S UNIVERSITY BELFAST)
MURNAGHAN, SHEELAGH MARY (*SEE P. 228*) (LIBERAL, QUEEN'S UNIVERSITY BELFAST)

General Election, 1969 (52 seats) ———————————

Polling Day: 24 February 1969

Women Elected

DEVLIN, JOSEPHINE BERNADETTE (PEOPLE'S DEMOCRACY, LONDONDERRY SOUTH)
DICKSON, ANNE LETITIA (UNIONIST (O'NEILL), CARRICK)

(Josephine) Bernadette Devlin, later McAliskey

DATE/PLACE OF BIRTH: 23 APRIL 1947/COOKSTOWN, COUNTY TYRONE

PARTY: PEOPLE'S DEMOCRACY (PD) INDEPENDENT, 1970-74

CONSTITUENCY: MID-ULSTER

FAMILY: MARRIED MICHAEL MCALISKEY, 1973

EDUCATION: QUEEN'S UNIVERSITY BELFAST (PSYCHOLOGY)

PUBLICATIONS:

Devlin, B., *The Price of My Soul*, London: Pan, 1969. Elliott, S. and N.D Flackes, *Northern Ireland: A Political Directory 1968-99*, Belfast: Blackstaff, 1999.

BERNADETTE DEVLIN entered public life during the civil rights campaign as a member of the People's Democracy (PD) movement. She took part in the student demonstrations in Belfast in the summer of 1968 and in Northern Ireland Civil Rights Association (NICRA) marches that year in Dungannon, Armagh and in Duke Street, Derry. She was also in the Belfast–Derry People's Democracy march in January 1969, when it was attacked by militant loyalists at Burntollet.

She lost her first election when she stood against Major Chichester-Clark (who was soon to become Prime Minister) in South Derry in February 1969. The next month she won a by-election in Mid-Ulster for Westminster, defeating the Unionist candidate in a poll of 92 per cent. She became the youngest woman ever to be elected to Westminster, and the youngest MP for fifty years. She took her seat on her twenty-second birthday.

She made her maiden speech an hour after taking her seat. In it she attacked the Unionist government of Captain Terence O'Neill and said that an extreme, but possible, solution would be the abolition of Stormont. The Home Secretary, James Callaghan, spoke of her brilliance and said that he looked to the day when she might be standing at the Government despatch box. Newspapers hailed her as the voice not only of NICRA, but of the student generation.

In the 'Battle of the Bogside' in Derry in August 1969, she became the focus of world attention by encouraging the Bogsiders to raise their barricades against the police. The Scarman Tribunal report described how she was involved in telephone conversations to the Prime Minister and the Minister of State at the Home Office at the height of the violence on 13 August 1969. Scarman also noted that she was seen to be actively defending Rossville Street barricades.

In August 1969, on a trip to the US, she raised £50,000 for relief in Northern Ireland. In December 1969 she was sentenced to six months' imprisonment at Derry Magistrates Court for incitement to riot and obstruction and disorderly behaviour arising from the Bogside incidents. She went to Armagh Prison in June 1970, after she had increased her Mid-Ulster majority to nearly 6,000 in the general election; there were protest marches and demonstrations in many parts of Northern Ireland and a protest march in London

In January 1972, in the House of Commons, Bernadette Devlin punched the Home Secretary, Reginald Maudling, alleging that he was lying about the events of 'Bloody Sunday' in Derry in which thirteen people had died. She said that the reaction to the incident showed a lot about the English; it had created more popular outrage than the Derry shootings.

In the February 1974 general election she lost her Mid-Ulster seat. She helped to found the Irish Republican Socialist Party (IRSP) at the end of 1974. When the 1975 feud developed between the Official IRA and the Irish Republican Socialist Party, she strongly denied that the Irish Republican Socialist Party had a military wing. On a lecture tour of the US in 1976 she attacked the Peace People and said that she would not tell the Provisional IRA to stop fighting as they were fighting British imperialism in the only way they knew how. In the 1979 European election she championed the case of the republican prisoners engaged in protests at the Maze prison to secure political status, but Provisional Sinn Féin did not support her, and urged voters to boycott the election. She was eliminated on the third count.

On 16 February 1981 she and her husband were seriously injured when they were shot in their home at Derrylaughan, County Tyrone, by loyalist gunmen. An army patrol arrived quickly and she later acknowledged the value of emergency treatment given by the soldiers.

In 1980 and 1981 she was the main spokeswoman of the National H-Block/Armagh Committee.

In 1982 she stood unsuccessfully in the Republic's two general elections as People's Democracy candidate. She campaigned for a seat in Dublin North Central, the constituency of Charles Haughey. In 1987 and 1988 she campaigned against extradition from the Republic. In the 1992 general election she supported the Provisional Sinn Féin candidate in Fermanagh–South Tyrone. In 1992 she spoke at a founding meeting in Derry of a group defending Articles 2 and 3 of the Irish Constitution. She said that no one would make 'a Palestinian' out of her.

In July 1993 she won a judicial review against the BBC decision — under the direct broadcasting ban — to use sub-titles for her voice in the *Nation* programme of the previous September. In October she was a witness for James Smyth, a Maze Prison escapee, who sought to avoid extradition from California.

She gave an early lead to the wider republican movement to reject the Downing Street Declaration.

Anne Letitia Dickson, née McCance

DATE/PLACE OF BIRTH: APRIL 1928/LONDON

PARTY: UNIONIST

CONSTITUENCY: CARRICK

FAMILY: MARRIED TO JAMES JOHNSTON DICKSON; THREE DAUGHTERS, ONE SON

EDUCATION: RICHMOND LODGE SCHOOL, BELFAST; BELFAST COLLEGE OF TECHNOLOGY

OCCUPATION: FULL-TIME PUBLIC REPRESENTATIVE

CAREER:
Leader, Unionist Party of Northern Ireland (UPNI), 1976-81. Member, Newtownabbey Urban Council 1964-9; Vice-chairman, 1967-9. Member, County Antrim Library Committee 1967-73. President, South-East Antrim Unionist Association; President, Jordanstown and Greenisland branches; Vice-president, Ballyclare branch. Member, Northern Ireland Chamber of Commerce, 1969-73; Salvation Army Advisory Board, 1971. President, Newtownabbey Operatic Society, 1972. Founder Member, Rosstula Special School management committee. Member, Royal Overseas League; Royal Automobile Club. Chairwoman, Northern Ireland Consumer Council 1985-90.

ADDRESS: BALLINASCREEN, SHORE ROAD, GREENISLAND, COUNTY ANTRIM

ANNE DICKSON was first elected to Stormont parliament for the constituency of Carrick in 1969 as the Official Unionist candidate. She won the nomination in preference to the sitting member, Captain Austin Ardill.

Prior to the 1973 Assembly elections she was involved in a dispute over the selection of Official Unionist candidates in South Antrim. She was the choice of a group of South Antrim delegates who left the party's selection meeting. Captain Ardill was nominated by those who remained. Both she and Captain Ardill contested the election in the constituency and both were described on the ballot papers as Official Unionist. Anne Dickson had the support of the party leader, Brian Faulkner, and the party Secretary, J.O. Bailie, though not the support of the Unionist Council officers.

In the Assembly election of 1973 she was elected in South Antrim without the support of the Unionist Party headquarters. She was a strong supporter of Terence O'Neill as premier. She supported the power-sharing Executive, and was also elected to the Convention from South Antrim in 1975. When Brian Faulkner gave up the leadership of UPNI in 1976, she succeeded him as the first woman leader of a Northern Ireland political party. In 1979 she unsuccessfully contested North Belfast in the Westminster election. In October 1981 she presided at UPNI's final conference, when it was decided to wind up the party after a series of poor election results.

General Election to the Northern Ireland Assembly, 1973 (78 seats) ————————————————

Polling Day: 28 June 1973

Women Elected

CONN, SHENA ELIZABETH (UNIONIST, LONDONDERRY)

COULTER, ROSE JEAN (INDEPENDENT UNIONIST (LOYALIST COALITION), BELFAST WEST)

DICKSON, ANNE LETITIA (*SEE P. 232*) (INDEPENDENT UNIONIST (UNOFFICIAL CANDIDATE), ANTRIM SOUTH)

PAISLEY, EILEEN EMILY (DEMOCRATIC UNIONIST PARTY, BELFAST EAST)

Shena Elizabeth Conn

PLACE OF BIRTH: BELFAST

PARTY: UNIONIST

CONSTITUENCY: LONDONDERRY

FAMILY: MARRIED TO DOUGLAS CONN (PRESIDENT, NORTH LONDONDERRY UNIONIST ASSOCIATION); ONE SON, ONE DAUGHTER. DAUGHTER-IN-LAW OF MRS W.E. CONN (VICE-CHAIRMAN, LIMAVADY RURAL DISTRICT COUNCIL)

EDUCATION; QUEEN'S UNIVERSITY, BELFAST (BDS)

OCCUPATION: SCHOOL DENTIST, ROE VALLEY

CAREER:

District Commissioner, Limavady Girl Guides Association.

ADDRESS: CLAGGAN, LIMAVADY, COUNTY DERRY (ADDRESS AT TIME OF SERVICE)

SHENA CONN, in contesting an Assembly seat, was taking part in her first election for a public body. For many years her family were active in Unionist organisation and in local politics in the North Derry area.

Jean Coulter

PLACE OF BIRTH: SHANKILL, BELFAST

PARTY: INDEPENDENT UNIONIST (LOYALIST COALITION)

CONSTITUENCY: WEST BELFAST

EDUCATION: GIRLS MODEL SCHOOL, BELFAST

OCCUPATION: SOLICITOR'S CLERK

CAREER: SECRETARY, COURT WARD UNIONIST ASSOCIATION

ADDRESS: 20 DUNLUCE AVENUE, LISBURN ROAD, BELFAST (ADDRESS AT TIME OF SERVICE)

JEAN COULTER, was a founder of the West Belfast Loyalist coalition which was formed in June 1973, before the Assembly election, to oppose the then Official Unionists under Brian Faulkner. On the resignation of Brian Faulkner as leader of the Official Unionist Party in January 1974, Jean Coulter again became a supporter of the official leadership.

She was opposed to the power-sharing Northern Ireland Executive and the proposed Council of Ireland, and went to Sunningdale in December 1973, in order to protest against the absence of loyalist representatives at the negotiations.

Eileen Emily Paisley, née Cassels

DATE/PLACE OF BIRTH: 1934/BELFAST

PARTY: DEMOCRATIC UNIONIST PARTY

CONSTITUENCY: BELFAST EAST

FAMILY: MARRIED TO REV. IAN PAISLEY (LEADER, DEMOCRATIC UNIONIST PARTY; MEMBER, ASSEMBLY
FOR ANTRIM NORTH; WESTMINSTER MP FOR ANTRIM NORTH); MOTHER OF IAN PAISLEY JR, MLA;
THREE DAUGHTERS, TWIN SONS

EDUCATION: LOCAL SCHOOLS

OCCUPATION: HOUSEWIFE

CAREER:

Member, Belfast City Council, 1969-73; Education Committee, Library Committee, Transport Committee; Primary and Secondary Education Sub-Committees. Member, Board of Governors, Fleming Fulton Special School; Mitchell House Special School; College of Domestic Studies, Belfast.

ADDRESS: BEECHWOOD, 423 BEERSBRIDGE ROAD, BELFAST

EILEEN PAISLEY was elected to Belfast City Council as Protestant Unionist in 1969 and served on the Council until the reorganisation of the local authorities and the elections in 1973. In 1982, she was a member of a joint UUP-DUP publicity team visiting the US, standing in for her husband, who had been refused a US visa.

General Election to the Northern Ireland Constitutional Convention, 1975 (78 seats) ———

Polling Day: 1 May 1975

Women Elected

CONN, SHENA ELIZABETH (*SEE P. 233*) (OFFICIAL UNIONIST PARTY, UNITED ULSTER UNIONIST PARTY, LONDONDERRY)

COULTER, ROSE JEAN (*SEE P. 233*) (OFFICIAL UNIONIST PARTY, UNITED ULSTER UNIONIST PARTY, WEST BELFAST)

DICKSON, ANNE LETITIA (*SEE P. 232*) (UNIONIST PARTY OF NORTHERN IRELAND, ANTRIM SOUTH)

PAISLEY, EILEEN EMILY (*SEE P. 234*) (UNITED ULSTER UNIONIST PARTY, EAST BELFAST)

General Election to the Northern Ireland Assembly, 1982 (78 seats) ————————————————————————

Polling Day: 20 October 1982

Women Elected

DUNLOP, DOROTHY (OFFICIAL UNIONIST PARTY, EAST BELFAST)
McSORLEY, MARY KATHERINE (SOCIAL DEMOCRATIC AND LABOUR PARTY, MID-ULSTER)
SIMPSON, MARY (OFFICIAL UNIONIST PARTY, ARMAGH)

Dorothy Dunlop

PARTY: OFFICIAL UNIONIST PARTY

CONSTITUENCY: EAST BELFAST

FAMILY: GRANDDAUGHTER OF SIR ROBERT WOODS (UNIONIST MP AT WESTMINSTER FOR TCD)

EDUCATION: QUEEN'S UNIVERSITY BELFAST (BA)

OCCUPATION: MEMBER OF STAFF OF BBC TALKS DEPARTMENT; TEACHER IN SEVERAL BELFAST SCHOOLS
AND IN THE PRISON EDUCATION SERVICE

CAREER:
UUP Assembly Member for East Belfast 1982-6. Chairwoman, Health and Social Services Committee; Member, Education and Security Committees. Belfast City Council, 1975. Deputy Lord Mayor, 1978-9.

DOROTHY DUNLOP was one of five Belfast UUP councillors who lost the party whip in 1987 for failing to support the anti-Anglo-Irish Agreement adjournment policy; later that year she lost her place as chairwoman of East Belfast Unionist Association. She stood unsuccessfully as Independent in East Belfast in 1992, and joined the Conservatives as a lifelong integrationist soon after the election.

Mary Katherine McSorley, MBE

PARTY: SOCIAL DEMOCRATIC AND LABOUR PARTY. INDEPENDENT

CONSTITUENCY: MID-ULSTER

CAREER:
SDLP Assembly Member for Mid-Ulster, 1982-6. Member, Magherafelt Council, 1978-93. Party spokeswoman on tourism. Member, local government Staff Commission, 1985.

MARY KATHERINE McSORLEY became the first SDLP-elected representative to accept a royal honour, when she accepted an MBE in 1989. The party, unhappy with her decision, said that she could not run as SDLP candidate in the May 1989 District Council elections. However, she held her seat as an Independent. She retired at the May 1993 election.

Mary Simpson

PARTY: OFFICIAL UNIONIST PARTY

CONSTITUENCY: ARMAGH

CAREER:

UUP Assembly Member for Armagh, 1982-6. Member, Environment Committee; Vice-chair, Education Committee. Member, Craigavon Borough Council, 1977-89; first Lady Mayor, 1981-2. Honorary Secretary, Central Armagh Unionist Association, 1974-83. Founding Member, Craigavon and District Housing Association, 1980; Chair, 1990

Northern Ireland Senate, 1921-72 ──────────────────

The Government of Ireland Act, 1920 also set up the Senate, which consisted of twenty-four Senators elected on the principle of proportional representation by Members of the House of Commons for a term of eight years. The Senate continued independently of the life of Parliament; half of the elected Senators retired at the end of each fourth year. There were also two ex-officio Senators — the Lord Mayor of Belfast and the Mayor of Derry. Procedure in the Senate was akin to that of the House of Lords.

Northern Ireland Senate, 1950-58 ──────────────────

Women Members

GREEVES, MARION JANET

Marion Janet Greeves, née Cadbury, MBE, JP

DATE/PLACE OF BIRTH: 1894, ENGLAND

PARTY: NON-PARTY

FAMILY: MARRIED TO WILLIAM E. GREEVES. MEMBER OF CADBURY FAMILY, CHOCOLATE MANUFACTURERS

EDUCATION: ST JAMES SCHOOL FOR GIRLS, MALVERN, ENGLAND

OCCUPATION: JUSTICE OF THE PEACE

CAREER:

Member, Armagh County Council, 1946. Chief Commissioner, Ulster Girl Guides, 1952; Elder, Society of Friends (Quakers). Served in the Friends Ambulance Unit. Member, Committee of Friends School, Lisburn; Teacher, Sunday School. Minister, Moyallon Meeting. Founder, Rathvarna home for elderly Friends.

DATE OF DEATH: 1979

ADDRESS: ARDEEVIN, PORTADOWN, COUNTY ARMAGH

MARION JANET CADBURY moved to Northern Ireland on her marriage to William E. Greeves.

By-election, 1970 ——————————————

Women Elected

TAGGART, EDITH ASHOVER

Edith Ashover Taggart, neé Hind

DATE/PLACE OF BIRTH: 11 NOVEMBER 1909/NOTTINGHAM, ENGLAND

PARTY: UNIONIST

FAMILY: NIECE OF JOHN ANDREWS (FIRST PRIME MINISTER OF NORTHERN IRELAND AND WORLD GRAND MASTER OF THE ORANGE ORDER), JIM ANDREWS, (FIRST NORTHERN IRELAND LORD CHIEF JUSTICE) AND THOMAS ANDREWS, (OF TITANIC FAME). GRANDNIECE OF LORD PIRRIE (LORD MAYOR OF BELFAST, DIRECTOR OF HARLAND AND WOLFF). MARRIED TO REDMOND THIBEAUDEAU TAGGART; TWO DAUGHTERS, ONE SON

EDUCATION: AT HOME; WEST HEATH, ENGLAND; EASTBOURNE DOMESTIC SCIENCE COLLEGE (HEAD GIRL)

OCCUPATION: HOUSEWIFE.

CAREER:

Life President, Unitarian Presbyterian Women's League. Member, Clifdon House (old people's home) Committee. Member, Northern Ireland Forum/entry to negotiations.

EDITH ASHOVER TAGGART was only the second woman Senator since 1921.

Northern Ireland Forum Election: 30 May 1996 (110 seats) ——————————————————

In January 1996, after the Mitchell Commission report recommended that talks and decommissioning should happen in tandem, the UK Prime Minister, John Major, proposed an election to a forum as a method of enabling the parties to enter into talks. The elections were to produce a body of politicians from whom the party negotiators could be drawn.

Ninety members were to be elected using the eighteen parliamentary constituencies and party lists of candidates, with voters choosing a party list. Another twenty seats were to be allocated equally to the ten parties with the most votes overall. Talks delegates were to be nominated from the Northern Ireland Forum but were not dependent on it. The Forum held its final session on 24 April 1998.

Women Elected

EAST ANTRIM: MARY STEELE (UUP), MAY BEATTIE (DUP)

SOUTH BELFAST: JOAN PARKES (DUP)

WEST BELFAST: ANNE MCGUINNESS (SINN FÉIN), ANNE ARMSTRONG (SINN FÉIN)

SOUTH DOWN: MARGARET RITCHIE (SDLP)

NEWRY AND ARMAGH: MARIA CARAHER (SINN FÉIN)
STRANGFORD: IRIS ROBINSON (DUP)
UPPER BANN: BRÍD RODGERS (*SEE P. 197*) (SDLP), MICHELLE O'CONNOR (SINN FÉIN)

Northern Ireland Assembly
25 June 1998–11 February 2000 (suspension),
30 May 2000 to date ————————————————————

The first elections to the Northern Ireland Assembly were held on 25 June 1998. The elections followed a referendum held in Northern Ireland on 22 May 1998. That referendum endorsed the earlier Belfast/Good Friday Agreement of 10 April 1998. Support for the Agreement was expressed by 71 per cent of those who voted in the referendum; 81 per cent of those eligible to vote cast their votes.

A referendum on the 1998 Belfast/Good Friday Agreement was also held in the Irish Republic. Just over half (55.5 per cent) of those eligible to vote took part, and the vote was overwhelmingly in favour of the Agreement (94 per cent voted Yes and 6 per cent voted No, when asked if they supported the Agreement). The Belfast/Good Friday Agreement envisages that the next elections to the Assembly will be in May 2003; thereafter elections will take place quadrennially.

The Assembly has 108 members, who are elected using the Single Transferable Vote system of proportional representation (which has been used in Northern Ireland for elections to the European Parliament since 1979). There are eighteen constituencies — the same number as for the Westminster Parliament — and six members are elected to each.

Women Elected

BELFAST SOUTH
HANNA, CARMEL, SDLP
MCWILLIAMS, PROF. MONICA, NIWC

WEST BELFAST
DE BRÚN, BAIRBRE, SF
RAMSEY, SUE, SF

NORTH DOWN
BELL, EILEEN, ALL.
MORRICE, JANE, NIWC

FERMANAGH AND SOUTH TYRONE
CARSON, JOAN, UUP
GILDERNEW, MICHELLE, SF

FOYLE
NELIS, MARY, SF

Carmel Hanna

DATE/PLACE OF BIRTH: 26 APRIL 1946/WARRENPOINT, COUNTY DOWN

PARTY: SDLP

CONSTITUENCY: SOUTH BELFAST

EDUCATION: OUR LADY'S GRAMMAR SCHOOL, NEWRY; ROYAL MATERNITY HOSPITAL, BELFAST

OCCUPATION: NURSE; OFFICE ADMINISTRATOR; ASSESSOR, SOUTH AND EAST SOCIAL SERVICES TRUST, BELFAST SOCIAL SERVICES. MEMBER, NIPSA TRADE UNION

CAREER:
Member, Belfast City Council, 1997. Deputy Chair, Environment Committee. Member, Health, Social Services and Public Safety Committee. *Particular policy interests*: health, environment, Third World development. *Other interests*: reading, walking, travelling.

Monica McWilliams

DATE/PLACE OF BIRTH: 1955/KILREA, COUNTY DERRY

PARTY: NORTHERN IRELAND WOMEN'S COALITION (NIWC)

CONSTITUENCY: SOUTH BELFAST

FAMILY: MARRIED TO BRIAN; TWO SONS

EDUCATION: QUEEN'S UNIVERSITY BELFAST (MA), UNIVERSITY OF MICHIGAN

OCCUPATION: LECTURER; PROFESSOR OF SOCIAL POLICY AND WOMEN'S STUDIES, UNIVERSITY OF ULSTER

CAREER:
Founder Member, NIWC, 1996. Member, Northern Ireland Forum and Castle Buildings talks, 1996-8. Member, Higher & Further Education, Training and Employment; Health, Social Services and Public Safety Committees; Assembly Business Committee. *Particular policy interests*: Civic Forum, rights of violence victims, women's equality.

ADDRESS: 50 UNIVERSITY STREET, BELFAST BT7 1HB (CONSTITUENCY OFFICE)

MONICA MCWILLIAMS grew up in a Catholic nationalist family and joined the civil rights movement when she was a schoolgirl in 1968. She was on Magilligan Strand in Derry when marchers were beaten back by the British army. As a student in Queen's University in the early 1970s, she witnessed a number of murders. While she was cycling down the Lisburn Road a man was shot dead opposite her in a random sectarian murder. During the Ulster Workers' Council strike in 1974, a college friend was murdered.

Monica McWilliams won a postgraduate scholarship to the University of Michigan and became an urban planner in Detroit. She returned to Northern Ireland in 1978. She was a founder member of the Northern Ireland Women's Coalition — a party that transcends the nationalist and unionist categories — and she and her NIWC colleague, Pearl Sagar, received many insults in the Northern Forum, including the following:

> *As long as I live, I'll have a mission, which is to teach these two women to stand behind the loyal men of Ulster.*

WILLIE McCREA (DUP)

> *Thank God only 7,000 idiots voted for these women.*

IRIS ROBINSON (*SEE P. 243*)

In November 1998 the NIWC held its first party conference and named Monica McWilliams as party executive.

Bairbre de Brún

DATE/PLACE OF BIRTH: 1954/DUBLIN
PARTY: SINN FÉIN
CONSTITUENCY: WEST BELFAST
FAMILY: SINGLE
EDUCATION: UNIVERSITY COLLEGE, DUBLIN (BA); QUEEN'S UNIVERSITY, BELFAST (PGSE)
OCCUPATION: SCHOOLTEACHER, INCLUDING AT NORTHERN IRELAND'S FIRST IRISH-MEDIUM
SECONDARY SCHOOL
CAREER:
Minister for Health, Social Services and Public Safety in the power-sharing Northern Executive, 29 November 1999-11 February 2000 (Executive suspended), 30 May 2000 (restoration) to date. Party spokesperson on policing and justice, late 1980s. International Secretary, 1990-1996. Member, Irish National Teacher's Organisation.

BAIRBRE DE BRÚN is fluent in Irish, which she taught, and French. She moved to Belfast in 1979 and participated in community politics. She emerged politically as a leader of the H-Block Committee before and during the hunger strikes at the Maze prison in 1980. Having joined Sinn Féin in 1984, she has been an ard-comhairle member since then. She came to prominence in the late 1990s mostly through her involvement in the Multi-Party Talks leading to the Good Friday Agreement, 1998, and her media interviews. She has been a staunch critic of the RUC.

Sue Ramsey

DATE/PLACE OF BIRTH: 13 SEPTEMBER 1970/SPRINGHILL, BALLYMURPHY

PARTY: SINN FÉIN

CONSTITUENCY: WEST BELFAST

EDUCATION: ST LOUISE'S COMPREHENSIVE SCHOOL; PORTRUSH CATERING COLLEGE

OCCUPATION: CHEF (1988-94)

CAREER:
Councillor, Lisburn Council, 1997. Deputy Chair, Public Accounts Committee. Member, Health, Social Services and Public Safety Committee.

Eileen Bell

DATE/PLACE OF BIRTH: 15 AUGUST 1943/DROMARA, COUNTY DOWN

PARTY: ALLIANCE

CONSTITUENCY: NORTH DOWN

EDUCATION: DOMINICAN COLLEGE; UNIVERSITY OF ULSTER, JORDANSTOWN (BA HISTORY & POLITICS)

CAREER:
Member, Shadow Commission. General Secretary, Alliance Party, 1986-90; spokeswoman on women's affairs, 1988-93; education, 1993; Delegate to Brooke/Mayhew Talks on political future of Northern Ireland, 1991-4. Member, North Down Council, 1993. Alliance Party Delegate, Dublin Forum, 1995-6. Vice-Chair, Alliance Party, 1995-7. Alliance Party Delegate to Stormont, 1996-8. Member, Northern Ireland Forum, 1996-8. Chair, Alliance Party, 1997-9. Member, Committee of the Centre; Education Committee. *Particular policy interests*: education, equality, family issues. *Other interests*: theatre, reading.

EILEEN BELL was active in the Alliance Party organisation as a member of the West Belfast executive (1981–4) before becoming party general secretary. In 1992 she became administrator of the Peace Train organisation. She contested Newry and Armagh in the 1992 general election.

Jane Morrice

DATE/PLACE OF BIRTH: 11 MAY 1954/BELFAST

PARTY: NORTHERN IRELAND WOMEN'S COALITION

CONSTITUENCY: NORTH DOWN

EDUCATION: ASHLEIGH HOUSE SCHOOL; METHODIST COLLEGE, BELFAST. UNIVERSITY OF ULSTER (BA, 1977)

OCCUPATION: BRUSSELS-BASED JOURNALIST WITH FRENCH PRESS AGENCY, 'EUROPEAN REPORT', ALSO CONTRIBUTING TO BBC WORLD SERVICE, 1980-86. MADE FILMS ON AFRICA FOR PRODUCTION COMPANY 'C91', 1986-7. JOURNALIST, BBC NORTHERN IRELAND (LABOUR RELATIONS AND BUSINESS CORRESPONDENT), 1988-92. TRAINEE, EC AGRICULTURE DIVISION, BRUSSELS, 1980

CAREER:
Founder member, NIWC; Member, party talks delegation. Head of European Commission Office, Northern Ireland, March 1992-7; Member, National Union of Journalists. Member, Ad Hoc Committee on Flags; Public Accounts; Enterprise, Trade and Investment Committees.

Particular policy interests: Europe; economy; environment; agriculture, arts/culture (NIWC spokeswoman): international affairs; North/South Relations. *Other interests*: Writing; music; swimming.

PUBLICATIONS:
The Lomé Convention: From Politics to Practice and The North-South Dialogue
(on Third World issues).

Joan Carson

DATE/PLACE OF BIRTH: 29 JANUARY 1935/ENNISKILLEN, COUNTY FERMANAGH
PARTY: ULSTER UNIONIST
CONSTITUENCY: FERMANAGH-TYRONE SOUTH
EDUCATION: GIRLS' COLLEGIATE SCHOOL, ENNISKILLEN; STRANMILLIS COLLEGE, BELFAST
OCCUPATION: TEACHER. PRINCIPAL, TAMNAMORE PRIMARY SCHOOL, 1982-88.
CAREER:
Member, Dungannon District Council, 1997. Member, Higher & Further Education, Training and Employment, and Environment Committees. *Particular policy interests*: environment, education, children, women. *Other interests*: ornithology, painting, reading.

Michelle Gildernew

PARTY: SINN FÉIN
CONSTITUENCY: FERMANAGH-TYRONE SOUTH
DATE/PLACE OF BIRTH: 28 MARCH 1970/BRANTRY, DUNGANNON, COUNTY TYRONE
EDUCATION: ST CATHERINE'S COLLEGE, ARMAGH; UNIVERSITY OF ULSTER, COLERAINE
CAREER:
Sinn Féin representative, Downing Street Talks, 1997-98. Deputy Chair, Social Development Statutory Committee, Ad Hoc Committee on Flags, Committee of the Centre. *Particular policy interests*: Environment, women's issues, rural development, housing. *Other interests*: Gaelic football, cinema, reading, scuba diving, socialising, travel

MICHELLE GILDERNEW was a member of the family in the Caledon squat, the first protest in the 1968 civil rights campaign which took place in Caledon, County Tyrone before her birth. Austin Currie, a nationalist MP, took possession of a council house which he claimed had been improperly allocated by Dungannon Rural Council to a young single Protestant woman, instead of to the Gildernew family; he was ejected by the RUC.

Mary Nelis

PARTY: SINN FÉIN
CONSTITUENCY: FOYLE
FAMILY: MOTHER OF NINE CHILDREN
OCCUPATION: SHIRT FACTORY WORKER. TEACHER, ADULT LITERACY

CAREER:
Member, Sinn Féin delegation, Northern Ireland Forum, 1996-8. Member, Derry City Council, 1993. Deputy Chair, Culture, Arts and Leisure; and Higher & Further Education, Training and Employment Committees. Chair, Dove House Resource Centre. *Particular policy interests*: human rights, social issues.

MARY NELIS was active in the civil rights movement. She joined the SDLP and stood in district council elections in 1973. In 1976, her son was sentenced to sixteen years' imprisonment for IRA membership. When he joined the 'blanket' protest in the Maze Prison she with two others wore blankets and campaigned across Northern Ireland in support of prisoners' rights. She left the SDLP in 1977 and joined Sinn Féin in 1980.

Patricia Lewsley

DATE/PLACE OF BIRTH: 3 MARCH 1957/BELFAST

PARTY: SDLP

CONSTITUENCY: LAGAN VALLEY

EDUCATION: ST DOMINIC'S HIGH SCHOOL, BELFAST; UNIVERSITY OF ULSTER

OCCUPATION: 1994-5: INFORMATION/ADVICE CO-ORDINATOR. 1982-9 HEAD COOK

CAREER:
Member, Belfast City Council, 1993-7; Vice-chair, SDLP group; Chair, SDLP women's group. Member, Women's Political Forum. Member, Committee of the Centre; Enterprise, Trade and Investment; and Education Committees. Director, Community Work Programme; Shopmobility, Belfast. *Particular policy interests*: disability; special needs education; women's issues; women in small business. *Other interests*: walking, socialising.

Iris Robinson

DATE/PLACE OF BIRTH: 6 SEPTEMBER 1949/BELFAST

PARTY: DEMOCRATIC UNIONIST PARTY (DUP)

CONSTITUENCY: STRANGFORD

FAMILY: MARRIED TO PETER ROBINSON (DEPUTY LEADER, DUP; MP FOR EAST BELFAST SINCE 1979; ASSEMBLY MEMBER FOR EAST BELFAST, 1982-6). ONE DAUGHTER, TWO SONS

EDUCATION: KNOCKBREDA INT. SCHOOL; CASTLEREAGH TECHNICAL COLLEGE

OCCUPATION: 1969-70 SECRETARY TO DIRECTOR, SUPERMAC. 1971-3 SECRETARY TO DIRECTOR, ATKINSON TIES

CAREER:
Member Castlereagh Borough Council 1989; Mayor, 1992,1995; Alderman since 1997. Member, Northern Ireland Forum, 1996-8. Member, Assembly Business; and Health, Social Services and Public Safety Committees. *Particular policy interests*: health, education, housing. *Other interests*: walking, flower arranging.

ADDRESS: 2B JAMES STREET, NEWTOWNARDS BT23 4BY (CONSTITUENCY OFFICE)

IRIS ROBINSON served a prison sentence in 1988, at the same time as her husband, for refusal to pay fines arising out of protests against the Anglo–Irish Agreement and the public order laws.

Pauline Armitage

PARTY: ULSTER UNIONIST PARTY (UUP)
CONSTITUENCY: LONDONDERRY EAST
CAREER:
Member, Coleraine Council, 1985; Mayor, 1995-7. Member, Public Accounts; and Health, Social Services and Public Safety Committees. Former Member, Ulster Defence Regiment.

PAULINE ARMITAGE was commended for her co-operation, when Mayor, with SDLP Deputy Mayor, John Dallat. During the 1998 referendum campaign she was described as a 'soft no', but remained loyal to the leadership of David Trimble.

Northern Ireland
House of Commons at Westminster ————————————

The Government of Ireland Act, 1920, while establishing the two regional parliaments of Northern Ireland and Southern Ireland, also made provision for the continued representations of both parts of Ireland in the United Kingdom House of Commons at Westminster. The arrangements made for the south were superseded by the Anglo–Irish Treaty of 1921, but at each UK general election from 1922 onwards Northern Ireland has returned a number of MPs (varying from 12 to 17) to Westminster. The elections have been conducted, as in Great Britain, under the system of the single non-transferable vote, except in the Queen's University constituency, which operated under a system of proportional representation. However, this seat was contested only in 1945, and then by only two candidates; it was abolished by the *Representation of the Peoples Act, 1948*.

No women were elected in the general elections of 1922, 1923, 1924, 1929, 1931, 1935, 1945, 1950 or at by-elections during that period. No women were elected in the general elections in 1964, February and October, 1974, 1979, 1983, 1987, 1992 and 1997.

General Election, 1951
(12 Northern Ireland Seats) ————————————

Polling Day: 25 October 1951

No Women Elected

By-election, North Down ————————————————

15 April 1953

Women Elected
PATRICIA FORD (UNIONIST)

Patricia Ford

DATE OF BIRTH: 5 APRIL 1921

PARTY: UNIONIST

CONSTITUENCY: NORTH DOWN

FAMILY: DAUGHTER OF LIEUT-COL SIR W.D. SMILES, CIE, DSO (DEP-LIEUT AND MP, DROWNED *M.V. PRINCESS VICTORIA*, 31 JANUARY 1953). MARRIED DR LIONEL FORD (DEAN OF YORK AND HEADMASTER OF HARROW), 1941 (MARRIAGE DISSOLVED, 1956). MARRIED SIR NIGEL FISHER (MP FOR SURBITON) IN 1956

EDUCATION: BANGOR COLLEGIATE SCHOOL, GLENDOWER SCHOOL, LONDON AND ABROAD

CAREER:
Ulster Unionist and Conservative Member; Founder, Co-Chair of Women Caring Trust.

ADDRESS: 7 RUSSELL COURT, CLEVELAND ROW, ST JAMES, LONDON. PORTAVO POINT, DONAGHADEE, COUNTY DOWN (ADDRESS AT TIME OF SERVICE)

PATRICIA FORD was elected for North Down in April 1953 in succession to her father. She sat until she retired in 1955.

General Election, 1955
(12 Northern Ireland Seats) ——————————————

Polling Day: 26 May 1955

Women elected

MCLAUGHLIN, FLORENCE PATRICIA ALICE (UNIONIST, BELFAST WEST)

Florence Patricia Alice McLaughlin, OBE (1975)

DATE OF BIRTH: 23 JUNE 1916

PARTY: UNIONIST

CONSTITUENCY: BELFAST WEST

FAMILY: DAUGHTER OF CANON F.B. ALDWELL. MARRIED MAJOR W. MCLAUGHLIN, 1937

EDUCATION: BELFAST AND TRINITY COLLEGE, DUBLIN

CAREER:
Member, Executive Committee of Ulster Women's Unionist Council. Member, Executive Committee National Union. British Delegate to Conservative Assembly, Council of Europe. British Delegate to Western European Union. General Secretary, London Foundation for Marriage Education.

FLORENCE MCLAUGHLIN was elected for Belfast West in 1955 and sat until she retired in 1964. She unsuccessfully contested the 1970 election in the Wandsworth Central constituency.

General Election, 1959 ————————————————

Women Elected

MCLAUGHLIN, FLORENCE PATRICIA ALICE (*SEE P. 246*) (UNIONIST, BELFAST WEST)

General Election, 1966
(12 Northern Ireland Seats) ————————————

Polling Day: 31 March 1966

No women elected.

By-election: Mid-Ulster
17 April 1969 ————————————————————

Women Elected

DEVLIN, JOSEPHINE BERNADETTE (*SEE P. 230*) (UNITY)

General Election, 1970
(12 Northern Ireland Seats) ————————————

Polling Day: 18 June 1970

Women Elected

DEVLIN, JOSEPHINE BERNADETTE (*SEE P. 230*) (UNITY, MID ULSTER)

Bibliography

Publications by or about Women in Parliament

Carlton, Imogen (ed.), *The Directory of Northern Ireland Government 1999/2000*, Watford: Carlton Publishing, 1999.

Claffey, Una, *The Women who Won: Women of the 27th Dáil*, Dublin: Attic Press, 1993.

Clarke, Kathleen, *Revolutionary Woman: Kathleen Clarke, 1878–1972: An Autobiography*, (ed.) Helen Litton, Dublin: O'Brien Press, 1991.

Elliott, Sydney and Flackes, W.D., *Northern Ireland: a Political Directory 1968–1999*, Belfast: Blackstaff Press, 1999.

Fallon, Charlotte H., *Soul of Fire: A Biography of Mary MacSwiney*, Cork: Mercier Press, 1986.

Finlay, Fergus, *Mary Robinson: A President with a Purpose*, Dublin: O'Brien Press, 1990.

Haverty, Anne, *Constance Markievicz: An Independent Life*, London: Pandora, 1988.

Horgan, John, *Mary Robinson: An Independent Voice*, Dublin: O'Brien Press, 1997.

Kearns, Linda, *In Times of Peril: Leaves from the Diary of Nurse Linda Kearns from Easter Week 1916 to Mountjoy, 1921*, edited by Annie M.P. Smithson, Dublin: Talbot Press, 1922.

McCarthy, Justine, *Mary McAleese: The Outsider, An Unauthorised Biography*, Dublin: Blackwater Press, 1999.

McDowell, R.B., *Alice Stopford Green*, Dublin: Allen Figgis, 1967.

McQuillan, Deirdre, *Mary Robinson, A President in Progress*, Dublin: Gill and Macmillan, 1994.

Marreco, Anne, *The Rebel Countess: The Life and Times of Constance Markievicz*, London: Weidenfeld and Nicolson, 1967.

Norman, Diana, *Terrible Beauty: A Life of Constance Markievicz*, London: Hodder and Stoughton, 1987.

Ó Faoláin, Seán, *Constance Markievicz,* London: Cresset Women's Voices, 1987 [originally, London: Cape, 1934].

O'Leary, Olivia and Helen Burke, *Mary Robinson: The Authorised Biography*, London: Hodder and Stoughton, 1998.

O'Neill, Marie, *From Parnell to De Valera: A Biography of Jennie Wyse Power, 1858–1941*, Dublin: Blackwater Press, 1991.

O'Sullivan, Michael, *Mary Robinson: The Life and Times of an Irish Liberal*, Dublin: Blackwater Press, 1993.

Uí Thallamháin, Caitlín, Bean, *Ros fiain Lios an Daill [leabhar beathaisnéise ar Chuntaois Markievicz]*, Baile Átha Cliath: Clódhanna, 1967.

Van Voris, Jacqueline, *Constance de Markievicz: In the Cause of Ireland*, Amherst: University of Massachusetts Press, 1967.

Publications on Women and Politics

All-Party Oireachtas Committee on the Constitution: Second Progress Report: Seanad Éireann, Pn. 3835. Dublin: Stationery Office, 1977, p. 7.

Brown, Alice and Yvonne Galligan, 'Views from the Periphery: Changing the Political Agenda for Women in the Republic of Ireland and in Scotland', *West European Politics*, 16:2, 1993, pp. 165–89.

Browne, Vincent and M. Farrell, *The Magill Book of Irish Politics*, Dublin: Magill, 1981.

Carty, R.K., 'Women in Irish Politics', *Canadian Journal of Irish Studies*, 6:1, 1980, pp. 90–104.

Clancy, Mary, 'Aspects of Women's Contribution to the Oireachtas Debate in the Irish Free State, 1922–1937' in Maria Luddy and Cliona Murphy, *Women Surviving*, Swords: Poolbeg, 1989.

Clancy, Mary, 'Shaping the Nation: Women in the Free State Parliament, 1923–1937', in Yvonne Galligan, Eilís Ward and Rick Wilford (eds.), *Contesting Politics Women in Ireland, North and South*, Oxford: Westview/PSAI, 1999.

Coakley, John and Michael Gallagher (eds.), *Politics in the Republic of Ireland*, 3rd edition, Dublin and London: Folens; Limerick: PSAI Press, 1993.

Coulter, Carol, *The Hidden Tradition: Feminism, Women and Nationalism in Ireland*, Cork: Cork University Press, 1993.

Darcy, R., 'The Election of Women to Dáil Éireann: A Formal Analysis', *Irish Political Studies*, 3, 1988, pp. 63–76.

Donnelly, Seán, *Partnership: The Story of the 1992 General Election*, Dublin: Seán Donnelly, 1993.

Donnelly, Seán, *Elections '97*, Dublin: Seán Donnelly, 1998.

Donnelly, Seán, *Elections '99: All Kinds of Everything*, Dublin: Seán Donnelly, 1999.

Engstrom, R.L., 'District Magnitudes and the Election of Women to the Irish Dáil', *Electoral Studies*, 6:2, 1987, pp. 123–36.

European Commission, *Women in Power*: Final Report: Athens conference and summit. European expert network, 'Women in Decision-making', Brussels: European Women's Lobby, 1992.

Eurostat, *A Statistical Eye on Europe*, Luxembourg: Office for Official Publications of the European Communities, 1999.

Fawcett, Liz, 'The Recruitment of Women to Local Politics in Ireland: A Case Study', *Irish Political Studies*, 7, 1992, pp. 41–55.

Fearon, Kate, *Women's Work: The Story of the Northern Ireland Women's Coalition*, Belfast: Blackstaff Press, 1999.

Fitzgerald, Frances, 'Women, Empowerment and Contemporary Ireland', in O'Connell, Maurice R., *People Power: Proceedings of the Third Annual Daniel O'Connell Workshop, Cahirciveen, Ireland*, Dublin: Institute of Public Administration on behalf of DOCAL — Daniel O'Connell Association, 1993.

Flynn, William J., *The Oireachtas Companion and Saorstát Guide for 1928: Oireachtas Éireann, 1922–27*. Dublin: Hely's, 1928.

Flynn, William J., *The Oireachtas Companion and Saorstát Guide for 1929*, Dublin: Hely's, 1929.

Flynn, William J., *The Oireachtas Companion and Saorstát Guide for 1930*, Dublin: Hely's, 1930.

Flynn, William J., *Free State Parliamentary Companion for 1932*, Dublin: Talbot Press, 1930.

Flynn, William J., *Irish Parliamentary Handbook, 1939*, Dublin: Stationery Office, 1939.

Flynn, William J., *Irish Parliamentary Handbook, 1945*, Dublin: Stationery Office, 1945.

Gallagher, Michael, 'By-elections to Dáil Éireann 1923–96: The Anomaly that Conforms', *Irish Political Studies*, vol. 11, 1996.

Galligan, Yvonne, 'Women and the 1991 Local Elections' in Rafter, Kevin and Noel Whelan (eds.), *From Malin Head to Mizen Head: The Definitive Guide to Local Government in Ireland*, Dublin: Blackwater Press, 1992, pp. 16–20.

Galligan, Yvonne, Eilís Ward and Rick Wilford, *Women's Political Representation in Ireland in Contesting Politics: Women in Ireland, North and South*, Oxford: Westview, 1999.

Galligan, Yvonne, 'Women in Irish Politics' in John Coakley and Micheal Gallagher (eds.), *Politics in the Republic of Ireland*, 2nd edition, Dublin: Folens, and Limerick: PSAI Press, 1993, pp. 207–26.

Galligan, Yvonne, 'Party Politics and Gender in the Republic in Ireland' in Joni Lovenduski and Pippa Norris (eds.), *Gender and Party Politics*, Sage: London, 1993, pp. 147–67.

Galligan, Yvonne, 'The Legislature' in Alpha Connelly (ed.), Gender and the Law in Ireland, Dublin: Gill and Macmillan, 1993b, pp 28–46.

Galligan, Yvonne, 'From the Margins to the Mainstream: Fianna Fáil and the Women's Movement' in Philip Hannon and Jackie Gallagher (eds.) *Taking the Long View — 70 Years of Fianna Fáil*, Dublin: Blackwater Press, 1996, pp. 73–81.

Galligan, Yvonne, *Women and Politics in Contemporary Ireland: from the Margins to the Mainstream*, London: Pinter, 1998.

Gardiner, Frances, 'Political Interest and Participation of Irish Women, 1922–1992: The Unfinished Revolution', *Canadian Journal of Irish Studies*, 18:1, 1992, pp. 15–39.

Gardiner, Frances, 'Women in the Election' in Michael Gallagher and Michael Laver (eds.), *How Ireland Voted 1992*, Dublin: Folens and Limerick: PSAI Press, 1993, pp. 79–92.

Genovese, Michael A. (ed.), *Women as National Leaders*, London: Sage, 1993.

Hannon, Philip and Jackie Gallagher (eds.), *Taking the Long View — 70 Years of Fianna Fáil*, Dublin: Blackwater Press, 1996.

Inter-Parliamentary Union, Inter-Parliamentary Symposium on the Participation of Women in the Political and Parliamentary Decision-Making Process: Geneva, 20-24.X1.1989: reports and conclusions. Geneva: Inter-Parliamentary Union, 1989: reports and documents.

Inter-Parliamentary Union, *Men and Women in Politics: Democracy Still in the Making: A World Comparative Study*, Geneva: Inter-Parliamentary Union, 1997. Reports and documents (Inter-Parliamentary Union), no. 28.

Inter-Parliamentary Union, *Activities of the Inter-Parliamentary Union Concerning the Status of Women: Background and Results*, 88th Inter-Parliamentary Conference 1992, Stockholm. Geneva: Inter-Parliamentary Union, 1992.

Inter-Parliamentary Union, *Minutes of the Meeting of Women Parliamentarians: Sunday 20th and Friday 25th March, 1994*. Meeting of Women Parliamentarians, 1994, Paris. Geneva: Inter-Parliamentary Union, 1994.

Inter-Parliamentary Union, *Women and Political Power: Survey Carried Out among the 150 National Parliaments Existing as of 31st October, 1991*, Geneva: Inter-Parliamentary Union, 1992.

Inter-Parliamentary Union, *Women: What the IPU is Doing?* Geneva: Inter-Parliamentary Union, 1997.

Joint Committee on Women's Rights (Second), *First Report: Changing Attitudes to the Role of Women in Ireland: Attitudes towards the Role and Status of Women 1975–1986*, Stationery Office, Dublin, May 1988 [Pl.5609].

Kelly, Adrian, 'Women in Twentieth Century Ireland: Activism and Change', in Ilka Kangas, *SEW-Situation of Elderly Women*, Helsinki: STAKES, 1997.

MacDermott, Eithne, *Clann na Poblachta*, Cork: Cork University Press, 1998.

Manning, Maurice, 'Women in the Elections' in Howard R Penniman and Brian Farrell (eds.) *Ireland at the Polls 1981, 1982 and 1987: A Study of Four General Elections*, Durham NC: Duke University Press, 1987, pp. 156–66.

Manning Maurice, 'Women in Irish National and Local Politics, 1977–77' in Margaret MacCurtain and Dónal Ó Corráin (eds.), *Women in Irish Society*, Dublin: Arlen House, 1978, pp. 92f–102.

Marsh, Michael, 'Electoral Evaluations of Candidates in Irish General Elections 1948–82', *Irish Political Studies*, 2, 1987, pp. 65–76.

Meaney, Geraldine, *Sex and Nation: Women in Irish Culture and Politics*, Dublin: Attic Press, 1991.

Nealon, Ted, *Ireland: A Parliamentary Directory 1973–74*, Dublin: Institute of Public Administration, 1974.

Nealon, Ted, with Frank Dunlop. *Guide to the 21st Dáil and Seanad: Election '77*, Dublin, Platform Press, 1977.

Nealon, Ted, *Guide to the 22nd Dáil and Seanad: Election '81*, Dublin: Platform Press, 1981.

Nealon, Ted and Séamus Brennan, *Guide to the 23rd Dáil and Seanad: Election '82*, Dublin: Platform Press, 1982.

Nealon, Ted, *Guide to the 24th Dáil and Seanad: 2nd election '82*, Dublin: Platform Press, 1983.

Nealon, Ted, *Guide to the 25th Dáil and Seanad: election '87*, Dublin: Platform Press, 1987.

Nealon, Ted, *Guide to the 26th Dáil and Seanad: election '89*, Dublin: Platform Press, 1989.

Nealon, Ted, *Guide to the 27th Dáil and Seanad: election '92*, Dublin: Gill and Macmillan, 1993.

Nealon, Ted, *Guide to the 28th Dáil and Seanad: election '97*, Dublin: Gill and Macmillan, 1997.

O'Connor, Pat, *Women in Contemporary Irish Society*, Dublin: Institute of Public Administration, 1997

O'Neill, Thomas, *The Women of Fianna Fáil*, Dublin: Fianna Fáil, n.d.

O'Hegarty, P.S., *The Victory of Sinn Féin*, Dublin: Talbot Press, 1924.

O'Reilly, Emily, *Candidate: The Truth Behind the Presidential Campaign*, Dublin: Attic Press, 1991.

Parliament of the Commonwealth of Australia, *Women, Elections and Parliament: Report from the Joint Standing Committee on Electoral Matters*, Canberra: Parliament of the Commonwealth of Australia, 1994.

Ratter, K. and N. Wholan (eds.), *From Malin Head to Mizen Head: The Definitive Guide to Local Government in Ireland*, Dublin: Blackwater Press, 1992.

Randall, Vickey and Ailbhe Smyth, 'Bishops and Bailiwicks: Obstacles to Women's Political Participation in Ireland', *Economic and Social Review*, 18:3, 1987 pp. 189–214.

Smyth, Ailbhe, 'Women and Power in Ireland: Problems, Progress, Practice', *Women's Studies International Forum*, 8:4, 1985, pp. 255–62.

Smyth, Ailbhe, 'The Contemporary Women's Movement in the Republic of Ireland', *Women's Studies International Forum*, 11:4, 1988, pp. 331–41.

Smyth, Ailbhe, 'The Women's Movement in the Republic of Ireland' in Ailbhe Smyth (ed.), *Irish Women's Studies Reader*, Dublin: Attic Press, 1993, pp. 245–69.

Tweedy, Hilda, *A Link in the Chain: The Story of the Irish Housewives Association 1942–1992*, Dublin: Attic Press, 1992.

United Nations Human Development Report, 1998.

Urquhart, Diane, *Women in Ulster Politics 1890–1940: A History Not Yet Told*, Dublin: Irish Academic Press, 2000.

Valiulis, Maryann Gialanella, '"Free Women in a Free Nation": Nationalist Feminist Expectations for Independence, in Brian Farrell (editor). *The Creation of the Dáil*, Dublin: Blackwater/Radio Telefís Éireann, 1994.

Ward, Margaret, *Unmanageable Revolutionaries: Women and Irish Nationalism*, Dingle, County Kerry: Brandon, 1983.

Parliamentary Websites

Inter-Parliamentary Union: www.ipu.org/Statistics on Women in Parliament Worldwide [Links to National Parliaments]

Oireachtas (Irish Parliament): www.irlgov/oireachtas/default.htm

Northern Ireland Assembly: www.nics.gov.uk

European Parliament: www.europarl.eu.int

Index